# Nixon, Kissinger, and Allende

## U.S. Involvement in the 1973 Coup in Chile

Lubna Z. Qureshi

LEXINGTON BOOKS

A division of
ROWMAN & LITTLEFIELD PUBLISHERS, INC.
Lanham • Boulder • New York • Toronto • Plymouth, UK

LEXINGTON BOOKS

A division of Rowman & Littlefield Publishers, Inc.
A wholly owned subsidiary of The Rowman & Littlefield Publishing Group, Inc.
4501 Forbes Boulevard, Suite 200
Lanham, MD 20706

Estover Road
Plymouth PL6 7PY
United Kingdom

British Library Cataloguing in Publication Information Available

**Library of Congress Cataloging-in-Publication Data**

Qureshi, Lubna Z., 1974–
  Nixon, Kissinger, and Allende: U.S. involvement in the 1973 coup in Chile / Lubna Z.
Qureshi.
    p. cm.
  Includes bibliographical references and index.
  1. Chile—History—Coup d'état, 1973—Causes. 2. United States—Foreign
relations—Chile. 3. Chile—Foreign relations—United States. 4. Allende Gossens,
Salvador, 1908–1973. 5. Nixon, Richard M. (Richard Milhous), 1913–1994. 6.
Kissinger, Henry, 1923– 7. United States. Central Intelligence Agency. I. Title.
  F3100.Q74 2009
  327.8307309'047—dc22

2008032326

ISBN: 978-0-7391-2655-4 (cloth : alk. paper)
ISBN: 978-0-7391-2656-1 (pbk. : alk. paper)
ISBN: 978-0-7391-3210-4 (e-book)

Printed in the United States of America

∞™ The paper used in this publication meets the minimum requirements of American
National Standard for Information Sciences—Permanence of Paper for Printed Library
Materials, ANSI/NISO Z39.48–1992.

# Nixon, Kissinger, and Allende

For my parents,
Dr. M. Wahid H. Qureshi
and
Dr. Shahida Qureshi

# Contents

# Acknowledgments

First of all, I would like to thank my major professor, Dr. Diane Shaver Clemens at the University of California, Berkeley, for her inspiration, guidance, and encouragement. I would also like to express my appreciation to the other members of my dissertation committee: Dr. Waldo E. Martin, Jr., and Dr. Beatriz Manz. Many thanks should also go to my undergraduate professor, Dr. Stanley I. Kutler at the University of Wisconsin–Madison, who first stimulated my interest in the history of the Nixon administration and later encouraged me to listen to the Nixon Tapes. Dr. Richard Immerman at Temple University supervised my master's thesis on the Chilean coup, and gave me the chance to present a paper on the subject at the 2007 conference of the Society for Historians of American Foreign Relations.

John Powers at the Nixon Presidential Materials Project at the National Archives II in College Park, Maryland, and Señora Carmen Gloria Duhart at the *Archivo General Historico del Ministerio de Relaciones Exteriores* in Santiago, Chile, were both invaluable archivists.

Judge Juan Guzman and Jorge Arrate kindly took the time to share their experiences and insights with me.

Cervimex and the Spanish Center of Kenosha assisted with the translation of Chilean sources. Luke Rouser translated an article from the Italian.

My sister, Naheed Qureshi, made my stay in Washington, D.C., easier, as did Hervey Allen in Santiago. I am grateful to the history department at Berkeley for awarding me the Kathryn MacLeod Graduate Fellowship, but I am even more grateful to my parents for supporting me when the fellowship ran out.

My classmate at Berkeley, Osamah Khalil, provided constructive criticism.

I spent the 2007–2008 academic year as a visiting scholar at Northwestern University, where Professors Michael Sherry and Frank Safford provided sound advice. The librarians at the Northwestern University Library were helpful.

I am indebted to Tanya Harmer at the London School of Economics for sharing her excellent research on Chilean–Cuban relations.

Professor Margaret Power at the Illinois Institute of Technology gave my manuscript an extremely close reading. Her research on the Chilean military, as well as the impact of gender on Chilean politics, illuminated my own work.

Finally, I would like to thank my editor at Lexington Books, Julie Kirsch, for giving me the opportunity to publish my first book.

# Introduction

Responding to the command of his superior, President Richard M. Nixon, Director Richard Helms of the Central Intelligence Agency walked into the Oval Office on the afternoon of September 15, 1970. Nixon wanted to discuss the recent election of Dr. Salvador Allende to the presidency of Chile. The victory of a Marxist candidate in that Latin American nation infuriated the president.

Helms took his seat with two other presidential subordinates, National Security Advisor Henry Kissinger and Attorney General John Mitchell, who undoubtedly shared Nixon's fury. As his superior issued orders, Helms took notes like any good bureaucrat:

1 in 10 chance perhaps, but save Chile!
worth spending
not concerned with risks involved
no involvement of embassy
$10,000,000 available, more if necessary
full-time job—best men we have
game plan
make the economy scream
48 hours for plan of action[1]

Although the president posed in public as the leader of the free world, he revealed a far different agenda in the privacy of the Oval Office. Using primarily extralegal means, Nixon sought to undermine a free democratic election in a foreign country. In his memoirs, Helms expressed some reservations about the Chilean scheme. "Standing mid-track and shouting at an oncoming locomotive might have been more effective than attempting to inject caution into this fifteen-minute White House session," Helms recalled for posterity.[2]

The director's reservations were more practical than moral, but in any case, he followed his leader's command. At stake were $1.5 billion worth of North American investments in Chile.[3] On September 11, 1973, the president's dream of a military coup in Chile came true, and three decades after the fall of Allende, the question remains: Why did the foreign policy team of Nixon and Kissinger regard the Marxist as a threat? Thanks to the work of the National Security Archive's Peter Kornbluh and two distinguished journalists, Christopher Hitchens and John Dinges, we know *what* Nixon and Kissinger *did* to Allende's Chile, but it has not been fully clear *why* they did it.[4] *Why* did Washington so greatly fear Allende as a symbol of the Latin American left?

Historians of U.S. foreign policy such as John Lewis Gaddis attributed the actions of the Nixon White House to fears that Allende would transform Chile into an authoritarian "satellite" of the Soviet Union.[5]

In his marvelous study of the relationship between Richard Nixon and Henry Kissinger, Robert Dallek speculated that the two men moved against Allende because of domestic apprehension in the face of the upcoming 1972 U.S. presidential election, as well as anticipated losses for the American corporate community. Yet, like Gaddis, Dallek suggests that the president and his national security advisor were deeply concerned about potential disturbances to the worldwide balance of power that would favor Moscow. In truth, Dallek does not arrive at a definitive answer. "For such staunch advocates of foreign policy realism as Nixon and Kissinger," Dallek admitted, "it is difficult to understand their apocalyptic fears about an Allende government.[6]

Dallek's book provides a very broad examination of Nixon and Kissinger's foreign policy. Perhaps a singular focus on U.S. policy on Chile in the early 1970s will explain why the two men posed so virulent a challenge to Allende.

Blaming the Chilean president for what befell his country in 1973, as scholars Jonathan Haslam and Kristian Gustafson have done in their one-volume treatments, would not be a productive exercise.[7] Allende could never have matched the might and power of Washington and its reactionary Chilean clients.

Haslam's Allende was a man of poor political judgment who lacked any competence in economic matters. To make matters worse, Allende had a sentimental attachment to Moscow and its worldwide agenda. Apart from unfairly assessing the Allende legacy, Haslam does not give the motives of Nixon and Kissinger more than a cursory analysis.

For his part, Kristian Gustafson claims that President Allende dangerously threatened the "Western way of life."[8] This assertion is particularly outrageous because if any leader violated the standards of Western civilization, it was Allende's successor.

Among other things, Gustafson points to the pre-presidential contact Allende had with the Soviets.[9] While this matter is definitely worthy of study, it is more relevant to examine Allende's attitude toward Moscow, as well as toward Washington, once he assumed the leadership of Chile.

The questions need to be asked. Did Allende actually intend to follow the example of Cuban leader Fidel Castro or even Soviet leader Nikita Khrushchev? Did a Socialist regime in Santiago threaten the safety and physical security of the United States? Nixon and Kissinger answered these questions affirmatively, at least in public.

In this book, I will challenge these affirmations by arguing that national security was not the foremost consideration. Not only did Nixon and Kissinger possess a ruthlessly imperial disdain for Latin America, they also felt the pressure of U.S. business interests. I have tried to understand the mindset of the Nixon administration. I trust the reader to evaluate my effort.

## Notes

1. Document formerly posted on the website of the National Security Archive: www.gwu.edu/~nsarchiv.

2. Richard Helms, *A Look Over My Shoulder: A Life in the Central Intelligence Agency* (New York: Random House, 2003), 404.

3. Margaret Power, *Right-wing Women in Chile, 1964–1973* (University Park, PA: The Pennsylvania State University Press, 2002), 41.

4. See Peter Kornbluh, *The Pinochet File: A Declassified Dossier on Atrocity and Accountability* (New York: The New Press, 2003); John Dinges, *The Condor Years* (New York: The New Press, 2004); and Christopher Hitchens, *The Trial of Henry Kissinger* (New York: Verso, 2002).

5. See John Lewis Gaddis, *Strategies of Containment: A Critical Reappraisal of American National Security Policy During the Cold War* (New York: Oxford University Press, 2005).

6. Robert Dallek, *Nixon and Kissinger: Partners in Power* (New York: HarperCollins Publishers, 2007), 239.

7. See Jonathan Haslam, *The Nixon Administration and the Death of Allende's Chile* (New York: Verso, 2005), and Kristian Gustafson, *Hostile Intent: U.S. Covert Operations in Chile, 1964–1974* (Washington, D.C.: Potomac Books, 2007).

8. Gustafson, *Hostile Intent*, 29.

9. Gustafson, *Hostile Intent*, 31.

# CHAPTER ONE

—— ⚬⚬⚬ ——

# Nixon and Latin America

The evidence indicates the profound influence of multinational corporations on the administration's Chilean policy, but historical actions are rarely monocausal. It is important to understand why the president was so receptive to that influence in the first place. His attitude toward Chile was but a specific application of his attitude toward Latin America as a whole. Long before his arrival in the White House, his own experiences in that part of world shaped his outlook.

As a vice president frustrated by his lack of influence over President Dwight D. Eisenhower, Nixon made a goodwill tour of South America at the behest of his superior in 1958. Ironically, he bypassed Chile, where his South American policies later would bear the greatest weight, because that nation's president was on a state visit to the United States. Nixon and his wife, Pat, enjoyed reasonably calm tours of Uruguay, Argentina, Paraguay, and Bolivia, but hostility greeted them in Peru. While visiting San Marcos University in the capital city of Lima, Nixon heard the chants of "¡Fuera Nixon!"—"Go Home Nixon!" and even "¡Muera Nixon!"—"Death to Nixon!"[1]

More likely than not, the demonstrators merely viewed Nixon as a convenient target for their resentment of Washington policy. After all, the vice-president enjoyed no role in shaping that policy; Eisenhower had little confidence in him. Still, he could have at least tried to understand their frustration, but his version of dialogue was actually little more than a monologue. "I want to talk to you! Why are you afraid of the truth?" the young vice president shouted at the demonstrators. He had the truth; they did not.[2]

They responded with rocks, one of which broke the tooth of a Secret Service agent. Nixon's combative nature compelled him to react foolhardily: "As we drove away, I stood up in the convertible and shouted, 'You are cowards, you are afraid of the truth!'"[3]

Returning to his hotel, Nixon insisted on getting out of his car to confront yet another mob. One man with an obvious fondness for chewing tobacco spat right into the vice-president's face. Insecure and combative by nature, Nixon reacted by "planting a healthy kick on his shins. Nothing I did all day made me feel better."[4]

Nixon could have chosen not to react at all, but he was not the sort of man to handle any political challenge, civil or otherwise, with any degree of good grace. Just as he could not handle the tobacco-chewer without lashing out, he could not deal with Allende in a calm and reasonable manner twelve years afterward. Something intrinsic to the Nixon psychology compelled him to crush his opponents rather than work to resolve his differences with them. The hostility, resentment, and drive for power that characterized his personality were but a manifestation of his self-hatred. A man who cannot love himself must dominate others.[5]

In any case, Nixon's experience in Venezuela failed to instill in him any desire for conciliation with Latin Americans. After landing at the Caracas airport, the vice president and his wife stood at attention for the Venezuelan national anthem. "For a second it seemed as if it had begun to rain, and then I realized that the crowd on the observation deck just above our heads was showering us with spit," Nixon recalled in his memoirs. "It fell on our faces and our hair. I saw Pat's bright red suit grow dark with tobacco-brown splotches."[6]

Following his second salivary baptism, Nixon barely survived an attack by a vicious mob. The attack began with rocks, and then a man tried to smash the window with an iron pipe. "Then I realized that the crowd was rocking the car back and forth—slower and higher each time," Nixon wrote. "I remembered that it was a common tactic for mobs to turn a car over and then set it on fire."[7]

Miraculously, the car broke free from the clutches of the rioters. As horrifying as his close call was, the idea that the Venezuelan people might have had legitimate grievances against the United States did not occur to Nixon. Not only had the Eisenhower administration awarded Venezuelan dictator Perez Jimenez a medal, it had welcomed him and his chief of the secret police to the United States after his ouster.[8] Publicly and inaccurately, he attributed the violence to outside forces:

I held a press conference late in the afternoon and made the same point that I had made in Lima: that the men and women who had led the riots could not claim to be loyal to their country because their first loyalty was to the international Communist conspiracy. I said that it would be very dangerous to ascribe the riots to the fact that after ten years of repressive dictatorship the people did not know how to exercise restraint in enjoying their new freedom. Those mobs were communists led by Communists. And they had no devotion to freedom at all.[9]

It was convenient for Nixon, and for the nation he represented, to overlook the realities of Latin American nationalism, to publicly minimize Peruvian and Venezuelan aspirations by attributing them to the plotting of Soviet agents. Yet in private, Nixon did not blame the Soviet Union for troubles south of the border. Rather, he expressed ethnocentric assumptions about Latin Americans: that they were primitive, easily led, and lacking in the ability to govern themselves. Of course, U.S. policymakers widely shared these assumptions, and Nixon did not suddenly acquire them in 1958. Due at least in part to that ill-starred tour of the region, however, Nixon came to equate Latin American democracy with violence and irrationality. Thirteen years later, in fact, President Nixon doubted the capacity of speakers of all the Romantic tongues, not just Spanish, for self-government. In a taped conversation with Helms and Kissinger, Nixon complimented the authoritarian style of former French President Charles de Gaulle:

I mean France is, is, is a Latin country. It couldn't, even France, with all its sophistication, couldn't handle democracy. You can't. The Italians, that's their problem. They can't afford the [unintelligible] democracy. [Unintelligible] Spain, and no country in Latin America that I know of, except for Colombia.[10]

As a profound cynic, his scoffing of democracy anywhere should not be surprising. Indeed, his self-destruction in the Watergate scandal shows he extended that very cynical disregard to democracy in his own country, but his contempt for Latin American political processes was striking.

The Nixon psychology was a contradictory one. Not everything the president said was consistent or even logical. In spite of his disdain for all Latin peoples, Nixon showed greater respect for the European variety. He was more prepared to tolerate self-determination for the Latin countries of the Old World.

Portugal best demonstrates this attitude. At the beginning of his presidency, Nixon cultivated close ties with the right-wing authoritarian regime in Lisbon. Portugal was an important member of NATO, and Washington greatly valued its lease of the Lajes air base in the Portuguese Azores. So favorably did Nixon and Kissinger view the Portuguese government that they tolerated its brutal colonial presence in Mozambique, Angola, and Guinea-Bissau.

In 1974, the conservative Lisbon regime fell to a popular left-wing military coup. Even though the new socialist government that followed included communists, the Nixon White House did nothing to intervene.[11] Ironically, the new Portuguese administration was probably as progressive as the Chilean one had been in Allende's time. What was intolerable in Latin America was easily tolerated in Europe.

For example, when Fidel Castro came to power fifteen years earlier, Nixon took it for granted that the United States had the right to meddle in Cuban affairs. He justified North American support for Castro's predecessor, the notorious dictator, Fulgencio Batista: "From the U.S. point of view, Batista at least was friendly; Castro turned out to be an implacable and dangerous enemy."[12]

Nixon was not the first U.S. politician to favor repressive government in Latin America, but interestingly, he did not hesitate to make his preference publicly known later. As nervous as the advent of Castro made the Eisenhower administration, the president still wanted Nixon to feel him out. In April of 1959, the vice president met with Castro, who had come to Washington to speak before the American Society of Newspaper Editors. Nixon included his memorandum of that meeting in his memoirs. Although he could not even determine whether Castro was a communist, the vice president assumed he knew all the answers to Cuba's problems. While Nixon condemned Castro for his authoritarian methods, what he actually resented was the leader's strong support from his own people rather than his failure to hold elections:

> It was this almost slavish subservience to prevailing majority opinion—the voice of the mob—rather than his naïve attitude toward communism and his obvious lack of understanding of even the most elementary economic principles which concerned me most in understanding in evaluating what kind of leader he might eventually turn out to be. That is the reason why I spent as much time as I could trying to emphasize that he had a great gift of leadership, but that it was the responsibility of a leader not always to follow public opinion but to help direct it in the proper channels-not to give people what they think they want at a time of emotional stress but to make them want what they ought to have.[13]

Indeed, the Chilean coup was not the first in Latin America to earn Nixon's approval. He later acknowledged his awareness of Eisenhower's plot to overthrow Castro, foreshadowing President John F. Kennedy's disastrous

Bay of Pigs operation.[14] Although the vice president had minimal influence with Eisenhower, he shared the enthusiasm of far more important advisors for the scheme. He repeatedly pressured his liaison man with the CIA: "How are the boys doing at the [CIA]? Are they falling dead over there? What in the world are they doing that takes months?"[15]

Nine years later, when Nixon finally reached the pinnacle of power himself, he quickly seized control of the foreign policy apparatus from the State Department, but that abrupt and ruthless seizure was not a one-man operation. His assistant was his national security advisor, Dr. Henry Kissinger, a professor of government at Harvard University. In the public eye, the academic came to overshadow the president to such an extent that friction developed between the two men. Ultimately, however, Kissinger was a skilled and cunning courtier, and the negotiations for which he won such global acclaim, such as the overture to China and the SALT agreement with the Soviet Union, were made because the president wanted them to be made. Whether dealing with Europe or Asia, the president and his advisor worked as an effective team because they shared common ideological ground. Their shared disdain for Latin America enabled their joint campaign to destabilize the Allende regime in Chile.

Even before Allende became president, Kissinger tactlessly made that disdain plain to Chilean Foreign Minister Gabriel Valdes in June of 1969. Chile had recently hosted a meeting of the Latin American Coordinating Committee in the seaside town of Viña del Mar. The committee's resolution, dubbed the Consensus of Viña del Mar, called for the opening of the U.S. market to Latin American goods. Perhaps more controversially, the Consensus of Viña del Mar advocated the end of conditional credit from the United States. Beyond that, the Consensus favored the creation of an international fund to assist Third World nations in the interest payments for these loans. Knowing he had the support of twenty-one Latin American nations, Valdes complained to Nixon about the inherently exploitative nature of U.S. assistance. Kissinger confronted Valdes the next day: "Mr. Minister, you made a strange speech. You come here speaking of Latin America, but this is not important. Nothing important can come from the South. History has never been produced in the South. The axis of history starts in Moscow, goes to Bonn, crosses over to Washington, and then goes to Tokyo. What happens in the South is of no importance. You're wasting your time."[16]

To Kissinger, the profound issues of war and peace and national security only concerned Europe and Asia. Latin America did not count. Surely, the national security advisor did not acquire this attitude from Nixon. He had had enough time to ponder international relations in Cambridge's ivory tower.

As a graduate student in the early 1950s, he had mentally resided in the Europe of the early nineteenth century. In his maiden intellectual work, *A World Restored*, Kissinger celebrated the virtues of the imperial order, the so-called balance of power negotiated in the aftermath of Napoleon by the British foreign secretary, Viscount Castlereagh, and the Austrian minister, Prince Klemens von Metternich. While the topic of his dissertation may have seemed antiquated and remote, the young scholar meant to apply its theme to his own time. "He had become concerned about the challenge of Soviet communism, so he explored the threats posed during the early nineteenth century by a 'revolutionary' power, France, that defied the legitimate international system," Kissinger biographer Walter Isaacson observed.[17]

Although Kissinger, in his own mind, likened the destructive force of Napoleon to the influential presence of the Soviet Union, the treatment of defeated France at the hands of Metternich and Castlereagh bears strong resemblance to the way the Nixon administration handled Latin America in the 1970s. When the Tsar of Russia called for the holding of elections in France to replace Napoleon, Metternich successfully opposed the idea, advocating the restoration of the Bourbon monarchy instead. Like his conservative admirer Kissinger, Metternich valued order over justice. The Austrian feared democracy "because foreign powers could not appeal to the people in a dynastic question without undermining the existence of *all* thrones."[18]

Castlereagh and Metternich both denied their intention to interfere in French affairs, just as Kissinger denied any interference in Chilean affairs a century and a half later. Yet, that was precisely what they did. Essentially, Castlereagh and Metternich imposed another tyranny upon the French people in order to meet their own ends. They rejected the democratic alternative not for the security and protection of the Austrian and British people, but for the security and protection of the imperial status quo. Kissinger accepted this elitist reasoning uncritically: "An order whose structure is accepted by all major powers is 'legitimate.' An order containing a power which considers its structure oppressive is 'revolutionary.' The security of a domestic order resides in the preponderant power of authority, that of an international order in the balance of forces and in its expression, the equilibrium."[19]

Kissinger the scholar applauded a European arrangement that permitted strong nations to manipulate weaker ones; Kissinger the statesman applied the force and might of the United States against Chilean democracy.

Richard Nixon succeeded President Lyndon Johnson on January 20, 1969, he was determined to preserve the superpower status of the United States when the floundering war in Vietnam seemed to indicate its decline. Vietnam, China, and the Soviet Union ranked foremost in his mind, and Latin America only had a place in the back of it. As political scientist Abraham Lowenthal notes, Nixon's idea of an innovative Latin American policy was "cutting back U.S. programs, toning down U.S. rhetoric, and generally reducing the U.S. presence."[20]

In spite of his own diplomatic priorities, however, Nixon knew that the United States had $12 billion in assets in Latin America, a highly volatile region. "Latin America is barely holding its own in the race between production and population," Nixon had warned the elite Bohemian Club in 1967. "As it continues to fall further behind the rest of the world, it becomes a tinder box for revolution."[21]

So, Nixon probably believed he had no choice but to dispatch Governor Nelson A. Rockefeller of New York on several visits to Latin America. Rockefeller, who had served as assistant secretary of state for Latin American affairs in the Roosevelt administration, prepared a report in 1969 that called for a "special relationship" with Latin America.[22]

For an aristocrat born to privilege unimagined by the president himself in his own youth, Rockefeller had marked compassion for the average Latin American peasant: "The *campesino* goes to bed hungry every night of his life. He will probably never see a doctor, a hospital, a dentist, or a nurse. He has little hope of being vaccinated against smallpox, or inoculated against typhoid, tetanus, or yellow fever. If he becomes ill, there is no medicine; he trusts to fate that he will either get better, or die."[23]

Compared to the average North American, who could expect to live for seventy years at the time of the report, life for the common Latin American was hard. The life expectancy in Central and South America and the Caribbean was only fifty-seven years.[24] Given the lack of clean water and limited access to nutritious food, 20 percent of the children in many parts of the region could not even expect to live that long, perishing before their fifth birthday.[25] The severe disparity of wealth between the United States and Latin America did not bode well for the stability of the Western Hemisphere as a whole. "Forces of anarchy, terror and subversion are loose in the Americas," the report stated. "Moreover, this fact has too long gone unheeded in the United States."[26]

Rockefeller criticized the United States for permitting vested interests to dictate its Latin American policy. This rigid and one-sided approach profoundly damaged hemispheric relations. Furthermore, the United States held back Latin American potential: "Its assistance and trade policies, so critical to the development process of other nations, have been distorted to serve a variety of purposes in the United States having nothing to do with the aspirations and interests of its neighbors; in fact, all too often these purposes have been in sharp conflict with the goals of development."[27]

To help remedy the Latin American crisis, Rockefeller urged Nixon to pay proper attention to it. He recommended the creation of a secretary of Western Hemisphere affairs. This cabinet-level officer would report directly to the secretary of state and the president.[28] Rockefeller also called for the establishment of a Western Hemisphere Institute for Education, Science, and Culture through the already existing Organization of American States. He even wanted the United States to provide $100 million a year in order to promote literacy and education in Latin America.[29]

As today, many economists and policymakers in the 1960s bloodlessly approached development in a bloodlessly statistical manner. The annual 4.9 percent increase in Latin America's Gross National Product during that decade must have encouraged them. By contrast, Rockefeller and his team of researchers had the wisdom and the humanity to see beyond the statistics. They pointed out that the Latin American population grew by 2.9 percent simultaneously. At that rate, they calculated, the quality of life in Latin America would not improve until 2004. "That is not good enough," Rockefeller concluded.[30]

To encourage the kind of development that would lift the standard of living, Rockefeller favored granting trade concessions desired by Latin American governments. He resembled a left-wing proponent of dependency theory in his complaint that although almost two-thirds of exports from developed nations consisted of manufactured goods, raw materials comprised 87 percent of exports from Latin America.[31] This imbalance created a vast disparity in wealth, and the governor offered a solution not only for Latin America but for the entire Third World: "The United States should work out a balanced approach to the problem of expanding hemisphere trade in industrial products by moving to a system of tariff preferences for imports from all developing nations."[32]

In the aftermath of the 1993 North American Free Trade Agreement, the removal of trade barriers now carries a bad stench in progressive circles, but Rockefeller's proposal was, at least, a thoughtful one. He called for provisions for U.S. workers whose livelihoods would potentially be threatened by the flood of imports from developing countries.[33] In turn, Rockefeller sought to prevent U.S. domination of Latin American markets. Under his plan, Latin American countries would slowly lower their own existing barriers to U.S.

goods, perhaps even making the process as long as a decade or two. "In this way, their infant industries can grow to a stature in which they are fully competitive in world markets," Rockefeller noted.[34]

While the opening of markets would assist development, the governor realized Latin America also needed financial assistance from the United States and the rest of the developed world. High-interest loans from the multinational lending agencies, which were heavily influenced by the United States, had left Latin America mired in debt, so Rockefeller proposed lower interest rates and easier conditions for repayment. "The basic concern of the United States lies not in how much interest is paid, but whether or not the funds 'pay off' in helping a country develop," Rockefeller argued, taking the position opposite that of the World Bank and the International Monetary Fund.[35]

Ironically, Rockefeller made one specific proposal that later could have averted the financial blockade of Chile. His report stated, "The Executive Branch should seek the suspension or modifications of the Pelley, Conte, Hickenlooper, Symington and Roess amendments which affect the extension of assistance including cut-offs where countries purchase sophisticated weapons, or seize weapons, or seize United States fishing boats operating without a license, or expropriate without due compensation."[36]

Smarting after the Cuban revolution, Congress had attached the Hickenlooper amendment to the Foreign Assistance Act of 1961. At the discretion of the president, the Hickenlooper amendment denied aid to nations that confiscated property belonging to U.S. corporations or citizens in violation of established standards of compensation. Offending countries could lose assistance from the Inter-American Development Bank, the International Monetary Fund, and the World Bank, all international organizations that were heavily influenced by the United States.[37]

For a man whose family had extracted great wealth from Latin America, recommending either the suspension or modification of the Hickenlooper amendment was extraordinary advice. Standard Oil, a Rockefeller family concern, held a major interest in the Venezuelan and Peruvian petroleum industries, for example.[38] At the time, the expropriation movement presented a grave threat to Standard Oil, among other Rockefeller assets in Latin America. Rockefeller favored development even when it came at the expense of his own capitalist class. Unfortunately, the White House did not follow this advice once Allende came to power, using the Hickenlooper amendment to punish Chile.

Despite many of Rockefeller's sound recommendations, his report had some flaws. In retrospect, his portrayal of the Latin American military as a progressive force is risible. He probably exaggerated the impact of growing lower-class enlistment in the armed forces: "Increasingly, their concern and dedication is to the eradication of poverty and the improvement of the lot of the oppressed, both in rural and urban areas."[39]

As much as he advocated progressive change, Rockefeller paradoxically desired to revive the traditional dependency by providing the military with greater support. Thinking like a stereotypical realist, Rockefeller wanted the United States to work with Latin American dictators. "It should recognize that diplomatic relations are merely practical conveniences and not measures of moral judgement," he insisted. "This can be done by maintaining formal lines of communication without embracing such regimes."[40]

Rockefeller made clear his fear that Fidel Castro's experiment would inspire the rest of Latin America. He meant to provide an alternative to Marxism. A more cynical reader of his somewhat contradictory report might accuse Rockefeller of recommending reforms and minor sacrifices solely to prevent even greater losses for his own social stratum. In truth, Rockefeller does give the reader the impression that he would have preferred a regressive leader who served U.S. interests to a progressive one who did not. Nevertheless, if Nixon had taken Rockefeller's maxim seriously, and literally, he would have allowed Allende to complete his presidential term unhindered: "The United States cannot allow disagreements with the form or the domestic policies of other American governments to jeopardize its basic objective of working with and for their people to our mutual benefit."[41]

Historians blessed with a vivid imagination can easily hear the president's snort upon his receipt of this report. Perhaps he simply did not want to believe what Rockefeller had to say. A passionate student of foreign affairs, he strictly adhered to the tutelage of Kissinger, who fixated solely on the Soviet Union, Western Europe, China, and Japan.[42] Rockefeller was not surprised that his report had no apparent impact on policy. Before attaching himself to Nixon during the 1968 campaign, Kissinger had served as the governor's foreign policy advisor during his own presidential runs. "It was not, Rockefeller ruefully concluded, entirely Nixon's fault," his speechwriter recalled. "Nelson had never been able to infect his friend Henry Kissinger with his own passion for Latin America; and Henry was now largely shaping the Nixon foreign policy."[43]

In actuality, Nixon's neglect of Latin American problems amounted to a refusal to alter the status quo, to question his country's domination of the region. When the president bothered to think about Latin America at all, he failed to produce any constructive ideas, for he wished to preserve North American influence, even at the expense of the Latin American people.

In contrast to Rockefeller who, for all his intellectual and philosophical limitations, had a sincere concern for Latin Americans, Nixon just went through the motions. Reflecting aloud on Latin American development for the benefit of a speechwriter in 1971, he made a fumbling attempt at eloquence: "We cannot have change. Change alone, without peace, is wrong, and peace without change is wrong. It must be that we live in a changed world. The Latin American countries particularly are changing, the Americas. The young people demand change. They demand progress for many people. And the other thing is that the enormous importance of stability in that part of the world by peaceful change."[44]

As Nixon gathered his thoughts, his condescension to Latin Americans yet again came to the fore:

> You know how the Latins are. They love to look to the flowery language. The president deeply believes in the Americas. He is all, he is for what they are. He watches these programs personally. He puts his true endorsement behind them. . . . And then, finally, the idea that we're, we in America are, that that that I believe that above everything else, in the relations between us and the American family, the key word is dignity. That we must recognize the individual dignity of every country large and small, and that we cannot have dignity without self-reliance.[45]

For all his rhetoric about dignity, Nixon still did not believe Latin American people merited the dignity of self-government. "Look at Latin America," Nixon said later that year. "They all followed the American constitution. Making a country in Latin America is making it dead. The only one that's really making it at the moment is Brazil . . . but it's now a dictatorship."[46]

Military dictators in the region enjoyed the president's wholehearted support. "When you look at Latin America, not a very encouraging place to see, except those countries that got dictators in it and successful dictators, they're all in a hell of a mess," Nixon confided to the chairman of the Joint Chiefs of Staff, Admiral Thomas Moorer.[47]

What probably intensified his paranoia about Allende's *Unidad Popular* and other Latin American nationalist movements was the most successful one of all, Castro's Cuban experiment. If Cuba could relinquish its status as a U.S. client, what would stop her sister states from doing the same? Allende's warm overtures to Castro certainly did not soothe Nixon's anxieties. "We throw in the towel on the Cubans and the effect on the rest of Latin America could be massive, encouraging the [unintelligible] Communists, Marxists, Allende, or call it what you will, to try for revolutions," Nixon told

CIA Director Helms.[48] Advising the president, Helms remained committed to treating Cuba as a pariah: "Sir, [unintelligible] a year ago on this question, and I gave you the answer then that I was opposed to the idea of relenting on Cuba. I'm just as opposed today, in fact, even more so. I think what's happened to Chile makes it even more advisable to keep a tough line on Cuba. I think that if you give the impression that we're now soft on Cuba in the middle of these things, I think that what I'm afraid is the wave of Latin America anyway is going to crash on the beach a lot faster."[49]

Nixon was determined to protect the beach from the crashing wave. Contrary to the standard Cold War rhetoric of the day, the administration did not truly fear that a Marxist presence in Latin American would directly result in a Soviet takeover of the region. "Latin America is of relatively priority for the Soviet Union," a National Security Study Memorandum noted in 1969.[50] The NSC Memorandum, which was directly submitted to Kissinger himself, hardly portrayed Castro as an agent of a Soviet plot to overrun the United States: "Castro has no hesitation in opposing local Communist parties which appear too 'orthodox' and Moscow-oriented, and he will consciously seek to steal the allegiance of their members."[51]

The Joint Chiefs of Staff, while generally paranoid about the Soviet Union, also viewed Latin America as a region with little potential for major conflict. "If the U.S. and the USSR are engaging in a technologically explosive arms race," the Joint Chiefs reported, "and if the Middle East is witnessing, in the constant effort to upset weapons parity, at least an arms walk, then Latin America is engaged at most in an arms crawl."[52] In fact, the generals ridiculed their counterparts to the south for exploiting Cold War tensions for more arms and equipment: "The spectre of the monolithic, continental communist threat they visualize has been used by some Latin American military leaders as a 'bogeyman' in hopes of influencing U.S. opinion."[53] Even more importantly, the Joint Chiefs all but dismissed the idea of the Soviet menace. "Military leaders continue to emphasize the external threat," they observed in the evaluation of the Latin American armed forces, "even when the U.S. considers it largely a product of their imagination (Chile, Ecuador) or of their own self-aggrandizing invention (Peru)."[54] Admittedly, the Joint Chiefs made their report one year before the election of Allende, but their dismissal of Soviet infiltration is striking.

Although the NSC, in its own memorandum, did point to a few factors that potentially made Latin America relevant to national security, they were not vital ones. It was unlikely that any foreign power would attack the United States from the Caribbean nations, despite their close location. The Cuban Missile Crisis of 1962, which involved the Soviet placement of medium-range and intermediate-range ballistic missiles in Cuba, was largely a defensive reaction against U.S. aggression in the Bay of Pigs invasion and other assorted CIA plots. Moreover, the Soviet Union's intercontinental ballistic missiles made the concept of Cuban Missile Crisis II obsolete. The interests emphasized by the NSC study were psychological and economic. The pretentious wording of the study alone indicated that it simply felt good to have "the diplomatic support for our worldwide policies represented by 23 nations generally submissive to U.S. leadership, at least on 'East-West' issues."[55] It was an exercise in geopolitical superiority. Nor did the NSC overlook the "approximately $12 billion in U.S. direct investment, a favorable balance of payments, and a flow of important raw materials."[56]

In order to promote these interests, the Nixon administration not only provided Latin American friends with military aid, but economic support as well. Nixon resented the efforts of the State Department and the international lending agencies to make respect for human rights a condition for loans. Conversing with Kissinger, Nixon had harsh words for International Monetary Fund President Pierre-Paul Schweitzer and World Bank President Robert S. McNamara, as well as Secretary of State William Rogers:

> You were right and Bill's wrong. . . . They are playing the role of God in judging not just the economic viability of loans, but whether or not loans should be made to nations that aren't [sic] live up to the moral criteria that we think governments should live up to. I don't think that has anything to do with a loan. The same argument that he argues is that it does, on the ground, that affects stability and so forth. Do you show me, on the other hand, see my view, if a loan's to be made, maybe a dictatorship is the most stable damn country to make it to, and if it is, make it to a dictatorship.[57]

Tellingly, Nixon did not advocate generous aid for Latin American democracies that could meet its financial obligations. A president who befriends dictators generally has little concern for those subject to their brutal rule. If he did not regard loans as a means of uplifting for the Latin American people, why did he favor their use at all? Obviously, financial aid greatly assisted repressive governments, whose maintenance served U.S. interests, or at least U.S. interests as the Nixon administration saw them. In the end, the administration desired easy access to the raw materials of the Americas.

This desire was emphasized at an Oval Office meeting with Kissinger, Treasury Secretary John Connally, and Robert McNamara on the importance of international lending agencies. Connally, a trusted presidential advisor, reminded McNamara that Europe was emerging as a competitor for the natural resources of the Third World:

> But there's, there's a feeling now in the international monetary field . . . that European community that they're, they're trying to build an economic base that is much stronger than the United States and that's fine, nothing wrong with ambition; if they desire it, they should do it. But more than that, you have more [unintelligible] job because the United States in the next decade, in the next twenty-five years, is going to become more and more reliant on raw materials from other, from other lands, [unintelligible] and that's become increasingly more true each day.[58]

Agreeing with Connally, McNamara pointed to Latin America, which he described as "a hotbed of expropriation without adequate compensation today."[59] Nevertheless, McNamara advocated cooperation with other members of the First World in order to contain economic nationalism in the Third. "It can't be done overnight and there are some conflicts of interest between Japan and the U.S. and Germany and the U.S. and France and the U.S., but in the long run, no one of these countries should stand alone," McNamara said, differing with Connally. "Nor can we at the international institutions stand alone."[60] If Nixon's most important associates had genuinely feared Soviet penetration of Latin America, it seems that they would have welcomed Western European investment as a financial bulwark. This was not the case. Their concerns about the area were economic rather than military.

In response, Kissinger duly noted a recent presidential order, which required the American member of each multinational bank to vote against loans to any country that had expropriated American property, unless the treasury secretary requested otherwise. To Kissinger, this stringent policy justly kept developing nations, including the Latin American states, at the service of the "advanced" ones. Most importantly, the policy ensured American predominance. "I think from the American side, by having the secretary of the treasury now in charge of the votes in international institutions, so that unless someone can convince them to vote yes, the vote is no in expropriation cases," Kissinger observed. "I think we have the control."[61]

In its promotion of U.S. economic interests in Latin America, the Nixon administration went beyond manipulating the multinational lending agencies. The president himself directly offered his support to corporate heads. For example, when Charles Bluhdorn of Gulf + Western paid an Oval Office visit in 1971, Nixon gave him a warm reception. Bluhdorn sought to protect Gulf + Western property in the Dominican Republic, which featured railroads, sugar plantations, a hotel, and an automotive parts plant. Alarmed by the leftist rise in Latin America, Bluhdorn maintained a firm friendship with the dictator of the Dominican Republic, Joaquin Balaguer. In fact, the friendship was so firm that Balaguer had entrusted Bluhdorn with a letter to Nixon. At the meeting, Bluhdorn emphatically disapproved of turbulent change in Chile, Peru, and Bolivia. In a tone lacking in deference for presidential authority, Bluhdorn lectured Nixon not to tolerate any challenge to the America's unofficial empire:

> I think that the most important single thing for the United States, being born here myself, is respect for the Americans and for the American flag. And I don't believe that this type of an attitude does anything certain except to encourage these people to go forward and forward and to continue a trend, which in my opinion, will destroy whatever is left of the Monroe Doctrine because we have those subversive elements moving in. The Chilean foreign minister has been in Moscow. You've been to Russia. I've been to Russia. I know for a fact, sir, that there's great pride, great pride in Russia, that they think they're infiltrating the Western Hemisphere.[62]

Like the Latin American generals, Bluhdorn may have cynically used the legend of the Soviet bogeyman just to frighten Nixon, but the president's lengthy response does not reveal any Cold War paranoia on his part. Economics, not national security, determined his Latin American policy. Nixon's personal bogeyman was expropriation, not infiltration. He feared leftist regimes would discourage U.S. investment. "How can we expect American business to go in?" Nixon wondered aloud. "John Connally pointed out . . . that under this whole gang [economic nationalists] . . . we lost a billion dollars because of expropriation."[63]

Nixon gave Bluhdorn no reason to doubt his sympathy. As he had with his own associates, the president expressed his distaste for idealism in foreign policy: "I have no patience with those that are against the Dominican Republic. That is the attitude of the State Department. It's not mine. They're against it because they consider it a dictatorship. I don't give a damn what it is. I'm for 'em. Is that clear?"[64]

The president assured Bluhdorn that he would maintain a hard line against leftists in Latin America: "Friends of the United States will be rewarded. Enemies of the United States will be punished. And that includes Peru, to the extent we can. It includes Bolivia, to the extent we can, and it includes, by all means, Chile, to the extent we can. Now that's the way the game has to be played."[65]

As much as Nixon demanded Latin American nations, friendly or otherwise, to fulfill the economic needs of his own country, he did not feel obligated to offer anything substantial in return, such as an open market for their goods. In fact, the president suddenly and effectively narrowed access to the U.S. market with an import surcharge in August of 1971.[66] For Latin America, there were no real rewards.

## Notes

1. Richard Nixon, *RN: The Memoirs of Richard Nixon* (New York: Grosset & Dunlap, 1978), 186–87.

2. Nixon, *RN*, 188.

3. Nixon, *RN*, 188.

4. Stephen E. Ambrose, *Nixon: The Education of a Politician, 1913–1962* (New York: Touchstone, 1987), 469.

5. For a psychologically perceptive study of Nixon, see Fawn M. Brodie, *Richard Nixon: The Shaping of His Character* (New York: W.W. Norton & Company, 1981).

6. Nixon, *RN*, 189.

7. Nixon, *RN*, 190.

8. Lars Schoultz, *Beneath the United States: A History of U.S. Policy toward Latin America* (Cambridge, MD: Harvard University Press, 1998), 353.

9. Nixon, *RN*, 191–92.

10. Conversation #462-5. 8:30a.m.–10:15a.m., Oval Office. March 5, 1971, *Nixon Tapes*, Nixon Presidential Materials Project, National Archives II, College Park, Maryland.

11. Mario Del Pero, "I limiti della distensione. Gli Stati Uniti e implosione del regime portoghese," in *Contemporanea* 8, no. 4 (October 2005).

12. Nixon, *RN*, 203.

13. Nixon, *RN*, 202.

14. Nixon, *RN*, 202.

15. Ambrose, *Nixon: The Education of a Politician*, 550.

16. Seymour M. Hersh, *The Price of Power: Kissinger in the Nixon White House* (New York: Summit Books, 1983), 263, and Albert L. Michaels, "The Alliance for Progress and Chile's 'Revolution in Liberty,' 1964–1970," *Journal of Interamerican Studies and World Affairs* 18, no. 1 (February 1976): 93.

17. Walter Isaacson, *Kissinger: A Biography* (New York: Simon & Schuster, 1992), 75.

18. Henry A. Kissinger, *A World Restored: Metternich, Castlereagh and the Problems of Peace, 1812–22* (Boston: Houghton Mifflin Company, 1957), 123.

19. Kissinger, *A World Restored*, 145.

20. Abraham F. Lowenthal, *Partners in Conflict: The United States and Latin America in the 1990s* (Baltimore: Johns Hopkins University Press, 1990), 41.

21. Hal Brands, "Richard Nixon and Economic Nationalism in Latin America: The Problem of Expropriations, 1969–1974," *Diplomacy and Statecraft* 18 (2007): 218.

22. Lowenthal, *Partners in Conflict*, 41.

23. Nelson A. Rockefeller, "Quality of Life in the Americas," page 121 of *Report of a U.S. Presidential Mission for the Western Hemisphere*, NSC Meetings, Box H-24, Folder 2, Nixon Presidential Materials Project, National Archives II, College Park, Maryland.

24. Rockefeller, "Quality of Life in the Americas," 121.

25. Rockefeller, "Quality of Life in the Americas," 119.

26. Rockefeller, "Quality of Life in the Americas," 49.

27. Nelson A. Rockefeller, *The Rockefeller Report on the Americas: The Official Report of the United States Presidential Mission for the Western Hemisphere*, ed. the *New York Times* (Chicago: Quadrangle Press, 1969), 21.

28. Rockefeller, *The Rockefeller Report on the Americas*, 45.

29. Rockefeller, *The Rockefeller Report on the Americas*, 115.

30. Rockefeller, *The Rockefeller Report on the Americas*, 68.

31. Rockefeller, *The Rockefeller Report on the Americas*, 72.

32. Rockefeller, *The Rockefeller Report on the Americas*, 75.

33. Rockefeller, *The Rockefeller Report on the Americas*, 76.

34. Rockefeller, *The Rockefeller Report on the Americas*, 75.

35. Rockefeller, "Quality of Life in the Americas," 77.

36. Rockefeller, "Quality of Life in the Americas," 77.

37. Brands, "Richard Nixon and Economic Nationalism," 217. Foreign Assistance Act of 1964, P.L. 88–633 § 301(d)(4) (1964). 78 Stat. 1009, 1013. 22 U.S.C.A. § 2370 (e)(2).

38. Peter H. Smith, *Talons of the Eagle: Dynamics of U.S.-Latin American Relations* (New York: Oxford University Press, 2000), 75–78. See the North American Congress on Latin America newsletter *The Rockefeller Empire: Latin America*, April-June 1969.

39. Rockefeller, *The Rockefeller Report on the Americas*, 32.

40. Rockefeller, *The Rockefeller Report on the Americas*, 58.

41. Rockefeller, *The Rockefeller Report on the Americas*, 59.

42. Lowenthal, *Partners in Conflict*, 42.

43. Joseph E. Persico, *The Imperial Rockefeller: A Biography of Nelson A. Rockefeller* (New York: Simon and Schuster, 1982), 106.

44. Conversation #458-5. 3:46p.m.?–4:05p.m., Oval Office. February 25, 1971. *Nixon Tapes.*

45. Conversation #458-5. 3:46p.m.?–4:05p.m., Oval Office. February 25, 1971. *Nixon Tapes.*

46. Conversation #497-2. 11:20a.m.–11:51p.m., Oval Office. May 11, 1971. *Nixon Tapes.*

47. Conversation #490-14. 11:38a.m.–12:03p.m., Oval Office. May 4, 1971. *Nixon Tapes.*

48. Conversation #462-5. 8:30a.m.–10:15a.m., Oval Office. March 5, 1971. *Nixon Tapes.*

49. Conversation #462-5. 8:30a.m.–10:15a.m., Oval Office. March 5, 1971. *Nixon Tapes.*

50. *A Study of U.S. Policy Toward Latin America: Prepared by National Security Council Interdepartmental Group for Inter-American Affairs (NSC-IG/ARA),* March 1969, 6. National Security Study Memorandum 15, Box H-134, Folder 3. Nixon Presidential Materials Project, National Archives II, College Park, Maryland.

51. *A Study of U.S. Policy Toward Latin America,* 7.

52. *Response to National Security Study Memorandum #68: The Military Establishment in Latin America (C)—As of August 1969—Prepared by the Organization of the Joint Chiefs of Staff,* page 23. National Security Study Memorandum 68, Box H-159, Folder 4. National Archives II, College Park, Maryland.

53. *Response to National Security Study Memorandum #68,* 21.

54. *Response to National Security Study Memorandum #68,* 22.

55. *A Study of U.S. Policy Toward Latin America,* 3.

56. *A Study of U.S. Policy Toward Latin America,* 4.

57. Conversation #517-20. 2:05p.m.–2:38p.m., Oval Office. June 11, 1971. *Nixon Tapes.*

58. Conversation #593-10. 10:08a.m.–10:37p.m., Oval Office. October 15, 1971. *Nixon Tapes.*

59. Conversation #593-10. 10:08a.m.–10:37p.m., Oval Office. October 15, 1971. *Nixon Tapes.*

60. Conversation #593-10. 10:08a.m.–10:37p.m., Oval Office. October 15, 1971. *Nixon Tapes.*

61. Conversation #593-10. 10:08a.m.–10:37p.m., Oval Office. October 15, 1971. *Nixon Tapes.*

62. Conversation #523-4. Unknown time between 3:41p.m.–4:30p.m. June 16, 1971. *Nixon Tapes.*

63. Conversation #523-4. Unknown time between 3:41p.m.–4:30p.m. June 16, 1971. *Nixon Tapes.*

64. Conversation #523-4. Unknown time between 3:41p.m.–4:30p.m. June 16, 1971. *Nixon Tapes.*

65. Conversation #523-4. Unknown time between 3:41p.m.–4:30p.m. June 16, 1971. *Nixon Tapes.*

66. Lowenthal, *Partners in Conflict,* 42.

# CHAPTER TWO

—∞∞∞—

# Early U.S.–Chilean Relations

As profoundly as the United States feared challenges to its hegemony in many parts of the world, the superpower remained securely confident that Latin America belonged to its sphere of influence. In early 1970, Chile was definitely a part of that empire, but Washington was not the first power center to dominate the Latin American nation.

While Chile won the battle for political independence from Spain in 1818, London quickly gained economic control. "By 1849 some fifty British firms controlled most Chilean exports: nearly 50 percent of the value of these exports went to England," political scientist Brian Loveman observed, "and English goods accounted for 30 to 40 percent of the value of Chilean imports."[1]

While evading customs duties, British merchants managed to drive up the price of vital necessities and bring down the price of luxuries at the same time. This arrangement only benefited the Chilean upper class, causing great harm to the common people of Chile, whose quality of life descended to the standards of the late seventeenth century. "However, lacking the basic financial infrastructure and economic clout to compete in international markets," Loveman continues, "the Chilean economic elites, practically out of necessity, allowed themselves to be incorporated into the web of international commerce which the British spun throughout Latin America and elsewhere in the nineteenth century."[2]

Chile enriched the British Empire with its own abundant natural resources.

-eee-

The British purchased Chilean agricultural products such as hides and wool, in addition to wheat, corn and barley, even when Argentina, Australia, and the United States emerged as rival suppliers during the mid-nineteenth century.[3] What truly introduced Chile to the global economy, however, were its deposits of silver, copper, and nitrates. In particular, the British invested heavily in the nitrate mines, or *salitreras*, to the north, owning half of them. President Jose Manuel Balmaceda resentfully pointed his finger in 1890 at one British *salitrero*, John Thomas North, for seizing "the profit of native wealth . . . to give to other lands and unknown people the treasures of our soil, our own property, and the riches we require."[4]

The First World War devastated the nitrate industry, ending British patronage of Chile. Ironically, the European conflict, which required nitrate for explosives, simultaneously prevented Chile from exporting it. Even though nitrate production skyrocketed to three million tons by 1917, the British blockade eliminated Germany as a customer. Britain, on the other hand, remained one, but lost the ability to furnish Chile with imports.[5] The United States, emerging as the world's leading economic power, recognized the economic potential and assumed the formerly British role. With the aid of wartime allies, Washington kept the price of nitrates artificially low, ruining Chile's opportunity to profit from the war even as the North American power accumulated vast wealth.[6] Such is the nature of empire.

In any case, the German substitution of synthetic nitrates made the issue, and the Chilean industry itself, obsolete. Copper became Chile's most important export, and the United States became the most important consumer. The U.S. companies that quickly gained control of most of this profitable resource in the 1920s, Anaconda and Kennecott, retained it until the 1970s.[7] This investment was no minor issue for Chile, for Anaconda and Kennecott controlled 7 percent to approximately 20 percent of the country's Gross Domestic Product. Copper financed 10 percent to 40 percent of the public budget, and its exports comprised 30 percent to 80 percent of the national income in hard currency.[8] Ironically, no corporation or industry enjoyed such economic influence in the United States, that paragon of capitalism. "The Rockefellers and the Morgans with all their affiliates at their height were minor operators in comparison to the position that Anaconda and Kennecott occupied for half a century in Chile," noted scholar Theodore H. Moran.[9]

Chileans were not blind to the implications of this corporate phenomenon. The Chilean historian Francisco Encino described it as *denacionalización*, a threat to national integrity.[10] Another Chilean accused the

Anaconda-owned Chuquicamata, the largest open-pit copper mine in the world, of "annihilating the race." The copper towns, he believed, trapped its workers in lives of "misery, promiscuity, alcohol, and degeneration."[11] One resentful politician declared in 1927 that "the government of Chile is subordinated to North America bankers and it cannot undertake any guarantee or sign any loans without the approval of these bankers."[12]

That does not mean that Chile never asserted itself against the wishes of the United States. During World War II, Chile resisted declaring war against the Axis powers until February of 1945.[13] Chilean policymakers, feeling the weight and strength of North American muscle, probably questioned the Allied portrayal of the war as a desperate struggle against German and Japanese tyranny. Moreover, they regarded Washington's promises to safeguard Chile with skepticism. President Franklin D. Roosevelt, after all, expected Chile to join the conflict even as he denied it military aid. In response to a U.S. pledge to secure the Chilean coastline with its own fleet, Foreign Minister Gabriel Rossetti asked, "What fleet? The one sunk in Pearl Harbor?"[14]

Indeed, as the Chileans watched Germany make stunning gains early in the war, some quietly favored the Axis, hoping to break the traditional Anglo-American hold on their country. The Chilean ambassador in Berlin opposed entering the conflict, explaining that "by breaking ties with the Axis we cut the secular ties of vital importance with this continent and we will deliver ourselves to only one of the belligerents."[15]

During the Second World War, Chile's new relationship with the North Americans worked to its disadvantage. Chile lost the opportunity to profit from the hostilities, as it did during the Great War. Chile could not even exploit the increased demand for copper. "Practically all of Chile's copper . . . was marketed through subsidiaries of United States copper firms established in Chile—for whom the Allied governments fixed a ceiling price upon copper products during the course of the war," Loveman reported.[16] In the end, a potentially profitable war cost Chile $100 million to $500 million.[17]

After the surrender of the Axis powers, the United States exploited a growing rivalry with another European power, the Soviet Union, to further impose its will on Chile. The United States insisted that Chile join the "Free World" in opposition to Communism.[18] Amidst growing social unrest, U.S. policymakers feared the impact of Communism on the labor movement. To weaken the collectivist influence, Washington funded the Socialist groups within the Chilean Workers Federation, or CTCH. More ruthlessly, the United States targeted the Communist ministers of Radical President Gabriel Gonzalez Videla when he was vulnerable to the strength of the Communist party.[19] Fearing a Communist takeover of the coal mines, President Gonzalez Videla approached the United States for an emergency supply of coal. "I suggest situation set forth above [reference to a general strike scheduled for late June 1947] be taken into consideration in connection with Chile's request for coal stockpile in its struggle to combat Communism," Ambassador Claude Bowers advised the secretary of state.[20] Once Gonzalez Videla, grasping the expedience of a stronger anti-Communist posture, began to dismiss the Communists from his own Cabinet, the United States made a generous offer of coal.[21]

Gonzalez Videla, who quickly suppressed the labor unrest with police and military assistance, did not rest in his campaign to please his patrons in Washington. Not only did the president end diplomatic relations with the Soviet Union, he arranged for the passage of the Law for the Permanent Defense of Democracy, which banned the Communist party, essentially gutting the labor movement. The president did not spare the agricultural workers from his regressive politics. Law 8891 eradicated the fledgling labor movement in the countryside.[22] Indeed, the policies of Gonzalez and his Radical predecessors radically, and adversely, affected the most vulnerable sectors of society. Between 1938 and 1952, the real income for urban and rural workers alike declined, and more than one-third of Chilean youngsters never received an education.[23]

Gonzalez Videla's immediate successors failed to alleviate the suffering of the working classes, or to break the stranglehold of the United States on the Chilean economy, now mired in recession. The invitation extended by President Carlos Ibañez to the Klein-Saks Mission, an economic advisory group from the United States, indicated that the long dependency would continue. To combat the astronomic inflation of the day, the mission warned the Chilean government not to permit wage increases to match the rise in the cost of living. As orthodox economists, the Klein-Saks team attributed the inflation to disproportionate consumer demand. In addition to wage controls, Klein-Saks advised the Chileans to slash the public budget as well as available bank credit, and to do away with state support of basic consumer goods and services. As devastating as this plan would be for Chilean workers, one suggestion made by Klein-Saks, progressive taxation, displeased the Chilean upper class, and was rejected by the conservative Congress. The legislators accepted the rest of the Klein-Saks blueprint, which aggravated the recession. Although inflation did decline somewhat, meeting expectations, so did industrial growth.[24] In the phrasing of world systems theorist Immanuel Wallerstein, the mission's advice, in the end, reinforced the ability of the capitalist core to exploit peripheral Chile. Despite Chile's efforts to develop its industrial base, the nation remained one of the "hewers of wood and carriers of water," a deliver of raw materials to the more developed world.[25]

By 1958, inflation and economic stagnation remained issues for the politicians to resolve. In that year's presidential campaign, the three major candidates were Dr. Salvador Allende from the left, Eduardo Frei from the center, and Jorge Alessandri from the right.

Of the three candidates, Allende was the most interesting. The senator for the provinces of Antofagasta and Tarapacá, Allende represented the working-class Popular Action Front, or FRAP, which was a coalition of the candidate's own Socialist party and the Communists. A widely accomplished man, he had distinguished himself long before entering the Senate. A physician by training, Allende had joined the administration of President Pedro Aguirre Cerda as minister of health in 1939. During his year-long tenure at the Ministry of Health, Allende had published a book, *La Realidad Médico-Social Chilena*, or the Chilean Medico-Social Reality, which presented the devastating health effects of poverty in Chile.[26]

Amazingly, Washington had had a high regard for Allende in the early 1950s, and the good doctor seemed to reciprocate that regard. Even though Allende had criticized the Law for the Defense of Democracy, Ambassador Bowers described him as "able and decent," as well as an "able physician."[27] It is only when Allende turned against U.S. policy in Latin America that Washington turned against him. When the United States pressured the Organization of American States to pass an "anti-Communist" resolution in Caracas in March of 1954, Allende mocked it. Allende regarded the resolution as little more than propaganda that left the

> impression that the mountains of [our] countries are infested with communists, that our coasts are full of communist ships, that the small country of Guatemala threatens the existence of the largest of the bourgeois countries. Like David and Goliath. But Guatemala does not have a sling. Its only sling is showing the road to follow for introducing progress and liberty in the nations of America.[28]

Disregarding Allende's concerns for the sovereignty and integrity of Latin American nations, the U.S. embassy in Santiago now smeared him as a "Communist," a "commie-liner," and a "dupe."[29]

In June, the U.S.-sponsored coup against Arbenz radicalized Allende further. He realized that when Latin American nations would not submit willingly to Washington's dictates, force would be readily applied. Without a doubt, Allende knew that if Washington could destroy democracy in Guatemala, it could also do so in Chile. Seeking new friends for his country, Allende spent several months not only in Western Europe, but also the Soviet Union and China.[30]

Allende returned to Chile profoundly enlightened by his travels. He conceived of a new *vía pacífica*, or peaceful way to socialism, and he was fully prepared to challenge the United States for blocking that radical path. By the time of the presidential campaign of 1958, Allende openly and emphatically said, "The [U.S.] Department of State insists upon a policy that is odious and anti-popular. . . .We Chileans demand the right to seek our own solutions and to follow the roads that best suit our habits and traditions."[31] Indeed, by 1958, Washington knew that Allende would simply not do.

Like his Socialist rival, Eduardo Frei also opposed U.S. intervention in Guatemala, but he was more willing to work within a system dominated by Washington. As a Christian Democrat, he symbolized the bourgeois attempt to reconcile capitalism and socialism.[32] Alessandri, for his part, embraced capitalism as a nominal independent, but he relied on the support of the rightist Liberal and Conservative parties. In the end, Alessandri emerged as the winner. Still, he could hardly claim his victory, 31.6 percent of the vote, as an enthusiastic endorsement from the Chilean people. Allende, who finished in second place, only lost to Alessandri by 33,500 votes.[33]

Alessandri took office firmly convinced that the principles of laissez-faire would cure Chile of its financial malaise. His remedy for inflation, which had jumped from 17 percent to 33 percent since the previous year, angered the major labor organization, *Central Única de Trabajabadores*, or CUT.[34] As much as the new president celebrated the virtues of free trade and the free market, he tightly restricted the aspirations of the labor movement. Like the Klein-Saks Mission, the new president felt the need to keep wages down, and proposed only one wage increase proportionate to the level of inflation. After that 1959 pay raise, Alessandri insisted that wage increases would have to match increases in economic productivity.[35] Hoping to stabilize inflation in 1960, the president rejected the workers' call for a wage increase on a par with the preceding year's 38 percent inflation rate. Instead, Alessandri offered a wage increase of 10 percent. The CUT, outraged by the president's apparent obliviousness to the struggles of the working class, commenced a twenty-four-hour general strike. The defiance did not end there, indicating that popular opposition to Alessandri extended far beyond union politics bureaucracy: "It was followed by a series of strikes by individual unions in hopes of breaking the stabilization program: 40,000 workers went on strike from the copper and coal mines; telephone and electricity services; metal, textile, and construction industries; 40,000 teachers also went on strike. The government called the strikes all part of a 'subversive' plan."[36]

That November, the Labor Committee of the Chamber of Deputies, or the lower house of the Chilean congress, amended the readjustment bill's 10 percent wage increase to 38 percent. Reacting in a less than politic fashion, the president removed the bill from legislative consideration altogether. Protestors from the CUT embarked upon a vandalizing journey toward *La Moneda*, the presidential palace.[37] Encountering a barrage of police bullets, thirty-five demonstrators sustained wounds and two met their deaths. As a result, the FRAP and the CUT organized another twenty-four-hour general strike as well as a protest memorializing the "martyrs against the stabilization program."[38] The president made his sympathies clear when he not only protested that a more substantial wage increase would exhaust the public treasury and raise prices, but that "readjustments made by the private sector have been at the cost of profits."[39]

As little as Alessandri empathized with the struggles of the working class, he could ill-afford to ignore its highly successful strike, which crippled transportation, mining, and other vital industries, not to mention the public sector. Feeling the pressure, Alessandri made the barely perceptible concession of a 15 percent wage increase.[40] The 1961 congressional election, which ended the Liberal-Conservative majority in the Senate, indicated the president's own profound vulnerability. After their humiliating defeat, even the right-wing Liberals and Conservatives realized that laissez-faire capitalism had lost its appeal to the Chilean electorate. The system required reform. With the addition of the Radical party to the ruling coalition, the government now increased wages by 16.7 percent, and then implemented the popularly demanded 100 percent wage increase for the year 1963.[41]

Alessandri's strategy to combat inflation collapsed, but that was not his sole encounter with failure. The president also could not fulfill his promise to revive private investment and industry in Chile. As a laissez-faire capitalist, he endorsed as well as observed the principles of free trade. Arguing that international competition would stimulate the economy, Alessandri steadily reduced tariffs from 1959.[42] In consequence, imports, U.S. goods in particular, overwhelmed the Chilean market. Paradoxically, the president's scheme to empower the Chilean economy only reinforced its dependence on the United States.[43]

With his acceptance of U.S. loans, Alessandri ensured that Chilean reliance on that powerhouse to the north would last for many years. A grand total of $130 million traveled southward from the U.S. banking industry, the U.S. Treasury Department, the International Monetary Fund, and the International Cooperation Agency, which was a forerunner of the Agency for International Development.[44] Neither the public nor the private sectors of the United States would deal so generously with the Allende administration more than a decade later. At this point in time, however, the Alessandri administration offered much to please Washington in return. In his effort to draw North American corporations to his country, Alessandri did not stop at weakening trade barriers. He also rewarded foreign investors with tax breaks.[45]

By 1962, it was clear that Alessandri's stabilization policy had not worked. The rampant inflation and deadening stagnation had many causes. Chilean dependence on the U.S. economy played a great role in the crisis. Expectations that the business-friendly climate would stimulate direct investment in Chile did not materialize due to a recession in the United States, which was apprehensive anyway about financial dealings with a Latin American nation in the aftermath of the Cuban Revolution.[46] Furthermore, the astonishing rise in imports, 86 percent from early 1959 to late 1961 alone, created a severe trade deficit, contributing to the devaluation of the *escudo*, the Chilean currency. In addition, governmental manipulation of the *escudo*'s exchange rate did not help matters.[47]

Alarmed by the prospect of ever-worsening inflation, workers insisted on an adequate wage increase, and expressed their anxiety in the most direct and effective way: they ceased their labor. Indeed, 1962 alone would see 400 strikes.[48] When the administration finally proposed a 15 percent wage increase, the CUT arranged for a general strike. Participants came from the private and public sectors, including employees of copper mines, the steel industry, the State Bank, and the National Health Service.[49] Soon, the slum dwellers of Santiago showed solidarity with the strikers by obstructing streets. Most dramatically, the police, equipped with rifles and tear gas, encountered stone-throwing protesters holding up the train service. In the melee, six protestors died and many more were injured. When the Minister of Public Works toured the site afterward, he was overcome by the residents' grievances about nonexistent sanitation, roads in need of repair, and too few schools. Eduardo Frei feared for Chile's stability: "Are we building something positive in this country, or are we accumulating a foundation of hate in these people which tomorrow no one will be able to contain, neither one man nor any political party?"[50]

In the presidential campaign of 1964, Frei presented himself as a force of stability, running once again as a Christian Democrat. His party had evolved from a Catholic student group that had defected from the Conservatives three decades before. Never outgrowing its philosophical origins in Catholic doctrine, the Christian Democrats espoused an alternative to both communism and capitalism that would eliminate class conflict.[51] Like their rivals to the left, the Christian Democratic party fully supported the right of labor unions to exist. In theory, however, labor and business would share a mutually beneficial agenda. Through a moderate redistribution of corporate wealth and worker participation in corporate decision-making, theory would become reality.[52]

Although spiritually inspired, the party favored technical remedies to social ills, and proved particularly attractive to the university-trained products of the middle class. Furthermore, the Christian Democrats took care to broadcast a secular image to the masses. Designing their platform for mass appeal, they endorsed the construction of 360,000 houses, universal primary education, and in six years, the provision of 100,000 families with land. On the other hand, the Christian Democrats advocated a slow and graduated approach to inflation.[53] Reeling from the economic volatility of the Alessandri term, the workers undoubtedly wanted an instant solution, and could not have looked upon Frei's inflation policy with favor.

Frei's proposed copper policy proved most controversial and divisive, at least for his own party. In opposition to more left-leaning party members, who called for complete nationalization of the copper mines, Frei endorsed "Chileanization." Under this scheme, the government would buy a majority share of the mines, with the transferred funds used for the development of the copper industry within Chile itself.[54]

Beyond a sizable portion of the middle class, Frei could expect votes from his society's loftier ranks. Not that wealthy businessmen loved the Christian Democrat; they simply regarded him as a palatable, as well as the most likely, option to Salvador Allende, his only significant rival.[55] Chilean aristocrats were not alone in that view. Dreading the prospect of a Chilean counterpart to Fidel Castro, the United States government secretly provided the Frei campaign with far more than moral support. According to a 1975 report by U.S. Senate Select Committee on Intelligence, both the Kennedy and Johnson administrations dispatched their campaign contributions to the Christian Democrats, courtesy of the Central Intelligence Agency. "The Special Group authorized over three million dollars during the 1962–1964 period to prevent the election of a Socialist or Communist candidate," the Senate report noted.[56]

U.S. clandestine support for Frei stemmed directly from President John F. Kennedy's Latin American program, the Alliance for Progress. Introducing the program in 1961, Kennedy declared that it would "demonstrate to the entire world that man's unsatisfied aspiration for economic progress and social justice can best be achieved by free men working within a framework of democratic institutions."[57] The dashing leader addressed Latin American in noble cadences previously never uttered by any Cold War president. Foreshadowing Nelson Rockefeller's 1969 proposal to Nixon, Kennedy described the *Alianza para el progreso* as "a vast cooperative effort, unparalleled in magnitude and nobility of purpose, to satisfy the basic needs of the Latin American people for homes, work and land, health and schools."[58]

To provide the Latin American people with *techo, trabajo y tierra, salud y escuela*, the Alliance for Progress promised their governments $20 billion in public and private assistance over the next decade.[59] Despite the rhetorical idealism, the Kennedy administration designed the Alliance for Progress to make capitalism more durable in Latin America. Anything was preferable to the extension of Castro's revolution. Economist Walt Rostow, one of the many intellectuals at the Kennedy White House, endorsed modernization theory as an alternative. This philosophical approach to the Third World was in the height of fashion in the 1960s. Essentially, modernization theorists sought to transform developing countries into smaller versions of the United States. To their biased perspective, the United States was the ideal modern society: capitalistic, technologically advanced, literate, and democratic. It was imperative for Washington not only to set a standard for traditional societies, but also to impose it.[60] Military operations were one application of modernization theory; economic investment was another.

Rostow argued that U.S. investment in Latin American societies would lead to the "take-off," the point at which those societies would have accumulated enough capital to sustain its own industry.[61] This new wealth would uplift the indigent, eventually.[62] Socialist alternatives were therefore unnecessary.

Rostow gave Washington's preferred system of free enterprise a very convenient defense. What the Kennedy administration could never admit, however, was that true progress in Latin America would not come without North American sacrifice. Raul Prebisch, the distinguished Argentine economist, made clear in his own work as director of the United Nations Economic Commission for Latin America that the region would remain poor if it only specialized in the production of raw materials for the benefit of the industrialized First World.[63] For their own economic advancement, therefore, the Latin Americans would have to control their own natural resources. If the Latin American economies had progressed enough to shift to large-scale manufacturing, the United States would have lost its traditional access to these raw materials. Furthermore, Latin American manufacturing would have reduced the need for North American imports. Kennedy had declared his own war against poverty in Latin America, but a more equitable allocation of regional wealth would have forced the bourgeoisie as well as the aristocracy to reduce their own purchases, including North American imports.[64]

Capitalism emphasizes profit over any human value, so even the altruism of the Alliance for Progress was limited. "Latin America may have received only about 70 to 75 percent of the $20 billion authorized," historian Stephen G. Rabe observed. "Even then, the net capital flow to Latin America did not amount to $14 to 15 billion, because Latin Americans had to repay principal and interest on pre-1961 loans and on short-term loans made in the 1960s."[65] Not only did the administration extend twenty-five-year loans with a mere five-year grace period, it insisted that the debtors buy U.S. materials for building programs.[66]

By the end of the 1960s, the Latin American standard of living had not improved at all.[67] Undeniably, Kennedy's twin goals of capitalism and social justice clashed, but the contradiction did not end there. "Also contradictory was Kennedy's counter-insurgency schools training Latin American officers in civic action, guerilla warfare, and virulent anti-communism," historian Albert L. Michaels wrote.[68] Rostow and other proponents of modernization regarded the armed forces as a useful tool. MIT's Center for International Studies, a think tank for modernization theory, argued that "armies in underdeveloped countries can perform many essentially civilian functions more effectively than the existing civilian institutions in these countries."[69] Not only was the military a technologically sophisticated organization, it emphasized "respect for authority and organization. The army can be a highly significant training ground for large numbers of men, preparing them for new roles in society."[70]

It would be disingenuous to deny the political impact within Latin America of Kennedy's support of the military. In fact, the Kennedy administration witnessed the toppling of six democratic regimes by its armed forces.[71] This military investment not only inhibited constitutional, civilian rule in Latin America, but also its economic development. "These increasingly important, expensive military forces would in themselves generate requirements whose fulfillment would contract the limited national resources available for schooling, internal investment, and debt servicing," Michaels explained.[72]

Washington extended military assistance to Latin America more to combat local insurgencies than to contain Soviet influence. In fact, the Joint Chiefs of Staff urged Kennedy to divert his attention from hemispheric defense to strengthening "the capability of indigenous forces to conduct counter-insurgency, anti-subversion, and psychological warfare operations."[73] What the Kennedy administration sought to contain was the political expression of the Latin American people themselves.

Well before the Alliance for Progress came to its cynical demise, the Kennedy administration regarded Frei's Christian Democracy as the panacea for Chile. Alarmed by the country's economic stagnation, the administration feared the right-wing intransigence of Alessandri would drive the Chilean

electorate to the dreaded Allende. That perennial Marxist candidate annoyed Washington for many reasons. The White House blamed Allende for
Chile's official disapproval of the Bay of Pigs invasion, and for its continued
warm relationship with Cuba. After all, Allende had pronounced that "any
aggression against Cuba is an aggression against the small nations of the
world, against Latin America, and against Chile."[74] Furthermore, U.S. business assets in Chile, including the copper mines were worth $700 million.[75]
The election of Allende in 1964 would have threatened those assets. Above
all, Kennedy wished to avert a public relations catastrophe, which would be
"a major setback for us if the Communists were to win an election in a democratic country when we have said that communism can remain in power
only by building a wall."[76]

In contrast to the radical Allende, Frei reassured Kennedy. In the fall of
1963, Kennedy saw the candidate in Washington. Indeed, the president even
planned a trip to Chile in 1964 as an indication of his support for Frei.[77]
Kennedy's planned journey to Chile, tragically prevented by another journey
to Dallas, would have been a generous official gesture, but it was the CIA's
unofficial backing that proved most effective. The Agency enjoyed the
wholehearted support of Kennedy, and his successor, President Lyndon B.
Johnson. The White House directed the CIA in a complex and expectedly
clandestine fashion. Operating on behalf of the White House, a task force
featured, among others, National Security Advisor McGeorge Bundy, Assistant Secretary of State for Inter-American Affairs Thomas Mann, the CIA's
Western Hemisphere Division Chief Desmond Fitzgerald, and presidential
aide Ralph Dungan, whom Johnson would later appoint ambassador to
Chile.[78]

Working in conjunction with the Office of Bolivian and Chilean Affairs
at the State Department, the task force also had its counterpart in Santiago,
which was comprised of the ambassador, the deputy chief of mission, the CIA
chief of station, and the heads of the Political and Economic Sections at the
embassy.[79] In fact, Washington supported any political party in Chile, as long
as it was not Allende's FRAP coalition. Once the Democratic Front, a conservative alliance, performed poorly in a by-election in the spring of 1964,
the Johnson administration shifted its attention exclusively to Frei. "The
CIA underwrote slightly more than half of the total cost of that campaign,"
the Select Committee discovered, even though it doubted Frei's own knowledge of this fact.[80] Still, it is hard to understand how any political candidate,
in any country, could be kept ignorant of major campaign contributors.

The newly released minutes of a task force or "Special Group" meeting
confirm the 1975 Senate finding that the Johnson White House failed to

maintain a scrupulous distance from the Frei campaign. If the administration did not operate at the behest of corporate America, their respective interests at least coincided. "[CIA Director] McCone referred to several meetings he had had in recent days with American industrialists with major interest in the Chilean economy," the recorder noted. "In one instance, David Rockefeller headed a group representing various companies."[81] Nelson's younger brother, the chairman of the Chase Manhattan Bank, had formed the Business Group for Latin America the year before. Along with the chief executive officer of the Anaconda Company, the executive committee of the Business Group featured top corporate men such as Harold S. Geneen of International Telephone and Telegraph and Donald M. Kendall of Pepsico, who would later star in the Chilean drama of the early seventies.[82]

In the meantime, Washington was determined to see Frei wear the presidential sash. The director of the CIA informed his compatriots of his meetings with David Rockefeller, as well as the Anaconda executives. The chairman of the Anaconda board, Clyde E. Weed, and the president, Charles M. Brinckerhoff, regarded the Allende candidacy as a threat to their company. McCone had also met a Chilean who had a stake in the copper industry, Augustin Edwards, the publisher of the El Mercurio newspaper. All three men had advised McCone of the necessity of providing financial support to Frei. Indeed, their Business Group for the Latin America was already doing so.[83]

After long deliberation, the Special Group determined after that McCone "would convey to Mr. Weed the U.S. decision not to become a partner with business interests in covert political action but at the same time to assure him that the U.S. was making every effort, on a priority basis, to prevent the election of Allende."[84] The Group then assigned Desmond Fitzgerald to the task of planning the disbursement of roughly $2 million to the Frei campaign. Fitzgerald knew that the original proposal was far from a fixed amount, however.[85]

The CIA certainly understood that more money was available when it requested $500,000 more that July. As one memorandum warned McGeorge Bundy, "We can't afford to lose this one, so I don't think there should be any economy shaving in this instance. We assume the Commies are pouring in dough; we have no proofs. They must assume we are pouring in dough; they have no proofs. Let's pour it on and in."[86]

The 303 Committee, which oversaw intelligence operations on behalf of the White House, quickly authorized the additional expenditure.[87] Whatever reservations McCone and the rest of the Special Group may have had about a partnership with the private sector, the CIA and interested corporations certainly worked in tandem. The 1975 Senate investigation found this to be the case: "A group of American businessmen in Chile offered to provide one and a half million dollars to be administered and disbursed covertly by the U.S. Government to prevent Allende from winning the 1964 presidential election."[88] Although the U.S. government turned down the offer on practical as well as ethical grounds, "CIA money, represented as private money, was passed to the Christian Democrats through a private businessman," the report pointed out.[89]

The embassy in Santiago kept Washington abreast of Frei's friendly attitude. For the sake of appearances, Frei officially declined financial assistance because he believed the "PDC was adequately supplied and in any case it was desirable that the Chilean people themselves be made to feel an obligation to contribute and thus feel selves as personally involved in campaign."[90] Despite that official refusal, Frei still expected to benefit from U.S. intelligence: "He hoped that we could assist him . . . through furnishing information on FRAP activities."[91] Probably, Frei also anticipated receiving U.S. financial assistance in an indirect manner.

Like policymakers in Washington, Frei did not fear the Allende candidacy for reasons of national security. He knew that the people of the Western Hemisphere would survive a Marxist victory in Chile. Preoccupied with economic issues himself, Frei based his appeal for help on the awareness that the United States shared his preoccupation:

> He made the interesting observation that he felt that among the reasons that it was necessary for him to win by a really large majority was the reassuring effect that this would have on potential private investment from abroad. A win by a mere plurality or by a very narrow majority would keep alive the suspicion in the United States and Europe that communism was still just around the corner in Chile and this would discourage the massive investments that he felt Chile needed.[92]

Tellingly, the National Security Council's contingency planning for an Allende victory did not even include the possibility that his election would alter the military balance of power between the "Free World" and the so-called Communist Bloc. The NSC only anticipated an escalation of the ideological and economic rivalry with the Soviet Union, not a military conflict. Indeed, NSC strategists attributed the Sino-Soviet split to the Chinese endorsement of revolution through violent conflict. As an NSC memorandum noted, "The Soviets will probably offer substantial financial assistance to Allende if we refuse, and may be even if we do not. But they would be inheriting an economy which is in serious difficulty as opposed to Cuba, where it was basically strong. In the Soviet-Chinese fight, Chile is extremely important to the Soviet thesis that communism can achieve power by peaceful means."[93]

In bald monetary terms, the U.S. impact on the 1964 election was worth $20 million.[94] Washington also dispatched a minimum of one hundred "special personnel" to Chile to help insure Allende's defeat. "U.S. government intervention in Chile in 1964 was blatant and almost obscene," an intelligence official later admitted. "We were shipping people off right and left, mainly State Department but also CIA with all sorts of covers."[95] The future CIA defector Philip Agee observed at the time: "The Santiago station has a really big operation going to keep Allende from being elected. He was almost elected at the last elections in 1958, and this time nobody's taking any chance."[96]

Direct subsidies of the Frei campaign only comprised part of the vast U.S. expenditure.[97] The campaign received at least $3 million from the CIA. To make that monetary contribution more comprehensible to North Americans, Karl Inderfurth of the Senate Select Committee offered an apt analogy: "The $3 million spent by the CIA represents almost 30 cents for every man, woman, and child in Chile. Now if a foreign government had spent an equivalent amount per capita in our 1964 election, that government would have spent about $60 million. . . . President Johnson and Senator Goldwater spent $25 million combined [in 1964], so this would have been about $35 million more."[98]

The CIA also sponsored a colossal propaganda drive in Chile. "Extensive use was made of the press, radio, films, pamphlets, posters, leaflets, direct mailings, paper streamers, and wall painting," the Select Committee reported of the CIA's attempt to connect Communist atrocities to Allende in the Chilean mind. "It was a 'scare campaign,' which relied heavily on images of Soviet tanks and Cuban firing squads and was directed especially to women."[99] It is also very likely that the CIA funded *Acción Mujeres de Chile* (Chilean Women's Action), an anti-communist group for ladies.[100] As historian Margaret Power has noted in her own excellent analysis of gender in Chile, Chilean women were generally more conservative than Chilean men. This political gender gap was the exact reverse of its North American counterpart. With a profound attachment to the hierarchies of the Catholic Church and the patriarchal family, these women were far less receptive to Allende's speeches on socialism and equality. On the other hand, they were highly receptive to posters with captions such as "Listen, as a mother, as a wife, as a daughter. Today you have a great responsibility. Have you thought of the unity of your home? The future of your children? Your children's happiness? Remember that which you value most in your life is in danger. And remember that the choice is Democracy or Marxism!"[101]

Yet, that poster was merely one of many. The CIA began production at an amazing volume. "During the first week of intensive propaganda activity (the third week of June 1964)," the Select Committee revealed, "a CIA-funded propaganda group produced twenty radio spots per day in Santiago and on 44 provincial stations; twelve-minute news broadcasts five times daily on three Santiago stations and 24 provincial outlets; thousands of cartoons, and much paid press advertising."[102] The CIA was satisfied by its work. "We believe that Frei will win by a clear majority," the Agency predicted, which meant that the Chilean Congress would not have to determine the victor in a runoff.[103]

That prediction proved correct. On September 4, 1964, Frei won 56 percent of the vote, defeating Allende, who only received 38.9 percent.[104] Even though Frei would have probably attained his ultimate goal without outside interference, a CIA study acknowledged that the candidate won a majority rather than a plurality of the votes because of it.[105] More than a decade later, the CIA looked back upon their prolific propagandistic pace with great pride.[106]

When Frei succeeded President Alessandri, he found himself beholden to supporters from every point on the political continuum. Frei's most conservative supporters had only turned to him as the only realistic alternative to Allende, and opposed any government intervention in economic affairs. Their centrist counterparts also celebrated the free market, but they urged the new regime to stimulate private enterprise with reforms and subsidies. Those on the left favored far more extensive change. Despite the differences between the moderate and radical blocs of the PDC, they initially backed Frei.[107]

Foreign control of the copper industry was the most volatile issue. Frei could hardly afford to ignore it. He was as pleased with his triumph as were his North American patrons, but the solidity of his political base depended on the success of "Chileanization." Obviously, Frei would never go so far as to nationalize the entire industry. Nevertheless, his conciliatory policy involved the government acquisition of 51 percent of Braden Copper, a holding of Kennecott, and 25 percent of the Anaconda concern in Chile.[108]

Although the arrangement seemed fair on paper, it left both companies wealthier than ever before. Braden Copper, whose entire book value was only $65 million, collected $81.6 million from the Chilean government for only 51 percent of the El Teniente mine, and one-fourth of two other mines. Nevertheless, the benefits of Chileanization for the U.S. companies extended far beyond the inflated return for that sale. According to investigative journalist Seymour Hersh, "Braden claimed that the book value was unrealistically low, but one reason for the low value was the Chilean government's willingness to permit the firm to depreciate its assets at a favorable rate, and thus pay lower taxes."[109]

Although the Anaconda Corporation, for its part, declined to sell any shares of Chuquicamata, its most important mine, it still permitted the Frei administration to purchase 25 percent of its Exotica mine. Anaconda assured the Chilean government that it would boost its production, but like its rival Kennecott, the corporation also demanded tax deductions from the government in exchange. Indeed, the Chilean government promised all the companies involved in the deal that there would be no tax increases for the next two decades. The state also bought 25 percent of the Cerro de Blanco Corporation's Rio Blanco mine.[110] In addition, both companies maintained the exclusive right to manage the extraction and sale of their copper. The investment of the state funds in the copper industry brought about a step-up in output. In the decade before Allende's presidential investiture, revenue for the U.S. companies leaped. Anaconda, for example, accumulated revenue of $500 million. Yet, even higher copper prices brought little benefit to Chile itself. Chileanization guaranteed the copper companies $100,000 of the revenue that directly resulted from the increase in prices.[111] Power over the copper industry stayed in foreign hands.[112]

As the United States escalated its war in Vietnam in 1965, creating a greater demand for copper, the superpower would not even permit Chile to immediately raise the world price by as much as two cents per pound.[113] The Johnson administration simply could not conceive of the idea of copper at 38 cents per pound instead of 36 cents. National Security Advisor McGeorge Bundy favored using the traditional carrot-and-sticks approach with Chile: We have our eye on the following possible sticks:

(1) Pending $80 million program loan.
(2) Hold-up on investment guarantees for $80 million Kennecott loan to Chile and $135 million new Anaconda investment with the result that there would be no expansion.
(3) Hold-up on pending Ex-Im [Export-Import] Bank applications for $135 million of loans to companies operating in Chile.
(4) Use of 700,000-ton U.S. stockpile to break world copper market.
(5) Use of government incentives to promote substitution of aluminum for copper.[114]

The carrot, of course, would be the free flow of U.S. loans. According to the minutes of a telephone conversation, the president evidently favored the Bundy strategy, for he said "he thought we should explain that if our economy goes bad we will not be able to give any loans."[115] Whether or not price increases on copper would have ruined the U.S. economy, the pressure applied to Frei by the Johnson administration worked. The Chilean president agreed to an arrangement by which his country could sell its copper to Europe at the desired price, while offering the United States a special discount.[116] In return, William F. Sater points out, "Washington lent Chile ten million dollars under such generous terms that it was tantamount to a gift."[117] U.S. beneficence also included an $80 million AID loan and a $23 million advance for the acquisition of two Boeing 727 jets.[118] In fact, Chile collected more than $1.5 billion in credit from the U.S. government and the multilateral development banks from 1961 to 1970. Astonishingly, only South Vietnam received more aid during this period.[119]

Yet that generosity compromised Chilean independence in international affairs. Tellingly, the letter from the Santiago embassy that detailed the copper arrangement for the State Department also detailed Chile's subservience in another realm, the United Nations: "During conversation Frei was informed by Dungan of uncertain GOC position on ChiCom representation issue. Frei reacted immediately. Went to telephone and ordered GOC representative to vote against admission Communist China."[120] Surely Frei had no significant quarrel with mainland China. Nevertheless, the Chileans found themselves endorsing a nonsensical policy of the United States for the sake of loans that effectively denied them the right to sell their own copper at a fair price. In reality, not much had changed since the Korean War. "Chileanization" was an utter misnomer.

Meanwhile, Washington did not cease its supervision of Chilean elections. The 303 Committee moved on to the 1965 congressional races. As pleased as they were with the presidential victory for the Christian Democrats, the committee members favored any candidate from any party that rivaled the FRAP, the pro-Allende coalition. A committee memorandum noted, "This proposal has the approval of Ambassador Dungan, who has reviewed the list of proposed candidates, and has agreed that covert support should be provided to most of them. The remaining candidates are under consideration and final selection will be made only with the approval of the Ambassador."[121]

In any case, Frei now had the opportunity to test his social theories with the full approval of the United States. True to their philosophical roots in Catholic ideology, the Christian Democrats attempted to ease class tensions with their espousal of a "communitarian" answer to the Chilean predicament. In theory, all members of a communitarian society, whether bourgeois or proletarian, shared a common agenda. All economic classes wanted to work together to create a just and humane social order. The Christian Democrats carefully eschewed the Marxian portrayal of the aristocracy as an exploiter of the common people.[122] Still, it is likely that Washington's influence played a greater role in Frei's political evolution than Catholic doctrine. Early in his career, Frei had condemned capitalism. Now, he embraced capitalists who came to Chile. "We have never confiscated foreign investments and have always guaranteed the persons and property of foreigners," Frei publicly declared.[123]

Despite their loud denials of class conflict, the Christian Democrats apparently favored some sectors of Chilean society over others. The Frei administration snubbed the CUT, declining to acknowledge the union as a legitimate agent for the working class. This rebuff deprived the CUT of any legal status. The Christian Democratic assault on the labor movement continued with an effort to legalize the open shop, which would have given workers the option of not joining a union. Had the Christian Democratic plan come to realization, the law would even have authorized more than one union at a single workplace.[124] President Frei also encouraged the growth of alternative labor organizations, going so far as to speak at May Day rallies intended to compete with the annual function hosted by the CUT.[125]

By 1966, tensions reminiscent of the Alessandri era had developed between labor and president. The celebrated Chileanization program had not increased job satisfaction among the copper workers themselves, and they resorted to a strike.[126] Contradicting his own denials of class conflict, Frei responded to the demands of the striking workingmen with military force. When soldiers disrupted a union meeting with gunfire on March 11, killing eight, the president gave the troops his public support, and blamed the Marxists for provoking the strike. Frei's attitude indicated how badly he had misread the national mood, for union membership, as well as the number of strikes, rose dramatically during this period.[127]

Despite the unrest, President Frei implemented several progressive measures that benefited labor. His agrarian reform program did provide 27,000 peasant families with farms through the compensated expropriation of land from large estates. This reform was vitally needed in a country where these estates controlled more than 80 percent of agricultural land.[128] In addition, Frei also promoted the unionization of the peasants. "The government also began to enforce the minimum wage laws and social legislation and to require wage payments in cash rather than in kind in order to raise the standard of living of the rural poor," Paul Sigmund observed.[129]

Unlike his predecessor, Frei did not begin his administration with the insistence that working class bear the burden of inflation control. He raised wages to match 100 percent of the inflation rate, to the undoubted pleasure of labor.[130] Price controls undoubtedly displeased capital, on top of the wage increases, so the president expected industrialists to compensate for the resulting decline in profits with a step-up in production. Moreover, the tax reform in 1965 targeted the rich. Barbara Stallings observes that the tax reform had a salutary anti-inflationary influence: "This had the effect of increasing government revenue so that it was not necessary to finance such a large part of government expenditure by printing money."[131] At least for the years 1965 and 1966, Frei's campaign to stabilize the economy seemed to work.[132]

By 1967, though, impersonal forces such as the drop in the international price of copper, drought, and the enormous foreign debt brought the Chilean economy to a standstill. Frei could have increased social spending to alleviate the recession, but the influence of Washington pulled him rightward.[133] His break with his original platform was now final. Following the advice of the International Monetary Fund and the World Bank, Frei instead trimmed the public housing and agrarian reform programs in an effort to combat inflation. Frei never kept his promise to construct 360,000 houses, building only a third as many.[134] Nor did he ever meet his original goal of establishing 100,000 family farms.[135] He also kept wage increases down to create an economy friendly and receptive to private investment, which the international lending agencies believed was the answer to the economic crisis.

Unfortunately, private investment did not resolve the crisis. Inflation affected the working classes most deeply by reducing the purchasing power of their wages. Although the Frei administration augmented wages by 36 percent in 1967, real wages only grew by 3 percent.[136] Civil unrest resulted. Abandoning the socioeconomic experimentation of earlier days, Frei grew more repressive than ever before toward an increasingly restive laboring class. The *Carabineros*, or national police, clashed bloodily with strikers and others on the left.[137] That November, the government dispatched troops to break up a strike at Anaconda's two major copper mines. The army arrested eight hundred workers, and twenty-two workers either died or sustained injuries in the confrontation. Frei also turned to the military when the rural peasantry expressed their dissatisfaction, an indication that he ultimately sided with property against the people. Beyond the countryside, an army encounter with unemployed shantytown dwellers resulted in nine deaths in March of 1969 in the port city of Puerto Montt.[138]

Frei's aggressive stance did not help matters. A deteriorating economy accompanied by worsening inflation distinguished the final two years of the Frei presidency.[139] Christian Democracy had not alleviated Chile's severe social inequality.

Forty percent of the Chilean population suffered from malnutrition. Compared to the United States, where the average person ate sixty grams of animal protein, the average Chilean consumed twenty-eight grams.[140] Those who subsisted on this inadequate diet were highly susceptible to diseases such as typhoid, pneumonia, diarrhea, and measles. To an affluent North American, these illnesses would not have seemed very serious, but they proved fatal to Chileans who lacked access to medical care. The poorest of Chile's children were most vulnerable to malnutrition, for it impeded their mental development.

While only 3 percent of the upper-class population was mentally retarded, 40 percent of poor children under school age had an intelligence quotient that fell below eighty.[141]

Malnutrition was so common because the distribution of income among the Chilean population remained wildly disproportionate. The richest 2 percent of the inhabitants collected nearly half of the Andean country's earnings, while the poorest 28.3 percent did not even earn 5 percent.[142] Yet the government came up with no remedies for the suffering masses of Chile. The U.S.-controlled multinational corporations, on the other hand, benefited immensely from the president's policies. Low taxes and deregulation of the import system drew more than one hundred corporations to Chile by 1970, but prosperity did not come with them.[143] According to Brian Loveman, "Foreign investment brought with it high technology, capital-intensive production units that made little contribution to the government's efforts to reduce unemployment. Indeed, for the decade 1960 to 1970, industry provided an average of only 15,000 new job opportunities per year—nowhere near enough to absorb the continuing tide of migrants from the countryside to the urban areas."[144]

Abandoning the socioeconomic experimentation of earlier days, Frei no longer tried to meet the needs of an increasingly restive laboring class.[145]

The losses sustained by the Christian Democrats in the congressional elections of 1969 were an official indication that Frei was losing his support. Amidst violent encounters with the left, the government also encountered hostility from the opposite direction. Foreshadowing his criminal role the following year, the fanatically right-wing Brigadier General Roberto Viaux directed a mutiny of the Tacna Army regiment that October. Although the government quickly crushed the abortive rebellion with widespread public approval, the "Tacnazo" revealed the sharpness of Chile's political polarization.[146] As the radical wing of the Christian Democratic drifted away from Frei, he could hardly appease them without further antagonizing conservatives. The Frei presidency had failed, and Chile needed an alterative. The upcoming presidential election of 1970 would provide that alternative, but the Tacnazo was an ominous warning. Frei's successor could reconstruct Chile only as far as the military would permit him.

Indeed, U.S. patronage of the military was a subtle threat during the Frei years. Although Washington saw no need to sponsor a coup in Chile, its generosity with the armed forces is illustrative. With the help of the Military Aid Program Agreement of 1952, the United States gradually became armed forces' principal patron and maintained that role throughout the next decade.[147] In 1963, for example, the U.S. bestowed $25 million on the military.[148] Unlike aid to the civilian sector, Washington did not require repayment of that lavish contribution. As the Frei presidency faded into history, U.S. support for the military remained firm. A report from the Joint Chiefs of Staff pointed to the dependency of the Chilean military:

> Total grant aid through FY 1969 has been approximately $93.0 million, along with surplus equipment valued at $23 million. Since the limited Chilean Defense budget has not been sufficient to support modernization to any significant degree, U.S. military assistance has been the primary means of modernizing Chilean Armed Forces although Chile is making some major purchases in the UK. Chile has received no military grant aid material assistance from any country other than the U.S.[149]

The United States offered the military far more than free loans, however. For the edification of Latin American officers, the Kennedy administration expanded a training program that already existed in the Panama Canal Zone, and renamed it the U.S. Army School of the Americas.[150] Officers also studied at military bases in the United States. In the seven years before the fall of Allende, these programs instructed 1,100 Chilean officers in counterinsurgency techniques.[151] Furthermore, the U.S. Military Assistance Advisory Group enjoyed the privilege of being the sole foreign military mission in Chile.[152] The setting-up of offices for the MAAG at the Chilean Ministry of Defense further indicated the intimacy between the armed forces of the two countries.[153]

Washington's interest in indoctrinating the Chilean military explains its deep commitment to military education. At that time, however, those in the highest ranks of the armed forces were frustratingly nonpartisan: "The Armed Forces refrain from imposing or expressing openly on non-military public policy, but Chilean officers' views on how to maintain progress with stability largely conform to prevail [sic] opinion in influential civilian circles. This includes respect for legality, free elections, and strong political parties as the essential elements of a system that is designed to produce solutions to national problems."[154]

The Joint Chiefs foresaw the disintegration of Christian Democracy, almost anticipating the electoral triumph of Allende. The Joint Chiefs predicted, "Within this context of social and economic instability, the military may well find themselves functioning as the brakes on change. With the lower classes claiming a larger share of the nation's economic resources, the possibility of disorders and a revolutionary answer to Chile's problem loom large."[155]

Washington regarded the Chilean military as an insurance against social reconstruction. For a Latin American country whose military only temporarily disturbed civilian authority three times since 1818, a coup would only be a "last resort."[156]

If that last resort were required, the Joint Chiefs could not think of one Chilean officer who could take charge: "No single military leader of national stature or with any significant tri-service following exists in Chile at present."[157] By continuing to work with the conservative officer corps in Chile, the United States would find such a leader, who would proceed to destroy Chilean democracy in 1973.

# Notes

1. Brian Loveman, *Chile: The Legacy of Hispanic Capitalism* (New York: Oxford University Press, 2001), 117.

2. Loveman, *Chile*, 117.

3. Loveman, *Chile*, 120.

4. William F. Sater, *Chile and the United States: Empires in Conflict* (Athens: The University of Georgia, 1990), 54.

5. Sater, *Chile and the United States*, 87.

6. Sater, *Chile and the United States*, 88.

7. Sater, *Chile and the United States*, 93.

8. Theodore H. Moran, *Multinational Corporations and the Politics of Dependence: Copper in Chile* (Princeton, NJ: Princeton University Press, 1974), 6.

9. Moran, *Multinational Corporations*, 7.

10. Moran, *Multinational Corporations*, 3.

11. Sater, *Chile and the United States*, 103.

12. Sater, *Chile and the United States*, 103.

13. Sater, *Chile and the United States*, 118.

14. Sater, *Chile and the United States*, 114.

15. Sater, *Chile and the United States*, 116.

16. Loveman, *Chile: The Legacy of Hispanic Capitalism*, 218.

17. Loveman, *Chile: The Legacy of Hispanic Capitalism*, 218.

18. Loveman, *Chile: The Legacy of Hispanic Capitalism*, 218.

19. Loveman, *Chile: The Legacy of Hispanic Capitalism*, 219.

20. Loveman, *Chile: The Legacy of Hispanic Capitalism*, 220.

21. Loveman, *Chile: The Legacy of Hispanic Capitalism*, 220.

22. Loveman, *Chile: The Legacy of Hispanic Capitalism*, 220.

23. Loveman, *Chile: The Legacy of Hispanic Capitalism*, 222.

24. Barbara Stallings, *Class Conflict and Economic Development in Chile, 1958–1973* (Stanford, CA: Stanford University Press, 1978), 33.

25. See Immanuel Wallerstein, *The Modern World-System: Capitalist Agriculture and the Origins of the European World-Economy in the Sixteenth Century* (New York: Academic Press), 1974, and Thomas J. McCormick, "World Systems," in *Explaining the History of American Foreign Relations*, ed. Michael J. Hogan and Thomas G. Paterson (New York: Cambridge University Press, 1991).

26. Mark T. Hove, "The Arbenz Factor: Salvador Allende, U.S.–Chilean Relations, and the 1954 U.S. Intervention in Guatemala," *Diplomatic History* 31, no. 4 (September 2007): 633. Stallings, *Class Conflict and Economic Development in Chile*, 79.

27. Hove, "The Arbenz Factor," 633, 651.

28. Hove, "The Arbenz Factor," 633, 635.

29. Hove, "The Arbenz Factor," 643.

30. Hove, "The Arbenz Factor," 643.

31. Hove, "The Arbenz Factor," 660–61.

32. Hove, "The Arbenz Factor," 631, and Stallings, *Class Conflict and Economic Development in Chile*, 65.

33. Stallings, *Class Conflict and Economic Development in Chile*, 79.

34. Julio Faundez, *Marxism and Democracy in Chile: From 1932 to the Fall of Allende* (London: Yale University Press, 1988), 110.

35. Stallings, *Class Conflict and Economic Development in Chile*, 82.

36. Stallings, *Class Conflict and Economic Development in Chile*, 82.

37. Stallings, *Class Conflict and Economic Development in Chile*, 83–84.

38. Stallings, *Class Conflict and Economic Development in Chile*, 84.

39. Stallings, *Class Conflict and Economic Development in Chile*, 84.

40. Stallings, *Class Conflict and Economic Development in Chile*, 84.

41. Stallings, *Class Conflict and Economic Development in Chile*, 85.

42. Stallings, *Class Conflict and Economic Development in Chile*, 86.

43. Stallings, *Class Conflict and Economic Development in Chile*, 87.

44. Stallings, *Class Conflict and Economic Development in Chile*, 87.

45. Stallings, *Class Conflict and Economic Development in Chile*, 87.

46. Stallings, *Class Conflict and Economic Development in Chile*, 87.

47. Stallings, *Class Conflict and Economic Development in Chile*, 88.

48. Faundez, *Marxism and Democracy in Chile*, 114.

49. Stallings, *Class Conflict and Economic Development in Chile*, 89.

50. Stallings, *Class Conflict and Economic Development in Chile*, 90.

51. Paul E. Sigmund, *The United States and Democracy in Chile* (Baltimore: Johns Hopkins University Press, 1993), 21.

52. Paul E. Sigmund, *The Overthrow of Allende and the Politics of Chile* (Pittsburgh: University of Pittsburgh Press, 1977), 30.

53. Sigmund, *The Overthrow of Allende and the Politics of Chile*, 32.

54. Sigmund, *The Overthrow of Allende and the Politics of Chile*, 33.

55. Sigmund, *The Overthrow of Allende and the Politics of Chile*, 34.

56. United States Senate Select Committee to Study Governmental Operations with Respect to Intelligence Activities, *Covert Action in Chile: 1963–1973* (Washington, D.C.: U.S. Government Printing Office, 1975), 14.

57. Sigmund, *The United States and Democracy in Chile*, 14.

58. Sigmund, *The United States and Democracy in Chile*, 14.

59. Stephen G. Rabe, *The Most Dangerous Area in the World: John F. Kennedy Confronts Communist Revolution in Latin America* (Chapel Hill: University of North Carolina Press, 1999), 2.

60. Nils Gilman, *Mandarins of the Future: Modernization Theory in Cold War America* (Baltimore: Johns Hopkins University Press, 2003), 3–5, 20.

61. Sigmund, *The United States and Democracy in Chile*, 14.

62. See Walt Rostow's *Stages of Economic Growth* (Cambridge, MA: MIT Press, 1960).

63. Gilman, *Mandarins of the Future*, 235.

64. Albert L. Michaels, "The Alliance for Progress and Chile's 'Revolution in Liberty,' 1964–1970," *Journal of Interamerican Studies and World Affairs* 18, no. 1 (February 1976): 76.

65. Rabe, *The Most Dangerous Area in the World*, 155.

66. Rabe, *The Most Dangerous Area in the World*, 154.

67. Rabe, *The Most Dangerous Area in the World*, 2.

68. Michaels, "The Alliance for Progress and Chile's 'Revolution in Liberty,'" 76.

69. Gilman, *Mandarins of the Future*, 189.

70. Gilman, *Mandarins of the Future*, 189.

71. Rabe, *The Most Dangerous Area in the World*, 2.

72. Michaels, "The Alliance for Progress and Chile's 'Revolution in Liberty,'" 76.

73. Rabe, *The Most Dangerous Area in the World*, 129

74. Rabe, *The Most Dangerous Area in the World*, 111.

75. Gilman, *Mandarins of the Future*, 110.

76. Gilman, *Mandarins of the Future*, 113.

77. Gilman, *Mandarins of the Future*, 113.

78. Select Committee, *Covert Action in Chile*, 16.

79. Select Committee, *Covert Action in Chile*, 16.

80. Select Committee, *Covert Action in Chile*, 15.

81. Chile Document 257. Memorandum for the Record. "Minutes of the Meeting of the Special Group, 12 May 1964," *FRUS, 1964–1968, Volume 31, South and Central America; Mexico.* www.state.gov/r/pa/ho/frus/johnsonlb/xxxi/36308.htm.

82. Hersh, *The Price of Power: Kissinger in the Nixon White House*, 260.

83. Chile Document 257. *FRUS, 1964–1968.* Hersh, *The Price of Power*, 260.

84. Chile Document 257.

85. Chile Document 257.

86. Chile Editorial Note 262. *FRUS, 1964–1968.*

87. Chile Editorial Note 262.

88. Select Committee, *Covert Action in Chile*, 16.

89. Select Committee, *Covert Action in Chile*, 16.

90. Chile Document 263. "Telegram from the Embassy in Chile to the Department of State," *FRUS, 1964–1968.*

91. Chile Document 263.

92. Chile Document 263.

93. Chile Document 264. "Memorandum From Robert M. Sayre of the National Security Council Staff to the President's Special Assistant for National Security Affairs," July 31, 1964, FRUS, 1964–1968.

94. Stallings, Class Conflict and Economic Development in Chile, 96. Hersh, The Price of Power: Kissinger in the Nixon White House, 260.

95. Stallings, Class Conflict and Economic Development in Chile, 96.

96. Margaret Power, Right-wing Women in Chile: Feminine Power and the Struggle Against Allende (University Park: Pennsylvania University Press, 2002), 91.

97. Stallings, Class Conflict and Economic Development in Chile, 96.

98. Power, Right-wing Women in Chile, 91.

99. Select Committee, Covert Action in Chile, 15.

100. Power, Right-wing Women in Chile, 78.

101. Power, Right-wing Women in Chile, 81.

102. Select Committee, Covert Action in Chile, 15.

103. Chile Document 268. "Memorandum Prepared in the Central Intelligence Agency," September 1, 1964, FRUS, 1964–1968.

104. Stallings, Class Conflict and Economic Development in Chile, 96.

105. Select Committee, Covert Action in Chile, 17.

106. Select Committee, Covert Action in Chile, 6.

107. Stallings, Class Conflict and Economic Development in Chile, 98.

108. Hersh, The Price of Power, 260.

109. Hersh, The Price of Power, 261n, Michaels, "Alliance for Progress and Chile's 'Revolution in Liberty,'" 85, and Susanne Bodenheimer, "Stagnation in Liberty— The Frei Experiment," in North American Congress on Latin America's New Chile (Berkeley, CA, and New York: Waller Press, 1973), 122.

110. Michaels, "Alliance for Progress and Chile's 'Revolution in Liberty,'" 85, and Stallings, Class Conflict and Economic Development in Chile, 107.

111. Hersh, The Price of Power, 259, and Bodenheimer, "Stagnation in Liberty— The Frei Experiment," 122.

112. Hersh, The Price of Power, 261n.

113. Sigmund, The United States and Democracy in Chile, 29.

114. Chile Document 262. Telegram from the President's Special Assistant for National Security Affairs (Bundy) to the Ambassador to Chile (Dungan), November 12, 1965, FRUS, 1964–1968.

115. Chile Document 284. Memorandum of Telephone Conversation between President Johnson and the Under Secretary of State for Economic Affairs (Mann), November 13, 1965, FRUS, 1964–1968.

116. Chile Document 287. Telegram From the Embassy in Chile to the Department of State, November 17, 1965, FRUS, 1964–1968 and Julio Faundez, Marxism and Democracy in Chile: From 1932 to the Fall of Allende (London: Yale University Press, 1988), 142.

117. Sater, Chile and the United States, 145.

118. Sater, *Chile and the United States*, 145.

119. Michaels, "The Alliance for Progress and Chile's 'Revolution in Liberty,'" 77.

120. Chile Document 287.

121. Chile Document 277. Memorandum for the 303 Committee. "Financial Support to Selected Candidates in the 7th March 1965 Congressional Elections in Chile," January 25, 1965, *FRUS, 1964–1968*.

122. Stallings, *Class Conflict and Economic Development in Chile*, 99.

123. Michaels, "The Alliance for Progress and Chile's 'Revolution in Liberty,'" 84.

124. Stallings, *Class Conflict and Economic Development in Chile*, 103.

125. Stallings, *Class Conflict and Economic Development in Chile*, 103.

126. Stallings, *Class Conflict and Economic Development in Chile*, 104.

127. Stallings, *Class Conflict and Economic Development in Chile*, 105.

128. Bodenheimer, "Stagnation in Liberty—The Frei Experiment," 118, and Sigmund, *The United States and Democracy in Chile*, 31.

129. Sigmund, *The United States and Democracy in Chile*, 131.

130. Stallings, *Class Conflict and Economic Development in Chile*, 105.

131. Stallings, *Class Conflict and Economic Development in Chile*, 105.

132. Stallings, *Class Conflict and Economic Development in Chile*, 105.

133. Michaels, "The Alliance for Progress and Chile's 'Revolution in Liberty,'" 89.

134. National Intelligence Estimate, Submitted by CIA Director Helms, January 28, 1969. NSC Files, HAK Office Files, Country Files, Box 128, Nixon Presidential Materials Project.

135. National Intelligence Estimate, Submitted by the Central Intelligence Agency, July 20, 1970. NSC Files, HAK Office Files, Country Files, Box 128, Nixon Presidential Materials Project.

136. National Intelligence Estimate, July 20, 1970.

137. Bodenheimer, "Stagnation in Liberty—The Frei Experiment," 122, and Stallings, *Class Conflict and Economic Development in Chile*, 114.

138. Michaels, "The Alliance for Progress and Chile's 'Revolution in Liberty,'" 89.

139. Stallings, *Class Conflict and Economic Development in Chile*, 114.

140. David J. Morris, *We Must Make Haste—Slowly: The Process of Revolution in Chile* (New York: Vintage, 1973), 239.

141. Morris, *We Must Make Haste—Slowly*, 178.

142. Hersh, *The Price of Power*, 259.

143. Loveman, *Chile: The Legacy of Hispanic Capitalism*, 239.

144. Loveman, *Chile: The Legacy of Hispanic Capitalism*, 239.

145. Stallings, *Class Conflict and Economic Development in Chile*, 114.

146. Stallings, *Class Conflict and Economic Development in Chile*, 120. See also Ruth Berins Collier and David Collier, *Shaping the Arena: Critical Junctures, the Labor Movement, and Regime Dynamics in Latin America* (Notre Dame, IN: University of Notre Dame Press, 2002).

147. The Organization of the Joint Chiefs of Staff, *Response to National Security Study Memorandum #68: The Military Establishment in Latin America—as of August*

*1969*, October 30, 1969, page 144. NSSM 68, Folder 4, Box H-159, Nixon Presidential Materials Project, National Archives II, College Park, Maryland.

148. Sigmund, *The United States and Democracy in Chile*, 19.

149. The Joint Chiefs of Staff, *The Military Establishment in Latin America*, 144.

150. The School of the Americas was relocated to Fort Benning, Georgia in 1984.

151. Ibid.

152. Ibid.

153. Sigmund, *The United States and Democracy in Chile*, 20.

154. The Joint Chiefs of Staff, *The Military Establishment in Latin America*, 138.

155. The Joint Chiefs of Staff, *The Military Establishment in Latin America*, 138.

156. Select Committee, *Covert Action in Chile*, 3 and The Joint Chiefs of Staff, *The Military Establishment in Latin America*, 140.

157. The Joint Chiefs of Staff, *The Military Establishment in Latin America*, 147.

# CHAPTER THREE

# Opposing an Election: 1970

Shaped by cultural prejudice and influenced by the legacy of his predecessors, Richard Nixon in 1970 looked on political developments in Chile with proprietary interest. Once again, Dr. Salvador Allende emerged as the leading leftist candidate for the presidential sash, and the increasing likelihood that he would wear it eventually preoccupied Nixon to the point of pathology.

This time, fate favored Allende, who had lost three times before. His competition featured the Christian Democrat Radomiro Tomic and Jorge Alessandri, who led a right-wing coalition in the hope of redeeming his failed presidency. Blessed with the common touch, Allende easily outcharmed them both. "He was familiarly known as *El Chicho*, a Chilean term for those with reddish curly hair," British journalist Hugh O'Shaughnessy recalled. *El Chicho* was a "hands-on politician, tirelessly campaigning the length and breadth of the country, picking up shovels and working side by side with the workers, and speaking eloquently to his chosen constituency."[1] Eschewing the royalist pretensions of many political figures, Allende presented himself to the electorate as their next *compañero presidente*, their friend as well as their leader.[2]

More crucially, Allende's coalition, *Unidad Popular* (Popular Unity), prevented conflicts among the various leftist parties by bringing them together in a common cause. Socialists, Communists, and most Radicals had no reason to dispute the UP platform: "Chile is a capitalist country, dependent on the imperialist nations and dominated by bourgeois groups who are structurally related to foreign capital and cannot resolve the country's fundamental problems—problems which are clearly the result of class privilege which will never be given up voluntarily."[3]

Furthermore, *Unidad Popular* attracted renegade Christian Democrats who were disillusioned by the Frei administration.[4] Uninterested in watching Tomic repeat the mistakes of the previous six years, these renegades agreed with the UP that Christian Democratic rule was "nothing but a new government of the bourgeoisie, in the service of national and foreign capitalism, whose weak effort to promote social change came to a sad end in economic stagnation, a rising cost of living, and violent repression of the people."[5] A committed centrist, Tomic could not expect to attract conservative voters, so these defections devastated his campaign.[6]

Although Tomic tried to entice the masses with the vow of comprehensive land reform, even that bold stand could not compare to the revolutionary sweep of the UP program. Allende planned to confiscate *all* haciendas possessing more than eighty irrigated hectares for redistribution among the peasants. Not only did the UP candidate promise to significantly increase social spending, he intended to socialize Chile's banking and insurance industries, with the suggestion of further expropriations. Allende envisioned a society in which the common people assume a more active role in governmental affairs, and wield greater control over the means of economic production.[7] Private enterprise would still have a place in Chile, but an Allende victory would bring about a major shift in power, a "peaceful transition to socialism" whose electoral legality would have far more potency in Latin America than Castro's revolution.

Washington was expending relatively little effort on the campaign at this point. The president seemed to take it for granted that Allende would lose. Certainly the reports from his ambassador in Santiago, Edward Korry, encouraged this complacency. Korry wrote to Washington that Frei's achievements would "keep Chile more or less on center and compatible in form and direction with our own system."[8] CIA Director Richard Helms, for his part, speculated later that the president had had an unrealistic, almost romantic expectation of what the CIA could accomplish with limited resources. Truly, Richard Nixon was a man so blithe, so confidently dismissive of Latin America that he could only envision easy manipulation of Chilean politics. Kissinger's own ignorance probably reinforced that of the president: "Latin America was an area in which I did not have then expertise of my own. I was lulled by the polls that predicted an Alessandri victory and by the consensus of the agencies—a consensus I would never have accepted so readily in an area where I had firsthand knowledge. And in the spring and summer Cambodia claimed much of my attention."[9]

Yet, in fairness to Nixon and Kissinger, the CIA did not always analyze Chilean domestic politics with accuracy. Helms's own Agency mistakenly reported to the White House that Alessandri was the front-runner.[10] So, the president was not the only man guilty of unwarranted optimism.

For the execution of this overly confident policy, the president turned to the top-secret 40 Committee, which supervised intelligence operations on behalf of the White House. Chaired by Kissinger, the supervisory body was comprised of Attorney General John Mitchell, CIA Director Helms, the chairman of the Joint Chiefs of Staff, and the deputy secretaries of state and defense.[11] At this point, the 40 Committee did not consider sponsoring a military coup because U.S. intelligence doubted that the Chilean military would block an Allende presidency. As Ambassador Korry reported to Washington, "With the GOC [Government of Chile] committed to buying arms and raising pay and with more opportunities for the promotions, there is no overriding impulse for the army to move."[12]

Instead, the 40 Committee resorted to a propaganda campaign: "The Embassy in Santiago, the Department of State and the CIA have agreed that the election of the UP candidate would be detrimental to the U.S. and that spoiling operations should be undertaken to influence a portion of the uncommitted vote away from the UP."[13] By way of radio, posters, and the press, the 40 Committee sought to discourage the undecided Chilean from casting a Marxist ballot. Since the White House cared neither for Alessandri nor Tomic, Allende's two opponents, it was a negative campaign in the truest sense: "It has also been agreed that the U.S. Government should not support either of the other two presidential candidates in the sensitive political environment currently found in Chile, since there is little to choose between them."[14] Back in 1964, Allende had condemned

the unprecedented squandering of money, a saturation of the media, a colossal disinformation attempt. This is no longer a simple case of propaganda; this is an example of violent, psychological repression. . . . They say we are enemies of the family, the home, the fatherland, religion, freedom, culture, and the spirit. These are all anticommunist lies.[15]

In 1970, Allende was just as outraged, and his defensive reaction against the posters and the misinformation connecting him not only to the Communist party in Chile but to the governments of Cuba and the Soviet Union attests to the impact of the CIA.[16]

In comparison to Washington's efforts in 1964, however, the 40 Committee's investment six years later seemed paltry. The CIA did the best it could with limited resources, but Richard Helms recalled his own frustration with the complacence of his superiors: "Several times, we warned the Nixon administration that if the United States were to undertake a serious covert action in the 1970 presidential election, we would have to get under way. It was not until March 1970—some six months before the election—that the 40 Committee authorized CIA to spend $135,000 on what it referred to as 'spoiling operations.' . . . In late June, the 40 Committee increased the budget to $300,000."[17]

Ultimately, the propaganda did not work. The returns came slowly on September 4, Election Day, but Allende emerged as the victor early the next morning thanks to a three-way split. His supporters took to the streets in their joy. It had been such a long, hard struggle. Some of the revelers expressed their sense of vindication with a cry that must have given Nixon many a nightmare: "Che Guevara, we are here."[18] Feeling threatened and embittered, the Nixon administration would make much of the Socialist's failure to win a majority of the vote. His collection of 36.6 percent of the ballot did seem unsubstantial when compared to the shares held by Tomic and Alessandri, 28.1 percent and 35.3 percent, respectively.[19]

While the election was extremely close, Allende was not the first presidential candidate in world history to win by a plurality. Alessandri had done so in 1958, and so had Richard Nixon ten years later, but that was irrelevant. Lacking the inclination for honest introspection, Nixon would never have likened himself to Salvador Allende, a Latin American politician. Nixon's contempt for Latin America was legendary. In this period of détente, the president could deal with Soviet and Chinese leaders on terms of relative equality and mutual respect, but he would compliment no Latin American official, let alone Allende, with prolonged consideration. His memoirs cover the entire Allende period in a scant two pages. One passage is particularly striking in its breeziness: "After three years of ineffectual administration, during which the Chilean economy suffered from a series of crippling strikes, Allende was overthrown by the Chilean military in September 1973, and according to conflicting reports, was either killed or committed suicide during the coup."[20]

What Nixon omitted in his memoirs were his own extensive efforts to undermine the "ineffectual administration" of Allende. Chile belonged to Washington's sphere of influence, so Nixon felt entitled, even compelled, to eliminate its government before moving on to more important matters. Even if Nixon felt neither military pressure from the Soviet Union nor legislative pressure from domestic politicians to act, he was not incognizant of the wishes of his corporate patrons such as Donald Kendall, the chief executive officer of Pepsico. Indeed, the beverage man seemed to expect the president to defer to his wishes. "I will tell the President he cannot stand for a Cuba in his administration," Kendall peremptorily informed Kissinger before he met with Nixon on September 14.[21] At the presidential meeting, Kendall was accompanied by Agustin Edwards, the right-wing proprietor of Chile's leading newspaper, El Mercurio.[22]

The next day, the two businessmen saw Kissinger and Attorney General John Mitchell in person before seeing Helms. Kendall and Edwards begged the CIA director to prevent the confirmation of Allende by the Chilean Congress. The Pepsico executive's easy access to the president was truly remarkable. Certainly, the two men had a professionally close relationship. Kendall had contributed lavishly to Nixon's political campaigns.[23] Furthermore, Pepsico was a client of Nixon's law firm during his hiatus from politics in the 1960s. Kendall even felt intimate enough with the president to introduce his elderly father to him on the same day as their fateful meeting.[24] In an effort to further explore the tie between Nixon and Kendall, I called Pepsico's public relations office to inquire if I might look at relevant documents from the period. I was told they were not available for public perusal.[25]

Kendall feared the election of a Socialist government in Chile for financial reasons. Pepsico did not want to lose its Chilean bottling plant to socialist expropriation. Like Nixon, he also dreaded what Allende represented for the rest of Latin America, and potentially for the entire world. With hands in the leasing and transportation industries, the Pepsico corporation not only produced soft drinks but food and sporting goods as well. In 1970, these various enterprises would generate over $1.1 billion in sales and revenue. Importantly, 19 percent of Pepsico's sales and revenue for 1970 and the following year came from foreign operations. A worldwide socialist trend could threaten those investments. In Washington, Kendall's fears were met with empathy. The chief executive of the United States responded promptly to the concerns of the chief executive of Pepsico. Nixon called Helms, Mitchell, and Kissinger for a meeting that very afternoon. This was the meeting at which Helms jotted down his infamous instructions quoted earlier in my introduction.[26]

Even though Helms had only thirty-eight days to carry out his order, he knew the president would not accept failure. Indeed, the chief executive's imperialist worldview did not escape him. "Truman had lost China. Kennedy had lost Cuba. Nixon was about to lose Chile."[27] At least in the president's mind, the Andean nation truly belonged to us.

The election shocked the White House, turning calm concern into desperation. Since the election lacked a solid majority, tradition dictated that the Congress choose the victor, which it would soon do on October 24.[28]

"Now we were forced to improvise while being confronted by a tight deadline and with no real preparations," Kissinger remembered. "With time running out our actions were inevitably frantic."[29] It was the determination of the Nixon administration to prevent the selection of Allende that led to corrupt and ultimately murderous acts.

First, the United States tried to bribe the Christian Democratic members of Congress.[30] Nixon did not deny this in his memoirs, justifying his unwarranted interference in the democratic process of a foreign country with the argument that Kennedy and Johnson had relied on the same methods. "Knowing this, and knowing that nearly two-thirds of the Chile's voters had rejected Allende, I directed the CIA to provide support for Allende's opponents in order to prevent his election by the Chilean Congress," Nixon wrote, conveniently forgetting his own narrow defeat of Vice-President Hubert Humphrey.[31]

For self-justification, the president borrowed a key argument of the realist school of foreign affairs. The underhanded tactics of foreign leaders justified his. Since the Soviet Union and its Communist satellites tampered with the democratic processes of foreign countries, he had an ethical obligation to counter that pernicious manipulation. "We live in a far from ideal world," Nixon opined.[32] Like Helms, the president claimed that the UP enjoyed the generous support of the Communist bloc without presenting specific evidence. Nixon claimed that this support gravely threatened the physical security of the United States. The capitalist superpower, could ill-afford another socialist state in our hemisphere: "I believed, as had my two predecessors, that a Communist regime in Cuba exporting violence, terrorism, and revolution throughout Latin America was dangerous enough."[33]

While Cuba was undeniably an annoyance for the United States, it is inconceivable that the small island nation ever truly endangered the lives of U.S. citizens. Even the most perilous moment of U.S.–Cuban relations, the Missile Crisis of 1962, had involved the *Soviet* placement of nuclear weapons on the island. Castro had eagerly authorized that special delivery, but the only real opponents in that geopolitical showdown had been the United States and the Soviet Union. If Castro had presented a threat, or seemed to have presented one to the United States during the Kennedy era, it was only with Soviet support. Since Castro's relationship with Moscow was not quite as warm a decade later, his potential for mischief was significantly diminished. In the case of Chile, the important question to ask was not whether Castro viewed an Allende presidency as a strategic asset, but whether General Secretary Leonid Brezhnev did. The president's foremost counselor on foreign policy, Henry Kissinger, indicated this in his own chronicle of the period, *White House Years*. "We were persuaded that it [Chile] would soon be inciting anti-American policies, attacking hemisphere solidarity, making common cause with Cuba, and sooner or later establishing close relations with the Soviet Union," the national security advisor wrote, linking developments in Chile to the Soviet use of a Cuban base for its nuclear submarines. Kissinger even went so far as to imply a connection between Allende and tensions in faraway Jordan.[34]

*White House Years* is a tremendously popular work, but it is also notorious for its selective and defensive version of events. The importance of Kissinger's memoir lies in what it conceals rather than reveals. A proper assessment of Allende within the Cold War context requires the use of additional sources.

Granted, a CIA analysis in June of 1970 did depict the Chilean election as an issue of critical concern to Moscow:

> The Soviet Union, while heretofore proceeding with the utmost discretion and generally maintaining a low silhouette in Chile, has now a vital stake in the forthcoming elections and in an Allende victory. Her interests manifest themselves in massive funding of the Allende campaign and in turning a deaf ear to all entreaties by Tomic to moderate the intransigent posture of the Chilean CP [Communist Party] which has refused in the most unambiguous terms to entertain any type of arrangement whereby the Chilean left would under certain conditions come to the support of Tomic whom they consider an American puppet.[35]

In addition, the USSR supplemented a Cuban donation of $350,000 to the *Unidad Popular*, even if the CIA did not know by how much. Although the Soviets probably felt ideologically obligated to provide moral support to *Unidad Popular*, an anti-capitalist movement, whatever money they may have spent to instate Allende counted for little when weighed against the money eventually spent by the United States to destroy him. One must note the vagueness of the CIA synopsis, lacking in solid evidence of a massive Soviet conduit to Allende. Furthermore, Korry noted the "neutrality of the Soviet embassy" in his lengthy, literary dispatches.[36] The ambassador pointed to the positive relationship that the Frei administration enjoyed with the Soviets, who gave Foreign Minister Valdes's "Opening to Cuba" their enthusiastic approval.[37] The Soviets had already gained entrée to Latin America; what more could the Soviet Union have gained from an Allende presidency?

"There is no country on earth that is so far from the two super-powers and Red China," the ambassador reflected. "It is not Poland nor is it Mexico."[38] On September 9, Korry lunched with a group of his ambassadorial counterparts presumably Latin American. He discussed the Chilean situation at length with a diplomat whose nationality is censored in the document. "We both agreed that the USSR had no stomack [sic] for another Cuban drain on its resources," the ambassador reported to Washington.[39] The fact that Korry could speak so dismissively of Chile's strategic importance is telling. Indeed, he seemed to reflect the president's own fears of what a Socialist state would bring: "While Allende Govt would move internally with initial prudence to seek a framework of constitutionality and legality, it would be committed, as Allende has stated, to policies that treated U.S. imperialism as public enemy number one in the Hemisphere, aside from nationalization of U.S. industries."[40]

Directly contradicting the conventional image of an international Communist conspiracy, the U.S.S.R. tried to discourage too much warmth between Santiago and Havana. The State Department's Bureau of Intelligence and Research reported that:

> A Soviet diplomat in Santiago reportedly cautioned that Allende should delay recognizing Castro until he can do so in concert with other Latin American countries, perhaps Peru and Bolivia, thereby avoiding unnecessary early difficulties for the UP administration. There are indications that the USSR does not want Chile to become dependent on trade with communist countries.
>
> Six months prior to the Chilean election two Soviet diplomats in Santiago reportedly said that the USSR could not logistically support an Allende government, and expressed the view that the policies of such a government would be completely different from those of Havana.[41]

In September, Castro had had no ambitions for Chile because he had not expected Allende to win. When news of the UP electoral triumph had come to Havana, the official newspaper, *Granma*, had featured the story with the headline "Defeat of Imperialism in Chile." Nevertheless, Castro had been astonished by the results.[42]

Most of the policymakers in Washington were not sure that an Allende presidency would gravely imperil the United States. For example, Viron Vaky, a Latin Americanist on Kissinger's National Security Council, voiced this uncertainty in a memorandum to the national security advisor: "There is no question that his victory would present problems to us. Whether that means a serious threat to U.S. security and national interest requires a better and more systematic judgment, because how serious we deem the threat to our interest to be will determine the risks we are willing to take to insure his defeat. I do not think we have reached sound conclusions yet, and certainly not a consensus."[43]

Had the United States faced an imminent threat in June 1970 as grave as the terrorist assaults of September 2001, would Vaky have written such an indeterminate assessment for Kissinger? Vaky disputed the argument of Ambassador Korry that it was far less dangerous to intervene directly in the Chilean election than to do nothing. Allende's approaching political victory had apparently led Korry to favor intervention. "The premise in Korry's proposal is that we cannot count on the Chileans themselves or private U.S. interests to do an adequate job against Allende, and we cannot afford to let them fail," Vaky wrote to Kissinger. "This is the basic premise and I am not sure it is proved."[44] Important sections of this document are now blacked out from public viewing, but certain passages imply Vaky's concern that his superiors would sponsor a military coup. Vaky favored the exercise of U.S. influence before the election. "But I recommend against the [censored] in the post electoral phase," Vaky counseled the national security advisor. "That is too dangerous, too antithetical to the concept of our general policy and of dubious effectiveness."[45] Furthermore, an NSC review of an internal study shows Vaky's vehement opposition to even the idea of a coup. "The only effective way of overthrowing him is by overt military intervention and the paper—correctly I think—judged that to be so unfeasible and costly as to be an unrealistic option," he warned Kissinger.[46] Vaky simply could not envision a menace serious enough to warrant a violent overthrow.

Recordings of presidential conversations further substantiate the idea that worries about national security did not drive U.S. antipathy to Allende, although Nixon's memoirs might give the reader the opposite impression. The White House tapes revealed no preoccupation with Cold War considerations. In reality, domestic concerns often trumped worries over national security during this period. Nevertheless, not one of the declassified conversations to which I listened even indicated presidential concern that right-wing members of Congress would exploit the existence of a Socialist Chile by attacking the White House. At least in the case of Chile, Nixon felt no need to demonstrate his fitness as a Cold Warrior, as he felt compelled to do in Southeast Asia. Talking with Kissinger in 1971, Nixon eschewed the notion of Soviet expansionism in the Western Hemisphere. What really worried him was the bad example Allende might set for other Latin American nations struggling for liberation from U.S. influence: "I know the argument, of course, that if we get out, we lose our [stroke?] there. The Russians will be happy to come in, and so forth and so on. But the fact is that he [Allende] is just gonna [wheel or reel?] us in, frankly, and also that treating him well is going to encourage others to go do likewise. That's what I'm more concerned about."[47]

Nixon was an intelligent man, and he clearly understood that an Allende victory could not have possibly resulted in a Communist conquest of Latin America. Once he left office, Nixon only sounded ridiculous when he claimed otherwise. The former president took a grilling from British journalist David Frost, which is worth quoting extensively:

> Nixon: I remember months before he [Allende] even came to power in 1970, that when it was thought he might run again . . . an Italian businessman came to call on me in the Oval Office and said, "If Allende should win the election in Chile and then you have Castro in Cuba, what you will in effect have in Latin America is a red sandwich. And eventually it will all be red." And that's what we confronted.
> Frost: . . . No, but surely, Mr. President, there's two . . . you've got little Cuba and little Chile . . . and all those enormous countries in between . . . it's like . . . if it's a red sandwich, it's got two pieces of bread here and here and an enormous bit of beef in the middle. I mean, are you really saying that Brazil should feel itself surrounded by Cuba and Chile?[48]

Back in 1970, the CIA also knew better. The Agency determined that an Allende presidency would not greatly enhance Russo-Chilean ties. In a 1969 National Intelligence Estimate, the CIA offered the following reasons why Santiago would continue to maintain some distance from Moscow, which are worth quoting in full:

a. An awareness of the strength of nationalist sentiment in the population generally, in the Congress, and in their own parties—a nationalism likely to be as strongly against subordinating Chile to the tutelage of Moscow (or Havana) as it has been against anything it considers subordination to Washington.

b. A realization that they must have and retain the support of political elements other than those that elected them if their administration is to be at all effective—especially since counsels would probably be divided in their own ranks on some aspects of both foreign and domestic policy.

c. A concern that if their administration tried to move too far and too fast, the Chilean security forces would unseat it.

d. An apprehension (and one which Moscow would probably share) that anything approaching a full embrace of communism in Chile would precipitate action on the part of Argentina, Peru, the U.S., and other countries-perhaps even direct military intervention.[49]

This National Intelligence Estimate not only bore the signatures of CIA Director Helms, but of his own deputy director, the director of the State Department's Bureau of Intelligence and Research, the director of the National Security Agency, and a representative of the Defense Intelligence Agency.[50]

One year later, the CIA produced a National Intelligence Estimate that portrayed Allende with slightly more crimson tones. The Agency suspected that Allende would side with Moscow against Washington: "When key issues in the UN, or in world affairs generally, involved in any kind of an East-West confrontation, an Allende administration would be openly hostile to U.S. interests or at best neutral."[51] Yet, even in this critical assessment, CIA was not predicting a Russo-Chilean military alliance. This was the age of détente, after all. In 1968, Allende had made his opposition to the Soviet intervention in Czechoslovakia quite clear. It is likely that what Langley meant by "an East-West confrontation" were differences over policies affecting the post-colonial world. The Soviets sometimes sided with Western Europe in its objections to U.S. positions on certain issues. Support of Palestinian rights, for example, or Vietnamse self-determination did not necessarily provoke an absolute split between the capitalist and communist blocs. Washington's concern was that Allende's representative in the United Nations, or anywhere else, would not endorse Washington's views.[52]

Whatever the CIA believed about Allende, what the president and his national security advisor thought was what ultimately mattered. The president and his national security advisor knew Chile was not an "East-West" issue. Perhaps Korry penetrated the motives of the Nixon White House more profoundly than his contemporaries. The ambassador raised the correct issue for an insecure administration fixated on issues of masculinity and toughness: "The Allende forces cannot escape the conclusion that if he is inaugurated that the U.S. has admitted its impotence."[53]

In order to keep the U.S. imperium in Latin America intact, Nixon had to prevent the election of Allende. So far, the attempted bribery of Chilean congressmen had not worked. Although Washington had no preference for any candidate, it had hoped to monetarily persuade the Christian Democrats to elect former President Jorge Alessandri, who would then resign and allow President Frei to succeed him. The United States suggested this idea because Chilean presidents cannot serve more than one consecutive term. Ambassador Korry had tried to involve the Chilean military in this scheme, but to no avail. The armed forces would not use its influence with the Christian Democratic legislators.[54] Now that Allende's final election seemed imminent, the president and his advisors moved on to a bloodier strategy. A coup d'etat by the Chilean military would serve the Nixon administration's interests nicely while concealing its involvement. Unfortunately for the administration, the CIA found that this alternative plan had a tremendous obstacle; namely, the deference of the Chilean armed forces to civilian processes: "We have no information now to indicate that the military will not accept an ALLENDE victory. Indeed, we have the word of General Rene SCHNEIDER, Commander-in-Chief of the Army, that he will accept the decision of the voters or the Congress. The formation of a unified group of officers dedicated to the prevention of a revolutionary Marxist state is not a realistic prospect."[55]

Although the Agency surmised some senior officers might oppose Allende on political grounds, the inclination of the captains and lieutenants was to honor the Chilean constitution rather than demolish it.[56] Clearly, General Schneider's strict constitutionalism foiled the Nixonian strategy.

At this point, the plot against Allende assumed two covert tracks. The first track, as we have seen, involved the attempted manipulation of the Chilean Congress. Ambassador Korry was a fully informed participant in this scheme. As much as he pretended otherwise in later years, Korry also worked to pressure the Chilean military into blocking the election of Allende.[57] The encouragement of a coup was known as Track II. From the beginning, Korry and the local CIA station had their eye on the retired veteran of the 1969 Tacna mutiny: "We cannot permit ourselves to pass over General Roberto Viaux."[58] With the CIA, Korry speculated that Viaux might intervene in the congressional runoff. Yet Korry went beyond mere speculation. A cable to the ambassador from Kissinger and Undersecretary of State U. Alexis Johnson reveals a diplomat clearly and culpably in the know of certain aspects of Track II:

> We understand from your previous messages that military are entirely aware that if Allende is elected they can expect no further MAP [Military Aid Program] or further assistance from us. If there is any doubt whatever in their mind in this regard, you should use the channels available to you to make this clear. You have also, in accordance with your recommendation, been authorized to inform them that we are already "holding in abeyance" all MAP, including military training and visits not already underway. You have also been informed that we are suspending action on all requests for processing munitions-control-export licenses for Chilean military.[59]

Obversely, the cable ordered the ambassador to notify the military that if it fulfilled the agenda of its Washington patrons, the largesse would never end.[60] Korry's threat did not work. The CIA observed that "the military remains reluctant to move against Allende despite their knowledge that the USG is considering cutting military aid to Chile and that no guarantees exist ensuring the positions of top military leaders."[61] Schneider had either given his subordinates backbone, or at least had frightened them into toeing an appropriate line.

Entailing bribery, Track I was an operation that was incompatible with the standards of international law. Track I, however, seems wholly aboveboard when assessed alongside Track II, for which the president appropriated $10 million. In contrast to Track I, the administration probably kept Korry ignorant of the ultra-classified operation in its totality.[62] Nixon would never completely trust his own ambassador, an appointee of Lyndon Johnson. As early as 1969, members of the presidential circle had discussed replacing Korry with a Republican.[63] With typical obsessiveness, Nixon complained that Korry's liberal Democratic politics made him partial to President Frei, whom Nixon detested for his previously close relations with Kennedy and Johnson. "Help him get another post," Nixon ordered Kissinger. "I don't care. Help him get any post that you can—Asia."[64]

Kissinger was a man profoundly talented in the art of pleasing his superior. In a memorandum to the president, the national security advisor echoed Nixon's own thoughts. Kissinger advised the chief executive not to rely on the ambassador's reports from Santiago, to maintain a skeptical attitude. "We cannot be sure of what the situation really is and how much Korry is justifying or camaflouging [sic]," Kissinger wrote.[65] He also warned Nixon against entrusting the ambassador with the most sensitive information: "Ambassador Korry is imaginative, but he is an "unguided missile." He is acting now as his own project chief and is trying to construct an operation all by himself. *This is dangerous from a professional intelligence-operations point of view,* and inefficient because there are so many inhibitions on his capacity to operate. *He is too exposed and visible to do this kind of thing,* and it may even affect his objectivity and analysis."[66]

Kissinger counseled the president to dispatch an intelligence expert to assume control of the conspiracy against popular government in Chile. Given the unhappiness of the CIA with Korry's amateurish direction, it is likely that this intelligence expert came from the Agency itself. As far as Kissinger was concerned, the replacement of Korry by a professional would only make Track II a more efficient operation. "In fast-moving situations some operational decisions may have to be made on the spot," the national security advisor predicted.[67]

Why was Track II too sensitive for Kissinger to fully reveal to the ambassador? The most significant aspect of Track II was the plan to violently remove that loyal constitutionalist, General Schneider. For all his own machinations in Santiago, Korry would not have been able to comprehend such an operation: "At the time, if you had asked me, I would have given you a considered opinion that it was out of the question, that it was inconceivable, that a man of Kissinger's intellectual abilities would get involved in a Mafia-type plot."[68]

According to Rene Schneider, Jr., his father believed the military had to keep its place. "During the time he was commander-in-chief, he said many times that the army should never hold political power," Schneider's son recalled three decades later. "If they did, he insisted, it would mean a dictatorship, the end of democracy."[69]

The Chilean commander-in-chief defied the stereotype of the goose-stepping career soldier. Beyond his strict adherence to the Chilean constitution, Schneider was at heart a progressive. In private conversations with his sons, the general expressed passionate yet thoughtfully nuanced opinions. He defended the violent Cuban Revolution as an appropriate response to societal injustice. "Of course, he would say that for Chile, such a way was not since our histories were significantly different," his sons recalled.[70] Unlike Cuba in the days of the Batista *dictadura*, Chile was a functioning democracy when Allende took office.

Indeed, as early as 1968, Schneider aligned himself with the radicals when a group of retired colleagues complained about political agitation at Chilean as well as French universities. "The world marches on toward a new type of society," he told them. "Like it or not, we must be prepared for these changes."[71]

If North American reactionaries grew to detest Schneider, he fully reciprocated the sentiment. Shortly after the assassination of Dr. Martin Luther King, Jr., a U.S. soldier told the Chilean general, "I think in the end it was for the better. He was causing major disruptions." Schneider, who deeply regretted the murder, was outraged.[72] He saw no justification for violence against peaceful men.

So, the compassionate and principled general was fiercely protective of the integrity of the Chilean political system, no matter who legitimately attained office from the left or the right. When it was nearly certain that Allende would emerge victorious in 1970, a conservative Chilean kidded the general: "When are the militants going to take power?" Schneider did not laugh. "I understand you are joking about this, but I resent that even as a joke," the general admonished the man. "We respect the constitution." Probably not liking what he was hearing, the man pressed Schneider further: "What if the left triumphs in the following elections?" The general made himself plain: "Either way the rules are the same for everyone."[73]

Meanwhile, our own men felt Schneider out. At a reception at the U.S. embassy, two North Americans interrogated General and Mrs. Schneider about their political views. "We better go," he said softly to his wife, "these men are probably CIA."[74]

Washington, through the Central Intelligence Agency, knew it did not have a friend in Schneider; the distinguished soldier had to be removed. For this dastardly assignment, the CIA employed several agents referred to as false-flaggers because of their counterfeit passports. These false-flaggers made contact with General Roberto Viaux, the veteran of the 1969 Tacna mutiny.[75] "Controlling factor in Viaux operation is that American hand not show in any manner," CIA Headquarters warned the Santiago station. With some apprehension, Headquarters approved subsidizing the extremist: "After funds handed over [censored agent's name] should explain that we willing move ahead but simply know more about Viaux plans and people."[76]

In mid-October, one of the false-flaggers extended $20,000 to Viaux, along with a pledge to provide the cashiered general with life and physical disability insurance.[77] The Santiago station informed Washington that "Viaux gave impression that request for drop and policies was bite-the-bullet-or-else proposition."[78] In effect, Viaux had to be bribed. This eagerness for self-aggrandizement suggests that policymakers in Washington wanted Schneider out of the way far more than any renegade Chilean officer did. In spite of support given to Viaux, U.S. intelligence had doubts about the cashiered general, who was linked with *Patria y Libertad*, a reactionary faction violently opposed to Allende.[79] Still, Viaux's mental instability probably would not have given the CIA a moment's pause were it not for the pessimism of Chileans such as General Camilo Valenzuela, a disaffected extremist who commanded the Santiago garrison. An intelligence report noted "Valenzuela believes that the military will not take over the government, and should General Viaux decide to move on his own, he would fail."[80]

Coming to the White House on October 15, the Agency's Thomas Karamessines warned Kissinger and his military aide, General Alexander Haig, that "Viaux did not have more than one chance in twenty—perhaps less—to launch a successful coup."[81]

Kissinger trusted Karamessines's judgment, and instructed the Agency to give Viaux the following order: "We have reviewed your plans, and based on your information and ours, we come to the conclusion that your plans for a coup cannot succeed. Failing, they may reduce our capabilities for the future. Preserve your assets. We will stay in touch. The time will come when you with all your other friends can do something. You will continue to have our support."[82]

Of course, Kissinger presented a completely different version of that meeting in his memoir: "I observed to the group that there appeared to be little that we could do to influence the Chilean situation one way or another. . . . The only remaining possibility was an amateurish plot organized by a General

Roberto Viaux to kidnap General Schneider and take him to Argentina. I reported to Nixon: 'I saw Karamessines today. That looks hopeless. I turned it off. Nothing would be worse than an abortive coup.' Nixon agreed. He was now resigned to an Allende presidency."[83]

The president himself also claimed later to have "turned-off" the coup at this point.[84] Even a quick study of the controversial life and career of Richard Nixon makes it obvious that this was not a man who would ever resign himself to the victory of any opponent, let alone Allende. In his destructive symbiosis with the president, Kissinger was no different. Furthermore, as the declassified minutes of that October 15 meeting have shown, Kissinger did not try to switch off the plot permanently but merely postpone it for a more convenient time. Nor did he express any moral reservations. Like a terrorist who, without hesitation, uses heinous means to reach desired ends, Kissinger did not bother to warn the kidnappers not to kill Schneider. Dead or alive, who cared as long as Schneider was out of the way? Therefore, the national security advisor had no compunction about furnishing unsavory characters with instruments of death.[85] In fact, his message gave Viaux every reason to believe that Washington would react with approval even if he acted prematurely but successfully.

By this time, the hopes of the White House now rested on General Valenzuela. Although U.S. intelligence turned to Valenzuela as an alternative to Viaux, their two gangs worked closely together.[86] Despite the clear connection between the two men, whatever doubts the CIA had about Viaux did not stop the Agency from extending him crucial aid. "Submachine guns and ammo being sent by regular [censored] courier leaving Washington 0700 hours 19 October due arrive Santiago late evening 20 October or early morning 21 October," CIA Headquarters informed the local station.[87] Colonel Paul M. Wimert, the U.S. Army attaché in Santiago, assisted with the delivery. One night, Wimert met a plane that had no markings: "I climbed up and handed the boxes out to the CIA chief and the plane was gone."[88] Presumably, the CIA chief Wimert referred to was Henry Hecksher. In any case, the CIA would eventually provide Valenzuela nine to ten untraceable submachine guns, six tear-gas grenades, and 500 rounds of ammunition. These untraceable submachine guns, colloquially known as grease guns, had their serial numbers wiped away with acid. As astounding as this undetectably deadly contribution may seem to the present-day reader, the Agency was only somewhat satisfied. "Unfortunately, were able to acquire only 500 rounds ammo on such short notice," Headquarters lamented. Nevertheless, the Agency was optimistic: "Should be sufficient for what they have in mind."[89]

Assisted by some of Viaux's henchmen, the Valenzuela gang made its first attempt at abduction on October 19. The plan was to nab Schneider on his way back from a stag dinner. "General Schneider will be abducted tonight while attending a party for military VIPs and flown to [classified location]," the CIA noted. "Valenzuela will then announce to the Generals that Schneider has disappeared and that General Carlos Prats will succeed him as Commander-in-Chief."[90] Although the Agency did not know how President Frei would respond to these planned events, it fully expected him to resign, making way for a military junta.[91] The Valenzuela faction did not accomplish its mission that night because Schneider did not take his command car.[92] "Schneider's car to [sic] fast and team became nervous due inexperience," the Santiago station reported. "Will try again evening 20 Oct."[93]

Schneider knew what was going on. Hostile telephone calls disturbed his home. Out of a sense of self-preservation, he took a pistol to his bed at night. Perhaps, too, for self-preservation, he also turned to humor. Observing his wife leaving for a dinner meeting, he quipped, "You better not go. One of these days you'll get back and find that I have been kidnapped."[94] In spite of his fear, Schneider dispensed with bodyguards. He just had a chauffeur to drive him around. 60 *Minutes* correspondent Bob Simon was amazed to learn years later that the commander-in-chief of the Chilean army had had no protection. Chile must have been a very special place, Simon concluded. "It was special," Raul Jr. agreed. "I believe Chile stopped being a special place with the death of my father. It was the first important political crime and it symbolized that something was changing."[95]

The CIA had no time to ponder the specialness of Chile, however. It was far too preoccupied with pressuring Valenzuela to make another effort, for obvious reasons: "The first step in this coup will be the abduction of General Schneider which was scheduled to take place last night."[96] The Agency transmitted a curious cable from its headquarters in Washington to its station in Santiago: "Station will understand that HQs must respond during morning October 20 to queries from higher levels."[97] No one ranked above CIA Director Richard Helms but Henry Kissinger and the president himself.

In any case, the CIA cable to Santiago did not turn off Track II after its initial failure, but encouraged its fruition. Headquarters anxiously pressed the local station: "Do you have indication that [censored] stag party actually took place? What is most likely way you would receive report if it did?"[98] This was not the message of an organization determined to prevent a crime, especially when it now had reason for confidence: "In recent weeks Station false flag officers and [censored] have made a vigorous effort to contact, advise, and influence key members of the military in an attempt to rally support for a coup.

Valenzuela's announcement that the military is now prepared to move may be an indication of the effectiveness of this effort."[99]

The bald language of the Agency's internal communications points to its tight entanglement with the Viaux-Valenzuela network, and evidence also suggests the involvement of Kissinger. This foreknowledge of a felonious assault against an innocent human being, confirms that members of U.S. intelligence, as well as the policymakers who supervised them from Washington, violated Chilean law. If the Rome Statute of the International Criminal Court had been in effect in 1970, they also could have been prosecuted for crimes against humanity, which are among the most serious offenses in international jurisprudence. Article 7 of the Rome Statute classifies the "enforced disappearance of persons" as a crime against humanity, and explicitly defines it: "the arrest, detention or abduction of persons by, or with the authorization, support or acquiescence of, a State or a political organization, followed by a refusal to acknowledge that deprivation of freedom or to give information on the fate or wheareabouts of those persons, with the intention of removing them from the protection of the law for a prolonged period of time."[100]

This definition perfectly matches the intrigue against Schneider. Colonel Wimert himself admitted later that the plotters had originally intended to whisk the unfortunate general away to Argentina.[101]

So far, the plan had not yet reached the operational stage. Disappointment with Valenzuela probably drove the CIA to again offer $50,000 each to Viaux and his partner, an admiral, who then made a move together on October 20 but failed. At the stroke of midnight on October 22, Schneider checked his watch and said, "Luckily the 21st is over." With tragic irony, he only had eight hours left to live.[102]

That morning, Viaux and his team, which included associates of Valenzuela, finally apprehended General Schneider by hitting his car. Then, according to a report by the Chilean military police, "five individuals, one of who, making use of a blunt instrument similar to a sledgehammer, broke the rear window and then fired at General Schneider, striking him in the region of the spleen, in the left shoulder, and in the left wrist."[103] Brave to the last, Schneider had taken out his revolver, but he proved no match to that gang of thugs. He died three days later. Despite the finding that the murderers employed their own handguns, an unidentified machine gun was discovered at the site.[104]

Despite the culpability of their patrons, only Viaux and Valenzuela paid for their crimes. A Chilean military court sentenced Viaux to twenty years in prison for subversion, followed by a five-year exile from Chile for the attempted abduction. For Valenzuela's own participation in the botched kidnapping, the court imposed a three-year exile.[105]

In the meantime, U.S. intelligence went to great pains to conceal its role in the murder. Colonel Wimert rushed to reclaim the money he had distributed. The admiral was a good sport, but Valenzuela, apparently also beneficiary, proved reluctant. The colonel then threatened him with his revolver: "I'll beat the shit out of you with this if you don't get me the money."[106] When Valenzuela still would not budge, Wimert recalled later, "I just hit him once and he went and got it."[107] Wimert also managed to locate the three submachine guns that had been furnished by the CIA. Accompanied by CIA Station Chief Henry Hecksher, Valenzuela raced to the oceanside city of Viña del Mar and tossed the weapons into the Pacific.[108]

Apologists for the U.S. intelligence apparatus might argue that it had only arranged for the abduction of General Schneider, not his murder. That argument would have no relevance in any court of law. As the elegant polemicist Christopher Hitchens observes, "You may not say, with a corpse at your feet, 'I was only trying to kidnap him.'"[109] Nevertheless, in a legal sense, one would err in calling Kissinger a war criminal for what befell Schneider, as the United States and Chile were not engaged in armed conflict.[110] Unfortunately, the Rome Statute bears no retroactive force, but Kissinger, at least in the moral sense, could be called a criminal against humanity.

Perhaps U.S. intelligence wanted Viaux and Valenzuela to do more than just kidnap Schneider. John C. Murray, the CIA branch chief for Mexico, felt uneasy about the extent of U.S. intelligence operations in Chile. Doing some detective work, he learned from one Agency source that some of the Santiago agents had never expected Schneider to survive the attack.[111] Furthermore, there is no evidence that the national security advisor reprimanded the CIA after the shooting. Presumably reflecting Kissinger's own attitude, CIA Headquarters cabled the Santiago station: "It agreed that given short time span of [censored] and circumstances prevailing in Chile a maximum effort has been achieved. Only Chileans themselves can manage a successful [censored] but the station has done excellent job of guiding Chileans to point today where a military solution is at least an option for them."[112]

Whether the CIA had wanted Schneider dead or alive, its sponsorship of that lethal assault backfired, at least temporarily. After Allende's victory, a Chilean contact warned the Santiago station that "any previous plans within the army to prevent Allende's ascent to power on 4 Nov had disappeared."[113] General Carlos Prats, who replaced the assassinated Schneider, shared the constitutionalist sentiments of his predecessor. In the long term, however, the killing of Schneider made the 1973 coup all but inevitable. Disgruntled Chilean officers now knew they would enjoy the full support of the United States if they staged a successful coup. At the same time, officers who remained loyal to the Chilean state knew what would befall them if they rose to its defense.

Indeed, it would be inaccurate to portray the Chilean military as a reactionary monolith. The extremely stratified armed forces reflected deep divisions within Chilean society. While the officers came from privileged families, the conscripts and non-commissioned officers were products of the peasantry or the urban working class. With the exception of progressive men such as General Schneider, the officers had a stake in the system of social inequality. Many non-commissioned officers and conscripts, on the other hand, wanted to change their lives and the lives of their families for the better.[114]

The navy illustrates political tensions that existed in Chile's armed forces. When Allende won the presidency, one sailor recalled that he "and all the other sailors jumped with joy, rifles in our hands. We yelled, 'Now the assholes are going to see what's what,' without really knowing who the assholes were."[115] The sailor soon learned that the naval officers felt quite differently about Allende: "They began to talk against the government and implement concrete plans to undermine the government. For example, they denied the sailors our weekly supply of food to take home to our families, and blamed the shortages on the government. They began to train us to put down riots and other disturbances; they told us that the workers were the enemy, along with the unions and all those forces that were trying to build a new Chile."[116]

Using such methods, the officers managed to effectively indoctrinate many of those under their command. The common soldiers and sailors who could dehumanize members of their own class as the enemy elevated their own standing. Those who were loyal to their own class eventually got into trouble.

As Chilean military officers struggled in their opposition to Allende, U.S. multinational corporations went to work. Pepsico was not the only company to pressure U.S. intelligence as it embarked on its project to undermine Chilean democracy. In particular, International Telephone and Telegraph worried that Allende, if elected, would expropriate Chiltelco, its telephone company in Chile. Allende had complained that Chiltelco only provided service to the wealthier areas of Santiago, and also critically pointed to its $13 million in revenue. His claim of excess profits resembled the charge he had lodged against the copper companies. Beyond a doubt, Allende terrified ITT with his argument that a nationalized telephone company would provide cheaper, more efficient service to all Chileans.[117]

Executives at ITT had good reason to believe that the White House would be receptive to their concerns. Indeed, Nixon's ties to the corporation predated his own presidency. Like Pepsico, ITT was a corporate client of Nixon's law firm.[118] After Nixon became president, he maintained a cordial relationship with the corporation. He even treated Harold S. Geneen, the company chairman and chief executive, to a meal on the *Sequoia*, the presidential yacht.[119] This rapport might explain why Nixon sided with ITT in 1971 against antitrust suits brought by Assistant Attorney General Richard McLaren. "I don't want McLaren to run around prosecuting people, raising hell about conglomerates, stirring things up at this point," Nixon warned Deputy Attorney General Richard Kleindienst. "Now you keep him the hell out of that."[120]

ITT had just purchased the Hartford Fire Insurance Company, as well as the Canteen and Grinnel Corporations. The president pressured the Justice Department into watering down its demands, so that ITT could at least hold on to the fire insurance company as well as a piece of Grinnel. While the out-of-court settlement forbade ITT from purchasing any company worth more than $100 million, it also allowed exceptions.[121] Even *Business Week*, a corporate-oriented publication was disappointed with the settlement:

> The ITT cases were promoted by the Nixon administration as an attempt to establish a clear judicial definition of the limits of corporate growth in a modern society . . . the government antitrusters have thrown away the chance to do that. . . . If McLaren and his lawyers feel that the mushroom growth of the conglomerate corporations threatens the U.S. economy and infringes the antitrust laws, then it is their duty to push the point with the courts until the law is established beyond question. It is not fair either to the companies involved or to the public to keep on brandishing the antitrust gun without even proving that it is really loaded.[122]

Was there a quid pro quo? In fairness, one must keep in mind that Nixon was a Republican, and his pro-business outlook made him sympathetic to large corporations, not just ITT.[123] Still, a grateful ITT did promise to help sponsor the 1972 Republican National Convention in San Diego with $400,000 in cash and services. In June of 1971, ITT lobbyist Dita Beard wrote a confidential letter to the corporation's executive representative for international trade: "I'm so sorry that we got that call from the White House. I thought you and I had agreed very thoroughly that under no circumstances would anyone in this office discuss with anyone our participation in the Convention, including me. Other than permitting John Mitchell, [California Lieutenant Governor] Ed Reinecke, [White House

Chief of Staff] Bob Haldeman and Nixon besides [California U.S. Representative] Bob Wilson . . . *no one* has known from whom that 400 thousand commitment has come."[124]

Another line in Beard's letter refers to the antitrust settlement: "Certainly the President has told Mitchell to see that things are worked out fairly."[125]

ITT denied the authenticity of the letter, but scientific analysis by the FBI contradicted that claim. In any case, the ITT executives found that their goals coincided with those of Washington to a remarkable degree. On September 20, Edward Gerrity, the senior vice president for government operations and public relations, met with William Broe, the head of the CIA's Western Hemisphere Division. Still, Broe later tried to minimize this contact in his testimony before the Senate Subcommittee on Multinational Corporations. "Did you discuss with Mr. Gerrity the feasibility of possible actions by U.S. companies to designed to create or accelerate economic instability in Chile?" inquired the subcommittee chairman, Senator Frank Church of Idaho. "I explored with Mr. Gerrity the feasibility of possible actions to apply some economic pressure on Chile: yes, sir," Broe responded cautiously.[126]

Among other things, Broe and Gerrity discussed the efficacy of cutting off economic and technical assistance to Chile. They also proposed cutting off deliveries, shipments of spare parts, and other commercial transactions. Broe admitted giving Gerrity a list of companies that might be encouraged to participate in this scheme. In effect, they planned an economic blockade against Chile. Church was clearly troubled by this, asking, "Was the objective of trying to create economic instability in the ways discussed to foment internal unrest which would lead the military to intervene and stop Allende from becoming President?"[127]

Broe responded that they had merely hoped that economic instability would encourage Christian Democratic members of the Chilean Congress to vote against Allende. He denied any intention of fomenting a military coup on the part of either Gerrity or himself.[128] Logically, Church found this hard to believe: "If this was not the objective, would you state what was the objective in attempting to create instability in Chile?" Broe repeated his denials.[129]

A few weeks after meeting with Gerrity, Broe also took the time to meet with with ITT's William R. Merriam. Disturbed by the prospect of an Allende presidency, Merriam feared that Washington would not deal with Chile firmly. To reassure him, Broe offered his "opinion that if Allende was elected the U.S. Government approach would be severe."[130] Broe did not elaborate on what he meant by "severe" in his Senate testimony. It is known that Merriam wrote to Kissinger, recommending that any aid "committed to Chile should be placed in the under review status in order that entry of money into Chile is temporarily stopped with a view to a permanent cut-off if necessary."[131] Did the Nixon administration later carry out this policy only coincidentally?

Internal memoranda from ITT indicate that the corporation had greater interest in Chilean military affairs than Broe was willing to admit. After lunching with a friendly employee of the CIA, Merriam reported to John McCone, the ITT corporate director, that the intelligence man was "very, very pessimistic about defeating Allende when the congressional vote takes place October 24. Approaches continue to be made to select members of the armed forces in an attempt to have them lead some sort of uprising—no success to date."[132]

Yet, ITT did not confine its lobbying of the CIA to the Washington area. A recently declassified CIA document affirmed that ITT kept in frequent touch with the Santiago station during this period.[133] ITT also monitored Ambassador Korry's actions with extreme closeness. A memorandum addressed to Gerrity resembled a classified CIA document more than a corporate transmission: "Late Tuesday night (September 15) Ambassador Edward Korry finally received a message from State Department giving him the green light to move in the name of President Nixon. The message gave him maximum authority to do all possible—short of a Dominican Republic-type action—to keep Allende from taking power."[134]

One might also speculate whether ITT favored the removal of Schneider as well. Clearly, the corporation regarded Schneider as an obstacle: "The armed forces boss, Rene Schneider, is fully aware of the danger of Allende moving in. But he will not budge an inch without Frei's okay. One retired general, Viaux, is all gung-ho about moving immediately reason or not, but Matte [Alessandri's advisor and ITT contact] said Schneider has threatened to have Viaux shot if he moves unilaterally."[135]

Whether ITT participated in Track II or not, the corporation was prepared to spend large sums of money to prevent Allende from coming to power. Harold S. Geneen, the chairman and chief executive of ITT, reluctantly acknowledged to the Senate subcommittee that the money was meant for the campaign of Jorge Alessandri.[136] McCone, the corporate director, was only somewhat more forthcoming in his own testimony. McCone admitted that ITT had offered the CIA a million dollars to spend against the UP. McCone, who had served himself as director of the CIA in the Kennedy and Johnson administrations, symbolized the close link between U.S. intelligence and the corporate world. In spite of this background, McCone insisted that Geneen only intended this contribution to be used for charitable purposes: "Well, what he had in his mind was not chaos. What he had in mind was what could be done constructively and channeled in such a way as to encourage the people who were in support of the institutions that were inherent in this country as opposed to the Marxist philosophy of Allende. What are they? Housing for one: technical assistance, assistance in agriculture, which is so badly needed in Chile, and I can go over a long shopping list."[137]

Senator Clifford Case of New Jersey rightly suspected that ITT had other motives. "There were only 6 weeks to go before the congressional election," Case asked McCone. "How would housing have had any valuable effect on the congressional elections?"[138] Case wondered if ITT desired a more direct influence on Chilean politics: "Bribing the legislature, was that discussed?"[139] Again, McCone could only respond evasively. The $1 million offer had been intended for precisely that purpose, and presumably ITT would not have vehemently opposed a coup as an alternate strategy.[140]

Kissinger, of course, knew of ITT's offer. "My own attitude was that any covert action in Chile should be carried out exclusively by our government; this was not a field for private enterprise," he later wrote.[141] The national security advisor wished to avoid any appearance of collusion. It was irrelevant that Kissinger did not accept the money directly. The CIA was still at the service of ITT. If the CIA would not function as a conduit for the multinational corporation, Broe assured Geneen that the CIA "would explore means for the secure financial infusion of funds." Henry Hecksher, the chief of station in Santiago, directed ITT operatives to a Chilean who could serve as a secret channel for the funds.[142] Thanks to the efforts made by public servants on government time, $1 million traveled from ITT coffers to Chilean recipients. Jorge Alessandri and his National party received at least $400,000 of this enormous corporate investment.[143] "This was not known at the White House or in the State Department," Kissinger claimed, "at any rate, it also was too late."[144]

Given both Nixon and Kissinger's notorious tendency to bypass Secretary of State William Rogers in all matters of foreign policy, the State Department's ignorance of the matter is plausible. It is hard to believe, however, that Kissinger knew nothing of the covert transaction. The CIA would not have dared to act without the approval of the national security advisor, who maintained a viselike control of all intelligence operations.[145] Furthermore, White House aide Charles Colson later described meeting Harold Geneen in the office of John Ehrlichman, a senior Nixon advisor. "Geneen was very happy to be in alliance with the CIA," Colson recounted. "He was bragging about all the money he had given to the Agency."[146]

The copper industry was involved as much as the telecommunications business. Jay Parkinson, the chairman of the Anaconda board, met with Ambassdor Korry to lobby on Jorge Alessandri's behalf. Obviously, Parkinson vehemently opposed the UP's Allende for his promise to nationalize the copper mines, and Tomic had made the same promise, even if he seemed more inclined to accommodate U.S. interests. "Mr. Parkinson states that it is 'widely known' that U.S. helped to elect Frei in 1964, yet goes on to assert we could become involved in the current campaign without risk of exposure," Korry reported to Washington.[147] Like Parkinson, Korry opposed Allende, but he feared the possible exposure of contributions from Washington: "Any significant sum arriving from the U.S. would be as discreet as a moon launch. Not only does the GOC [Government of Chile] have the advantage of its 1964 experience and knowledge, but I have had too many painful experiences in the past two years with supporters of Alessandri who believe that discretion signifies only telling their five closest friends."[148]

Therefore, it was discretion rather than morality that concerned Korry. The ambassdor had no real ethical objections to interfering in the constitutional procedures of another country. If he had any reservations about supporting Alessandri, it was only because he sought to avoid hurting Tomic. "I cannot see any theoretical advantage in helping one to fight the other with indirect benefits to Allende particularly when such a commitment could not be 'discreet,'" Korry advised.[149] All the same, the ambassador probably did not disappoint Parkinson: "I would understand a theoretical case to help both Alessandri and Tomic to defeat the Castroist Allende and to demonstrate a hedging U.S. sympathy to each."[150]

Apparently, Parkinson sought far more than theoretical support. One heavily redacted memorandum from CIA Director Helms to Kissinger indicates than a certain man of influence sought an appointment with Kissinger. This man, whose name is blacked out, was "advocating that the United States Government give a lot of financial help to the Allesandri [sic] campaign."[151]

As with Ambassador Korry, Helms had some reservations: "We in the Agency are worried about pouring money into the Allesandri [sic] campaign, because his political organization appears to be so diffuse that we are afraid it will have little impact."[152] Allende was rapidly gaining strength, however, so Helms sought Kissinger's guidance.[153]

Kissinger must have advised Helms to assist Tomic as well as Alessandri. As we have already seen, the CIA station in Santiago worked with Ambassador Korry to produce a contingency plan bribe the Chilean congress: "Financial help, if necessary, will be securely provided via third parties."[154] Our representatives warned Washington that the purchase of congressional votes would cost up to $500,000. At least, $250,000 was ultimately offered to the Chilean Congress by the U.S. government.

The embassy and the Santiago station hoped to convince the Christian Democrats to swing their support to Alessandri, who enjoyed greater support than Tomic. To the PDC legislators, they planned to present Alessandri as the lesser of evils, with Allende as the greater one. If such an argument did not work, the North Americans hoped that monetary persuasion would. Beyond that, there were other methods: "Armed forces preferences, appropriately enunciated, would have to be accorded their due weight in making up congressional minds."[155]

U.S. corporate interests very likely favored this approach. As for the legislators representing Radical Party, Washington's aim was to persuade them to their candidate, Alessandri. Normally, Chilean precedent dictated that the Congress, in the event of a runoff, would always approve the victor of the popular election. In addition to bribes, the North Americans hoped to remind the Radicals that an Allende presidency would not only lead to undesirable political change, but would also deny them political patronage.[156]

In the end, the North American plan backfired. Thanks to the stubborn integrity of the Chilean Congress, Allende won the presidency on October 24, 1970. The victor, who assumed the presidential sash on November 3, planned to radically restructure Chilean society through peaceful, constitutional means. Importantly, Allende sought to avoid the violence and repression of the Russian and Cuban revolutions: "We make the claim, and I say this in all modesty, that we are creating a different way and demonstrating that it is possible to make the fundamental changes on which the road to revolution is built. We have said that we are going to create a democratic, national, revolutionary and popular government which will open the road to socialism because socialism cannot be imposed by decree."[157]

Although the UP administration would leave ample room for private enterprise, this nonviolent transition to socialism would involve the public acquisition of a vital segment of the economy. In addition to the mining and communications industries, the government would manage the energy and transportation systems.[158] Allende also intended to broaden the agrarian reform program. The state would transform land expropriated from disproportionately large farms into collectives.[159] Wage reform, the expansion of social security and public housing, and socialized medicine were features of the UP program that would fit into any truly progressive agenda. Beyond that, Allende not only wanted to socialize but further democratize the Chilean order. He favored constitutional reforms, such as the replacement of the bicameral Congress with unicameral one. As striking as these proposals were, Allende knew he could not possibly implement them without challenging the iniquitous influence of the United States on his own country.[160]

As dismayed as the Nixon administration was, it did not fear for the safety and security of the American people. The CIA, which monitored the Soviet Union with claustrophobic closeness, did not foresee a strategic partnership between it and Allende's Chile. In fact, Helms believed that the new president would carefully strengthen ties with many countries beyond the Soviet sphere of influence. Allende anticipated that Western Europe and Japan would remain loyal customers of Chile's copper and iron, and also hoped that the Soviets would acquire a taste for this mineral bounty. The CIA director did not expect to witness the fulfillment of this hope: "As for the Soviet Union, Moscow is showing caution in dealing with the new government. In turn, the Chilean Socialists will want to avoid excessive dependence on Moscow, and the Chilean Communists— for the sake of their domestic appeal—will exercise restraint in promoting closer ties with Russia."[161]

Allende was a leftist, but Helms assured the National Security Council that it had no real reason to fear even the most radical members of the Socialist cabinet. The new foreign minister, Clodomiro Almeyda, was "so far to the left that his admiration for the Chinese Communists and the Cubans in the past has placed him in opposition to Moscow."[162]

Neither Kissinger nor his patron respected Secretary of State William Rogers, but perhaps they read a study submitted to the NSC by the State Department's Bureau of the Intelligence and Research. Like Helms, the bureau doubted that the new government would transform Chile into a Soviet satellite. Allende would not permit this, because "ideologically speaking, the Chilean Socialist Party has more in common with the leaders of the Third World, who follow a policy of non-alignment and anti-imperialism."[163]

Furthermore, the study pointed to tensions between the Socialist and Communist parties. Allende offered Moscow no knee-jerk support. In fact, he denounced Soviet brutality in Hungary in 1956 and in Czechoslovakia in 1968. The strength of anti-Communist sentiment in Chile would have made a takeover by Moscow impossible, even in the unlikely event of the Soviet invasion.[164] Even before the Chilean Congress confirmed Allende's victory, he was determined to demonstrate political independence from Moscow. This stand displeased the Chilean Communist party (PCCh). On October 4, 1970, a member of the PCCh Central Committee complained to Soviet Ambassador N.B. Alekseev that the Allende administration had decided not to appoint Communists to the important Ministries of Defense, Foreign Affairs, and the Interior. Aggravating the humiliation, Communists would not have the chance to serve as ambassadors to United States, Argentina, or even Cuba and the Soviet Union.[165]

Allende held no sentimental attachment to Moscow; he was simply searching for alternatives to Washington to aid his country's development. The Soviet delegation that attended the inauguration on November 4 had an unpleasant meeting with an Allende emissary, who "expressed his dissatisfaction toward the lack of concrete propositions concerning the development of collaborative economic and commercial expansion in Chile."[166] As much as Santiago wanted Soviet aid, it was not quite as eager to cultivate all the other members of the Warsaw Pact. As the Soviet delegation observed, "The representatives from the Democratic Republic of Germany [East Germany], complained about the lack of intention on behalf of Allende and his administration in the establishing of diplomatic relations between Chile and the DRG."[167]

Apparently, the U.S. State Department was correct to conclude that Allende would not subject himself to Moscow, but Kissinger devalued the views of our official foreign-affairs agency. The national security advisor took the opinion of the NSC's Viron Vaky far more seriously, though. Vaky had a somewhat more pessimistic view of the national security implications of the Allende regime than the State Department:

> An Allende Government in Chile does not in *itself* affect the world balance of power. However, it would present the potential for use of its facilities and territories by Soviet military power. Again, this in itself would not constitute a mortal threat to the United States, but would add incrementally to Soviet military capabilities and call for the development of counter capabilities on our part to preserve our present level of military authority in the South Pacific. It is also possible that an Allende Government would in time seek and receive Soviet military equipment and guidance for its own military institutions.[168]

The last sentence in the preceding passage is telling, suggestive of a concern that Allende would not use Soviet aid to enter Moscow's orbit but to break away from Washington's. Kissinger agreed that Allende was first and foremost a Chilean nationalist: "There is general agreement that Allende intends to . . . establish close relations with the USSR, Cuba and other Socialist countries, although he will try to avoid *dependence* on the Soviets.[169] Like Vaky, Kissinger worried that Chile would set a bad example for the entire region. "An Allende Government is likely to lead opposition to U.S. influence in the hemisphere, to promote policies counter to ours and to seek the adoption of a neutralist 'Third World' stance by Latin America," the national security advisor warned Nixon.[170]

Ironically, the most successful revolutionary in Latin America at this time was discouraging Allende from adopting a hostile attitude to the United States. The CIA reported that "Castro recommended that Allende move cautiously and not break diplomatic relations with the U.S."[171] The

CIA report predicted that Allende would try to maintain civil relations with Washington, and would never permit Soviet domination of his country. As much as the Soviet Union had discouraged close Chilean ties with Cuba, Castro warned Allende against excessive dependence on Moscow: "In order to use available funds for building your militia and defense against the possible threats of your neighbors it is best not to become an economic drain on the Soviet Union and to keep your dollar markets as open as long as you can."[172]

Based on their close relationship with Cuba, the Soviets had a far better read on Castro that the CIA did. Yet after Allende's daughter, Beatriz, visited Castro in Cuba, they came to the same conclusion as the CIA. The Soviet ambassador reported that Castro extended much counsel, through her, to Beatriz's father: "He suggested that Allende not pursue or initiate any revolutionary policies in Latin America . . . Castro also suggested Allende maintain Chilean copper within the dollar's orbit. Furthermore, he recommended that he accept compensation after the nationalization of the copper mine, if that was how the North American companies wanted it."[173]

More than anything, the interest of North American companies influenced Kissinger as he framed the U.S. policy on Chile. U.S. assets in the Latin America were worth roughly $800 million, more than half of which came from the mining industry.[174] "Allende will almost surely expropriate U.S. investments sooner or later," Kissinger cautioned the president, "whether he will also compensate adequately is not clear."[175] In addition, there was the worry that Chile would fail to pay back its loans from Washington and U.S. private banks.[176]

The Nixon administration had failed to stop Allende from taking office, but it was determined to prevent him from completing his term. Kissinger would not admit this publicly, of course: "Allende was elected legally, the first Marxist government ever to come to power by free elections. He *has* legitimacy in the eyes of Chileans and most of the world; there is nothing we can do to deny him that legitimacy or claim he does not have it."[177]

Therefore, Kissinger favored an approach that would be superficially "correct, but cold. Any public manifestion or statement of hostility would be geared to his actions to avoid giving him the advantage or arguing that he is the aggrieved party," he advised Nixon.[178]

It would be far more difficult for Allende to challenge covert hostility from Washington. Kissinger went on: "The question, therefore, is whether we can take action—create pressures, exploit weaknesses, magnify obstacles—which at a minimum will either insure his failure or force him to modify his policies, and at a maximum might lead to situations where his collapse or overthrow later may be more feasible."[179]

This passive-aggression would take several forms. Washington would stop new loans from the Agency for International Development and the Export-Import Bank, and also cut off investment and export guarantees.[180] The U.S. government would also use its tremendous influence within the Inter-American Development Bank and the World Bank to further deny loans to Chile.[181] The economic warfare did not end there. Since copper comprised 8 percent of Chile's exports, Nixon explored the possibility of driving the price of copper down by selling off the U.S. stockpile. This scheme would possibly have a devastating economic impact on Chile.[182]

Unfazed by the assassination of General Schneider, Nixon wanted to do more than manipulate the Chilean economy. The Chilean military concerned him just as much, if not more: "I will never agree with the policy of downgrading the military in Latin America. They are power centers subject to our influence. . . . We'll be very cool and correct, but doing these things which will be a real message to Allende and others."[183]

Still, Washington's approach toward the Chilean military did not come entirely with carrots. Sticks were also included. Following the threat made by Korry to the military, the Nixon administration postponed the delivery of promised tanks and processed the sale of C-130 and F-5 aircraft as slowly as possible.[184] This pressure made the Chilean armed forces understand that Washington's generosity depended on action against Allende. Moreover, the Defense Department expanded its Military Group, or Milgroup, program, which encouraged extensive contact between Latin American armed forces and personnel from the U.S. military.[185] On the intelligence side, CIA Headquarters ordered the Santiago station to maintain weekly contact with receptive members of the Chilean military.[186]

As 1970 drew to a close, Allende began his administration with an optimistic attitude. He hoped to arrange a *modus vivendi* with the United States. Allende dismissed the idea that Nixon and his policymakers would destroy his socialist experiment by either military or economic means. The good doctor believed that his "victory through the polling booths was the way to preempt any such policy, because their hands are tied."[187] Allende did not realize that his counterpart to the north had only renewed his determination to unseat him.

## Notes

1. Hugh O'Shaughnessy, *Pinochet: The Politics of Torture* (New York: New York University Press, 2000), 33.

2. O'Shaughnessy, *Pinochet: The Politics of Torture*, 34.

3. Brian Loveman, *Chile: The Legacy of Hispanic Capitalism* (New York: Oxford University Press, 2001), 246.

4. O'Shaughnessy, *Pinochet*, 34.

5. Loveman, *Chile*, 246.

6. Loveman, *Chile*, 247.

7. Loveman, *Chile*, 246.

8. Edward Korry, "When Klatch Means Country," Memorandum from U.S. Embassy in Santiago to Secretary of State, Confidential 307. NSC Files, Country Files, Latin America. Folder 1: Chile Wrap-up and Postmortem, Nixon Presidential Materials Project, National Archives II, College Park, Maryland.

9. Henry Kissinger, *White House Years* (Boston: Little, Brown and Company, 1979), 666.

10. "Presidential Politics in Chile: Waiting for Don Jorge?" CIA Memorandum, Office of National Estimates, August 6, 1969. Box 128, NSC Files, HAK Office Files, Country Files, Latin America, Nixon Presidential Materials Project. National Intelligence Estimate, presented by the Central Intelligence Agency, July 30, 1970. NSC Files, HAK Office Files, Country Files, Box 128, Nixon Presidential Materials Project.

11. Kissinger, *White House Years*, 660.

12. Korry, "When Klatch Means Country."

13. Frank Chapin, "Memorandum for Dr. Kissinger: Agenda Items for the 40 Committee Meeting, 25 March 1970." The White House, Washington. State Department Collection. Freedom of Information Act website, U.S. State Department, www.foia.state.gov. A warning to the researcher: The documents are only arranged chronologically in each collection.

14. Chapin, "Memorandum for Dr. Kissinger."

15. Margaret Power, *Right-wing Women in Chile: Feminine Power and the Struggle Against Allende* (University Park, PA: Pennsylvania State University Press, 2002), 84.

16. Memorandum for the 40 Committee, "Political Action Related to the 1970 Chilean Presidential Election," June 22, 1970, FOIA website.

17. Richard Helms, *A Look over My Shoulder: A Life in the Central Intelligence Agency* (New York: Random House, 2003), 400–401.

18. Juan de Onis, "Leftists Leading as Chileans Vote for a President," *New York Times*, September 5, 1970.

19. Barbara Stallings, *Class Conflict and Economic Development in Chile, 1958-1973* (Stanford University Press, 1978), 124. Also see both Nixon's and Kissinger's memoirs for their comments on Allende's close election.

20. Richard Nixon, *RN: The Memoirs of Richard Nixon* (New York: Grosset & Dunlap, 1978), 490.

21. Seymour M. Hersh, *The Price of Power: Kissinger in the Nixon White House* (New York: Summit Books, 1983), 273, and Telephone Conversation, Donald Kendall and Henry Kissinger, September 14, 1970, 10:20 a.m., courtesy of John Powers, Nixon Presidential Materials Project.

22. Hersh, *The Price of Power*, 260.

23. Stephen E. Ambrose, *Nixon: The Triumph of a Politician, 1962-1972* (New York: Simon and Schuster, 1989), 25.

24. Ambrose, *Nixon: The Triumph of a Politician*, 17–18, and Kendall/Kissinger Telcon, September 14, 1970.

25. When I first approached Pepsico in 2005, I was told Kendall's papers were not available. Three years later, I tried again. Ms. Julie Hamp of Pepsico Communications wrote me back: "The Pepsico CEO [Indra Nooyi] forwarded me your second request for access to Mr. Donald Kendall's 'papers' to enhance research you are conducting for your dissertation for publication. I regret to inform you we have nothing available to suite your needs for public perusal. This policy will not change." Message by electronic mail, April 22, 2008.

26. Helms note courtesy of the National Security Archive. 1971 Annual Report of the Pepsico Corporation, Historical Corporate Report Collection of the Library of the Walter A. Haas School of Business, University of California, Berkeley. Bob Woodward, *Veil: The Secret Wars of the CIA 1981-1987* (New York: Simon & Schuster, 1987), 56.

27. Richard Helms, *A Look over My Shoulder*, 404.

28. Richard Helms, *A Look over My Shoulder*, 404.

29. Kissinger, *White House Years*, 671.

30. Kissinger, *White House Years*, 671.

31. Richard Nixon, *RN*, 489.

32. Richard Nixon, *RN*, 489.

33. Nixon, *RN*, 489, and Helms, *A Look over My Shoulder*, 400.

34. Kissinger, *White House Years*, 654.

35. CIA Intelligence Synopsis/Summary, "Soviet Union: Maintaining a Low Profile in Chile," June 30, 1970.

36. Edward Korry, "Chile: Election Perspectives #4 (Part II), Telegram to the Secretary of State 765, July 1970. NSSM-97, Box H-172, Nixon Presidential Materials Project and United States Senate Select Committee to Study Governmental Operations with Respect to Intelligence Activities, *Covert Action in Chile: 1963-1973* (Washington: U.S. Government Printing Office, 1975), 20.

37. Korry, "Chile: Election Perspectives #4 (Part II).

38. Edward Korry, Cable to Secretary of State. Confidential Telegram 749, September 1970. Courtesy of the National Security Archive.

39. Edward Korry, Cable to Secretary of State, August 10, 1970.

40. Edward Korry, Cable to Secretary of State, August 10, 1970. Senior Review Group Meetings, Box H-47, Nixon Presidential Materials Project.

41. Jonathan Haslam, *The Nixon Administration and the Death of Allende's Chile* (New York: Verso, 2005), 74.

42. Tanya Harmer, "A Different 9/11: Cuba and the Chilean Coup of 1973," Annual Conference of the Society for Historians of American Foreign Relations, Chantilly, VA, June 21, 2007.

43. Viron P. Vaky, "Memorandum for Dr. Kissinger: Chilean Election," June 23, 1970. National Security Council, FOIA website.

44. Viron P. Vaky, "Memorandum for Dr. Kissinger: Chilean Election," June 23, 1970.

45. Viron P. Vaky, "Memorandum for Dr. Kissinger: Chilean Election," June 23, 1970.

46. Viron P. Vaky, "Memorandum for Dr. Kissinger: NSSM 97 – Chile," August 18, 1970. Senior Review Group Meetings, Box H-47, Nixon Presidential Materials Project.

47. Oval Office Conversation. June 11, 1971, 9:37a.m.–10:36a.m. Nixon, Haldeman, and Kissinger. Tape 517-4, Nixon Presidential Materials Project.

48. Sir David Frost with Bob Zelnick, Frost/Nixon: Behind the Scenes of the Nixon Interviews (New York: Harper Perennial, 2007), 287–288.

49. National Intelligence Estimate, submitted by CIA Director Richard Helms, January 28, 1969. NSC Files, HAK Office Files, Country Files, Box 128, Nixon Presidential Materials Project.

50. National Intelligence Estimate, January 28, 1969.

51. National Intelligence Estimate, July 30, 1970.

52. See Fredrik Logevall, Choosing War: The Lost Chance for Peace and the Escalation of War in Vietnam (Berkeley, Los Angeles: University of California Press, 1999). Avi Shlaim, The Iron Wall: Israel and the Arab World (New York: Norton, 2001).

53. Ibid. It is unlikely that Allende ever regarded the United States as impotent.

54. Viron Vaky, "Memorandum for Dr. Kissinger: 40 Committee Meeting, September 8– Chile," September 7, 1970, FOIA website.

55. CIA Memorandum for Deputy Director of Plans, "National Intelligence Estimate–Chile," July 29, 1970, FOIA website.

56. "National Intelligence Estimate – Chile," July 29, 1970.

57. The media helped to perpetuate this myth. See David Stout, "Edward Korry, 81, is Dead; Falsely Tied to Chile Coup," The New York Times, January 30, 2003.

58. Memorandum, "Phase II Planning," August 23, 1970. Attachment to "Presidential Politics in Chile: Waiting for Don Jorge?" CIA Memorandum, Office of National Estimates, August 6, 1969. Box 128, NSC Files, HAK Office Files, Country Files, Latin America, Nixon Presidential Materials Project.

59. "Eyes Only for Ambassador Korry from Dr. Kissinger and Alex Johnson," October 7, 1970. NSC Subject Files, Box 336, Nixon Presidential Materials Project.

60. "Eyes Only for Ambassador Korry."

61. CIA Report, "Track II," October 1970, FOIA website.

62. CIA Document, "Track II, October 25, 1974, FOIA website. Memorandum from P.M. Flanigan to Ambassador Korry, "Re: Ambassador Korry," April 8, 1969. White House Central Files, Special Files, Box 14. Ex Fo 2/CO 33 [1969-1970], Nixon Presidential Materials Project.

63. "Track II, October 25, 1974.

64. Oval Office Conversation. April 6, 1971, 10:05a.m.–11:03a.m. Nixon and Kissinger. Tape 517-4, Nixon Presidential Materials Project.

65. Memorandum from Henry A. Kissinger to President Nixon, "Subject: Chile," September 17, 1970. Courtesy of the National Security Archive.

66. "Subject: Chile," September 17, 1970.

67. "Subject: Chile," September 17, 1970.

68. "Schneider v. Kissinger," 60 Minutes, Columbia Broadcasting System, September 9, 2001.

69. "Schneider v. Kissinger."

70. Pio Garcia, Las Fuerzas Armadas y El Golpe de Estado en Chile (Mexico, Spain, and Argentina: Siglo Veintiuno Editores, 1974), 455.

71. Garcia, Las Fuerzas Armadas y El Golpe de Estado en Chile, 452.

72. Garcia, Las Fuerzas Armadas y El Golpe de Estado en Chile, 454.

73. Garcia, Las Fuerzas Armadas y El Golpe de Estado en Chile, 454.

74. Garcia, Las Fuerzas Armadas y El Golpe de Estado en Chile, 452.

75. Hersh, The Price of Power, 279.

76. Cable from CIA Headquarters to Santiago Station, October 11, 1970, FOIA website.

77. Cable from Santiago Station to CIA Headquarters, October 1970, FOIA website. Christopher Hitchens, The Trial of Henry Kissinger (New York: Verso, 2001), 262.

78. Cable from Santiago Station to CIA Headquarters, October 1970, FOIA website.

79. Hitchens, The Trial of Henry Kissinger, 57.

80. CIA Report, "Track II," October 1970, FOIA website.

81. CIA Memorandum of Conversation, "Dr. Kissinger, Mr. Karamessines, Gen. Haig at the White House," October 15, 1970, FOIA website.

82. "Dr. Kissinger, Mr. Karamessines, Gen. Haig at the White House," October 15, 1970.

83. Kissinger, White House Years, 676.

84. Richard Nixon, RN, 490.

85. Hitchens, The Trial of Henry Kissinger, 66.

86. Hersh, The Price of Power, 282.

87. CIA Cable from Headquarters to Santiago Station, October 18, 1970, FOIA website.

88. 60 Minutes, September 9, 2001.

89. CIA Cable from Headquarters to Santiago Station, October 20, 1970, FOIA website. Hersh, The Price of Power, 288, and 60 Minutes, September 9, 2001.

90. CIA, "Special Situation Report," October 19, 1970, FOIA website.

91. "Special Situation Report," October 19, 1970.

92. Hitchens, The Trial of Henry Kissinger, 63.

93. CIA Cable from Santiago Station to Washington, October 20, 1970, FOIA website.

94. Garcia, Las Fuerzas Armadas, 455.

95. 60 Minutes, September 9, 2001.

96. CIA Document, "Track II," October 20, 1970.

97. Cable from William Broe and David A. Phillips of CIA Headquarters to Santiago Station, October 20, 1970, FOIA website.

98. Cable from William Broe and David A. Phillips of CIA Headquarters to Santiago Station, October 20, 1970.

99. CIA Document, "Track II," October 20, 1970.

100. United Nations Diplomatic Conference of Plenipotentiaries on the Establishment of an International Criminal Court, *Rome Statute of the International Criminal Court*, July 17, 1998.

101. *60 Minutes*, September 9, 2001.

102. Garcia, *Las Fuerzas Armadas*, 453.

103. Hersh, *The Price of Power*, 290.

104. Gregory F. Treverton, *Covert Action: The Limits of Intervention in the Postwar World* (New York: Basic Books, 1987), 131, and *60 Minutes*, September 9, 2001. "The Interim Report: Alleged Assassination Plots Involving Foreign Leaders," The Select Committee to Study Government Operations with Respect to Intelligence Activities. Washington, DC: U.S. Government Printing Office, 1975: 226, 245.

105. Treverton, *Covert Action*, 132.

106. Hersh, *The Price of Power*, 289.

107. Hersh, *The Price of Power*, 289.

108. Hersh, *The Price of Power*, 293.

109. Hitchens, *The Trial of Henry Kissinger*, 64.

110. For clarification of these legal matters, the author would like to thank two specialists in international law, Professor Philippe Sands of University College, London, and an American scholar who wishes to remain anonymous.

111. Hersh, *The Price of Power*, 291.

112. "Maximum Effort in Circumstances Prevailing in Chile." Cable from CIA Headquarters to Santiago Station, October 23, 1970, FOIA website.

113. Cable from Santiago Station to CIA Director, October 30, 1970, FOIA website.

114. Margaret Power, "We Opposed the Coup: Chilean Military Resistance to the Overthrow of Salvador Allende," Annual Meeting of the American Historical Association, Washington, D.C., January 5, 2008, 3–4.

115. Power, "We Opposed the Coup," 5.

116. Power, "We Opposed the Coup," 8.

117. Testimony of Hal Hendrix. "Multinational Corporations and United States Foreign Policy," *Hearings before the Subcommittee on Multinational Corporations of the Committee on Foreign Relations, United States Senate, Ninety-Third Congress, on the International Telephone and Telegraph, 1970-1971,* (Washington: U.S. Government Printing Office, 1973), 128–129.

118. Robert Sobel, *I.T.T.: The Management of Opportunity* (New York: Times Books, 1982), 254.

119. Sobel, *I.T.T.*, 279.

120. Ambrose, *Nixon: The Triumph of a Politician*, 436. Anthony Sampson, *The Sovereign State of ITT* (New York: Stein and Day, 1973), 173.

121. Jack Anderson with George Clifford, *The Anderson Papers* (New York: Random House, 1973), 34–35. Anthony Sampson, *The Sovereign State of ITT* (New York: Stein and Day, 1973), 173.

122. Anderson, *The Anderson Papers*, 36–37.

123. Sobel, *I.T.T.*, 282–283.

124. Sampson, *The Sovereign State of ITT*, 201.

125. Sampson, *The Sovereign State of ITT*, 201.

126. Anderson, *The Anderson Papers*, 107. John Dean, *Blind Ambition: The White House Years* (New York: Simon & Schuster, 1976), 58. Testimony of William Broe. *Hearings before the Subcommittee on Multinational Corporations*, 250.

127. Broe, *Hearings before the Subcommittee on Multinational Corporations*, 251.

128. Broe, *Hearings before the Subcommittee on Multinational Corporations*, 251.

129. Broe, *Hearings before the Subcommittee on Multinational Corporations*, 251.

130. Broe, *Hearings before the Subcommittee on Multinational Corporations*, 254.

131. Anderson, *The Anderson Papers*, 117.

132. Anderson, *The Anderson Papers*, 115.

133. CIA, "ITT Funding in Chilean 1970 Presidential Election," FOIA website.

134. ITT Memorandum from Hal Hendrix and Robert Berrellez to Edward J. Gerrity, September 17, 1970. *Appendix to Hearings before the Subcommittee on Multinational Corporations*, 608.

135. Memorandum to Edward J. Gerrity, 612.

136. Testimony of Harold S. Geneen. *Hearings before the Subcommittee on Multinational Corporations*, 463.

137. Testimony of John McCone, 104.

138. Testimony of John McCone, 104.

139. Testimony of John McCone, 104.

140. David F. Cusack, *Revolution and Reaction: The Internal and International Dynamics of Conflict and Confrontation in Chile* (Denver: University of Denver Graduate School of International Studies, 1977), 109.

141. Kissinger, *White House Years*, 667n.

142. Hersh, *The Price of Power*, 267–268.

143. "Ambassador Korry Proposals and Requested 40 Committee to Endorse Them," October 23, 1970. CIA Collection, FOIA website.

144. Kissinger, *White House Years*, 667n.

145. Hersh, *The Price of Power*, 269.

146. Hersh, *The Price of Power*, 269.

147. "The Electoral Stakes, the Pot and the Jockey with the Money," telegram from American Embassy Santiago to Secretary of State, Wasington, D.C., April 28, 1970. Box 128, NSC Files, HAK Office Files, Country Files, Nixon Presidential Materials Project.

148. "The Electoral Stakes, the Pot and the Jockey with the Money."

149. "The Electoral Stakes, the Pot and the Jockey with the Money."

150. "The Electoral Stakes, the Pot and the Jockey with the Money."

151. Memorandum from Richard Helms to Henry Kissinger, June 16, 1970. NSC Files, HAK Office Files, Country Files, Box 101, Nixon Presidential Materials Project.

152. Memorandum from Richard Helms to Henry Kissinger, June 16, 1970.

153. Memorandum from Richard Helms to Henry Kissinger, June 16, 1970.

154. Memorandum, "Phase II Planning," August 23, 1970.

155. Hersh, *The Price of Power*, 278, Memorandum, "Phase II Planning," August 23, 1970.

156. Ibid.

157. Regis Debray, *Conversations with Allende* (Bristol, United Kingdom: NLB, 1971), 117.

158. Stallings, *Class Conflict and Economic Development in Chile*, 126.

159. Stallings, *Class Conflict and Economic Development in Chile*, 126–127.

160. Stallings, *Class Conflict and Economic Development in Chile*, 127.

161. Richard Helms, CIA Briefing for the National Security Council. November 6, 1970, FOIA website.

162. Helms, CIA Briefing, November 6, 1970.

163. State Department Research Study, "Chile: Is Allende the Prelude To a Communist Victory?" Bureau of Intelligence and Research. October 1, 1970, Senior Review Group Meetings, Box H-48, Nixon Presidential Materials Project.

164. "Chile: Is Allende the Prelude To a Communist Victory?"

165. A Conversation Between Ambassador N.B. Alekseev and Volodia Teitelboim, October 14, 1970, in "*Chile en los Archivos de las URSS* (1959-1973)," *Estudios Públicos* 72 (Spring 1998), 411.

166. Report of Soviet Delegation, October 31 to November 8, 1970, in "*Chile en los Archivos de las URSS*," 414.

167. Report of Soviet Delegation, October 31 to November 8, 1970.

168. Memorandum from Viron Vaky to Kissinger, "SRG Meeting–October 17 . . . . NSSM 97–Chile," October 16, 1970. Box H-048, Senior Review Group Meetings, Nixon Presidential Materials Project.

169. HAK Talking Points on Chile, November 6, 1970. NSC Meetings, Box H-29, Folder 8, Nixon Presidential Materials Project.

170. Henry Kissinger to President Nixon, "Chile – Immediate Operational Issues," NSC Document, FOIA website.

171. CIA Report on Cuban President Fidel Castro's Advice to Allende, October 6, 1970, FOIA website.

172. CIA Report on Cuban President Fidel Castro's Advice to Allende, October 6, 1970.

173. A Conversation Between Ambassador N.B. Alekseev and Volodia Teitelboim, October 14, 1970, in "*Chile en los Archivos de las URSS* (1959-1973)," 411.

174. Richard Helms, CIA Briefing for the National Security Council, November 6, 1970, FOIA website.

175. Henry Kissinger to President Nixon, "Chile – Immediate Operational Issues," NSC Document, FOIA website.

176. Memorandum from Viron Vaky to Kissinger, "SRG Meeting–October 17 . . . . NSSM 97–Chile," October 16, 1970.

177. Memorandum from Kissinger to President Nixon, "NSC Meeting, November 6–Chile," November 5, 1970. Box H-29, Folder 8, NSC Meetings, Nixon Presidential Materials Project.

178. "NSC Meeting, November 6–Chile," November 5, 1970.

179. Henry Kissinger to President Nixon, "Chile–Immediate Operational Issues," NSC Document, FOIA website.

180. Memorandum from Kissinger to President Nixon, "Status Report on Chile." Box H-220, Folder 2, NSDM 93, Nixon Presidential Materials Project.

181. "Status Report on Chile."

182. Memorandum of Conversation-NSC Meeting (NSSM 97), November 6, 1970. NSC Meetings, Box H-29, Folder 8, Nixon Presidential Materials Project.

183. Memorandum of Conversation-NSC Meeting (NSSM 97), November 6, 1970.

184. Memorandum from Kissinger to President Nixon, "Status Report on Chile."

185. Memorandum from Secretary of Defense Melvin Laird to President Nixon, "United States Military Representation in Latin America." NSDM-93, Box H-220, Folder 2, Nixon Presidential Materials Project.

186. CIA Cable to Santiago Station, November 1970, FOIA website.

187. Debray, Conversations with Allende, 126.

# CHAPTER FOUR

# Undermining the Chilean Experiment: 1971

President Allende began the year 1971 expressing no ill will toward the United States. Even though Nixon had refrained from congratulating Allende for his victory, the leader of Chile publicly expressed his desire for "friendly relations with the most powerful country in the hemisphere so long as it can admit disagreement and dissent."[1] He also insisted that his administration would "never permit the construction of a foreign military base by any power."[2] In conference with Ambassador Korry and Assistant Secretary of State for Inter-American Affairs Charles A. Meyer, the Chilean president gave his word that his country would not enter any entangling foreign alliances.[3]

Nixon did not care about Allende's promises. "We're still keeping our tough policy with regard to Chile," the president told Kissinger.[4] The Pentagon may have speculated that Socialist rule in Chile would make the Straits of Magellan vulnerable if the Panama Canal came under attack, but the United States really did not have to fear for its physical security.[5] To Nixon, Allende represented a loss for the United States rather than a gain for the Soviet Union. If Chile could break free from the North American empire, what would stop other Latin American countries from doing so? As I have noted in the previous chapter, Nixon admitted to Kissinger: "I know the argument, of course, that if we get out, we lose our [stroke?] there. The Russians will be happy to come in, and so forth and so on. But the fact is that he [Allende] is just gonna [wheel? reel?] us in, frankly, and also that treating him well is going to encourage others to go do likewise. That's what I'm more concerned about."[6]

Sharing his superior's attitude, Kissinger sarcastically dismissed Chile as "a dagger pointed at the heart of Antarctica."[7] Ironically, the national security advisor was merely repeating the assessment of Ernesto "Che" Guevara. The late Argentine revolutionary had studied the maps and determined that Chile was not a suitable pad from which to launch a revolution in the Southern Cone. Geograhically, Chile was but a slender strip caught between the Andes and the Pacific. The Atacama desert and an icy wonderland served as the northern and southern borders, respectively. In his planning, Guevara had favored Argentina, Peru, and Bolivia, the country where Guevara ultimately perished in 1967.[8]

No matter what Guevara had thought, it is unlikely that Allende would have struggled to liberate Chile from dependence on the United States only to subjugate his country to the Soviet Union, an empire potentially just as oppressive. The Chilean foreign minister, Clodomiro Almeyda, articulated a point that remains relevant today for Americans bewildered by international resentment of Washington policy: "It seems to me there exists a distinction between anti-imperialism and anti-Americanism. Actually, Chile's foreign policy is not aimed against any people of the world. Consequently, neither is it against the people of the United States. It is a policy designed to break the dependent relationship of Chile's economy with respect to interests which are not ours."[9]

Allende began to break this dependent relationship with the nationalization of the copper mines. Under the Allende administration, Jorge Arrate served as the chief executive officer of CODELCO, the public copper corporation. As a man of the left, Arrate did not think highly of President Frei, but he later commended the Christian Democrat for beginning the process of reform with his Chileanization program. "Probably, that's why the right in Chile baptized him as the Chilean Kerensky," Arrate observed.[10] Just as Alexander Kerensky inadvertently enabled the triumph of his more radical successor, Vladimir Lenin, in Russia in 1917, Frei performed the same function for Allende in Chile in 1970.

Truly significant change, however, only took place once Allende came to power. In the years since the coup, critics have attributed the failure of his Socialist experiment to political polarization within Chile. Yet, the politics of the Andean nation were not so polarized that Allende could not expropriate the copper mines through legal and constitutional means. In fact, on July 11 the Chilean Congress unanimously passed the constitutional amendment that made the nationalization possible. With justification, Allende felt triumphant: "Remember that in slightly more than 50 years more than $3 billion has left the country by way of copper profits. Now, with the nationalization, we will retain 90 million additional dollars annually. This will mean, in the next 20 years . . . 1.83 billion dollars."[11]

This amendment honored the principle of fair compensation, but allowed deductions from the compensation to copper companies for excess profits. Authorized by the amendment to determine the maximum profit level that was not in excess, Allende arrived at the figure of 12 percent. Consulting the register of profits for the U.S. copper corporations, which dated back to 1953, Allende made retroactive deductions.[12] Ultimately, the Chilean government would withhold $675 million from Kennecott and $364 million from Anaconda.[13] Arrate recalled: "So, when he applied, according to the constitution, the twelve percent backwards to the profits obtained by the companies, the amount that he had to deduct was more than the value of two of these four companies [mines], Chuquicamata [an Anaconda mine] and [Kennecott's] El Teniente, and very large in the case of [Anaconda's] El Salvador, the third mine, and almost nil in the case of the fourth mine, Andina, that was owned by Cerro Corporation [Cerro de Pasco, another U.S. company], and who got almost one hundred percent compensation of the book value."[14]

Besides Chuquicamata and El Salvador, Anaconda also lost its 75 percent share in the Exotica mine. Nevertheless, the new Chilean law allowed for fair consideration of corporate interests. Taking the constitutionally mandated course of action, the Chilean Comptroller General's office, or *contraloría*, awarded Cerro de Pasco $18 million in compensation upon determination that the company had not accumulated excess profits. The Chilean Special Court increased this award by almost $1 million the following year. Anaconda and Kennecott, of course, won nothing from the comptroller-general.[15] Despite this loss, the Allende administration assured the two corporations that it would deduct the excess profits solely from their own shares in the mines. After all, Frei's Chileanization scheme had left Anaconda with only 49 percent of Chuquicamata and El Salvador, and Kennecott with 49 percent of El Teniente.[16]

The Nixon administration could have reached an accommodation with Chile. In Santiago, the minister of the interior made an interesting communication to the U.S. ambassador. Korry reported to the secretary of state that "Allende wanted me to understand GOC's disposition to seek to avoid dispute over copper and that he had charged [Interior Minister] Toha with sounding me further on details."[17] Interestingly, Korry's own dispatches growing tolerance for Allende. It did not matter to Nixon. He was outraged by the expropriation, but Arrate believed that the president seized on the copper issue an excuse to torment the Allende government: "So, much time before

Allende came to government, or Allende nationalized copper, or Allende applied excess profits, or fixed the compensation of the copper companies, the U.S. policy was already punishing Chile. Certainly, the copper question became an additional question to reinforce U.S. policy, and I understand that because this decision by Allende of applying excess profits, to the excess profits concept, to the American companies had an international impact."[18]

Far more than the loss of the copper mines in Chile, Nixon feared the example the Chilean expropriations would set for the rest of Latin America, and indeed the entire Western Hemisphere. The president listened carefully to the advice of Treasury Secretary John Connally, who advocated a hard line. Connally eschewed the idea of cooperation with the rest of the world: "Foreigners are out to screw us. Our job is to screw them first."[19] Less crudely, Nixon explained Connally's viewpoint to Kissinger: "Now here's his argument. His argument is that, that for example, Guyana, we have $500 million worth of contracts with Guyana in bauxite and so forth. They're willing to expropriate. Chile is getting away with it. The Jamaicans, the Jamaicans are willing to expropriate and so forth and so on."[20]

In Connally's view, the United States had to regain control of Chile's copper. Connally wrote to Nixon that "it is in our interest to facilitate the development of the mineral resources of Chile. That country is practically unique in the resources it has under soil."[21] Apparently, it never occurred to the treasury secretary that the United States could have purchased Chilean copper on Chilean terms. Like the other members of the Nixon administration, Connally feared the example that Allende would set for the rest of the world, noting America's growing reliance on imported minerals.[22]

Kissinger feared that any concessions to Allende and his ilk in Latin America would lead to imperial decline. "We are sliding into the position of Great Britain around World War I," the former Harvard professor lectured in the Oval Office. "Yeah," Nixon replied with deference to Kissinger's erudition. "In the nineteenth century, they were so far ahead that no one could compete with them," the expert on European history continued. "It took them about thirty years to realize that they had become second-class."[23]

For a more succinct description of the White House mindset, one must turn to a scholar who remained active in his own academic field, Richard R. Fagen. "Once again, the specter of the dominoes arose, again with a global cast," Fagen wrote.[24] Just as President Nixon had senselessly committed himself to keeping the domino of South Vietnam erect in Asia, he now committed himself to preventing the fall of any Latin American dominoes after Chile. Nixon concealed his covert actions against Allende, but he intended his official policy on Chile to serve as a warning to its neighbors. Shortly after the confiscation of the copper mines, the president warned that in the case of any uncompensated seizures, the United States would "withhold its support from loans under consideration in multilateral development banks."[25] Treasury Secretary John Connally in particular pushed for this strategy. Connally placed enormous pressure on the president of the World Bank, former Defense Secretary Robert S. McNamara. Speaking to Nixon, Connally expressed his opinions in a forceful manner: "I'm gonna have lunch with Bob tomorrow to try to make him insist on a policy that no World Bank loan will be made to any country that has expropriated properties, and without some definite plans of compensation, and I think that's only fair."[26]

From 1964 to 1971, Chile had collected over $1 billion from the World Bank, the Inter-American Development Bank, the Export-Import Bank, and the Agency for International Development. Since the United States possessed 23 percent of the votes in the World Bank and dominated the Inter-American Development Bank, this meant an end to loans from these institutions.[27] Connally would forbid the American members of the development banks from approving any loans to Chile.[28]

In addition, credit would no longer come from the Agency for International Development or the Eximbank, which were both entirely controlled by the U.S. government.[29] The Exim Bank cut-off was particularly painful, for it affected a Chilean application for a $21 million loan needed for the procurement of one 727 and two 707 Boeing jets. LAN-Chile, the national airline, was a good credit risk. "The preliminary studies conducted by Boeing Co. show that this operation is commercially sound and that the aircraft services would produce enough revenues to cover the credits eventually agreed on for this purpose," the Chilean embassy pointed out.[30] The granting of the loan had been almost certain before the expropriation.[31]

Very disturbed by this sudden reversal, Chilean Ambassador Orlando Letelier met with Kissinger in Washington. Speaking for Allende, with whom he had conferred a few days earlier, Letelier expressed the preference for closer economic ties to the West than the East. According to the minutes of their meeting:

> The Ambassador indicated that if the Boeing planes were not available, the only real alternative Chile would have would be to buy Soviet planes. Chile needs long-range aircraft, and the only equivalent to the 707s were Ilyushin turboprops. He stated that a decision already had been made in principle to buy the Soviet planes, but that this would be a tragedy for Chile—the Soviet planes are much more expensive (around $100 million); LAN-Chile would have 50 percent U.S. planes and 50 percent Soviet planes, which would present problems and might even require shifting the fleet completely to Soviet planes.[32]

To the distinguished diplomat's face, Kissinger denied any involvement with Eximbank's abrupt turnaround, claiming "that his function was not to solve the problems of American business. He again reiterated that he did handle individual loans."[33] Letelier pointed out that Eximbank officers had admitted to him that their decision had been political rather than financial, "that they were concerned about the reaction of the Senate and other sectors." Letelier, who was probably too tactful to mention that Eximbank was also concerned about the reaction of the White House, asked the national security advisor to "clarify these political aspects so the loan could go forward."[34] Offering little encouragement, Kissinger only "indicated that . . . he would take a look at this matter, but emphasized that he had not taken an active role in this loan, and that he was not sure he wanted to get into these commercial matters."[35]

In fact, Kissinger was heavily invested in these commercial matters. Well before his confrontation with Letelier, Kissinger had conferred with an Eximbank official. The national security advisor later explained the retaliatory scheme to the president: "He can attach banking conditions, which, if they don't come across on expropriation, enable us to prevent the thing from coming through. What they would do is retrieve the application and process it over a period longer than the expropriation hearings."[36]

In many ways, this strategy was as covertly underhanded as the plotting against the late General Schneider. Kissinger warned Nixon that "an openly restrictive policy would be inconsistent with our public statements on Chile (and with our more forthcoming trade policies vis-à-vis the Soviet bloc and China), and would help Allende gain sympathy in Chile and abroad, thus making it easier for him to treat the U.S. companies unfairly."[37]

Kissinger's thinking matched that of the corporate world. That year, Secretary of State Rogers held a meeting with representatives of the companies most threatened by the Allende experiment: ITT, Anaconda, Ralston Purina, the Bank of America, and the First National City Bank. Several of the attendees, including Jack Guilfoyle and J.R. McNitt of ITT, lobbied for a punitive credit policy. The delegates from the First City National Bank and the Bank of America favored subtlety: "The bankers take the position that there should be no publicity, just not to approve the loan and let it slide along."[38] Kissinger did not arrive at this same passive-aggressive strategy by mere coincidence. Knowing where power rested in Washington, the corporations did not stop their lobbying with Secretary Rogers. They also met with Kissinger and his underlings. An internal Anaconda memorandum shows that the copper company worked closely with ITT to influence the national security advisor. "The idea is to keep the pressure on Kissinger and the White House," the memorandum stated.[39]

With this pressure, Chile did not get the loan for the jets, but the economic retribution did not end there. Kissinger embarked on total economic war, intending "to maintain economic pressure on Chile in order to contribute to Allende's economic problems and to help prevent the consolidation of his regime."[40] Through aggressive use of its own judicial system, the United States also froze stateside accounts belonging to the government of Chile.[41] Allende had anticipated that state control of the copper industry would enrich his country immeasurably, but the controversy now made the export of copper to the United States an absolute impossibility.

When the Chilean president turned to Western Europe as an alternative market, however, Kennecott worked to foil his plans. Taking legal action in France, Holland, Sweden, Italy, and Germany, Kennecott tried to block the copper sales. Although Germany did seize a shipment of copper, eventually a judge in Hamburg reversed this seizure. Chile was not so fortunate elsewhere. A French court agreed to freeze the profits from a shipment to the port of Le Havre, so Chile could not claim its entitled $1.3 million until the court determined if Kennecott was not still the rightful recipient. A delivery to Sweden was confiscated. At the port of Rotterdam, a Dutch court froze yet another copper shipment. Kennecott's campaign frightened other potential customers away. Furthermore, European banks now regarded Chile as a bad credit risk, and the beleaguered country lost $200 million in potential credit. The evidence suggests the possibility of collusion between Kennecott and the U.S. government. "Sure, we're in touch from time to time," a State Department spokesman admitted. "We're interested in solutions to problems. And you don't get solutions by sitting on your hands."[42]

As devastating as these legal actions were, their impact could not compare to the shortage of the machine components required for copper mining. Purchasing these components clearly had never been easy, as Arrate described the mining procedure "which started from the moment in which the mineral is extracted, to the process in which the mineral is crushed, and then when it's crushed, you have to concentrate the mineral, and once concentrated, you melt the mineral, and once the mineral is melted, you have to refine it. So, this continuous process of production demands very complex machinery, and for each machine there were hundreds of thousands of small things and parts and pieces."[43]

The United States had been the main supplier of these parts, but the expropriation put an end to that arrangement. The confiscation of Chilean assets in the United States forced CODELCO to procure these parts through intermediaries, which proved very expensive.[44]

Despite the widespread criticism of the UP economic program that continues to this day, the governmental operation of the copper industry was remarkably profitable, and its income grew by 8.3 percent in 1971 alone. More than three decades after the coup, CODELCO remains in state hands. Arrate estimated that the state-owned company's profits in the ten or fifteen years after expropriation equaled one-half of the Chilean national debt. "It's a public enterprise," Arrate noted with pride. "It's administered by people who are nominated by the government. And it works very well."[45] The never-ending campaign of certain businessmen to privatize CODELCO indicates its success. "That's obvious," the former CODELCO executive concludes. "This is big business. It's very good business. So, they like to privatize things in which they could earn a lot of money."[46]

Copper was not the only source of financial friction between Chile and the United States. In order to make telephone service more widely available in Chile, the Allende government assumed full control of Chiltelco, of which ITT owned seventy percent. As with the copper companies, the Chilean state and ITT could not agree over the value of the subsidiary. The Allende regime appraised Chiltelco at $24 million, while the corporation demanded $153 million in compensation. Interestingly, Chile might already have compensated ITT in 1966. The Frei administration had paid ITT $186 million to expand its service, even though another foreign corporation had outbid it. Of course, ITT would not see things that way. Like Kennecott and Anaconda, ITT would only resolve the issue to its advantage once the military junta came to power.[47]

Once relations with the United States reached the point of dysfunction, Allende desperately sought new, more equitable partnerships abroad. Breaking the dependence of the Chilean armed forces on the United States was an almost unrealistic project. Despite the economic blockade of Chile, the United States remained the main supplier of armaments to her military. Arrate recalled: "Allende made the attempt to orient the militaries to buy also Soviet weapons, and I think there was some official trips of military men to the Soviet Union to see weaponry, and see the possibilities of buying . . . but it was very difficult."[48]

Chile's economic diplomacy also met with little success. When Allende approached European countries such as France, Spain, Sweden, Holland, West Germany, and Finland for replacement of the credits that had been cut off by the United States, he found that such assistance would only come conditionally. European credit required the purchase of European goods.[49] The Chilean president also turned to the Kremlin for credit. The Soviet experience with Cuba made the socialist superpower disinclined to sponsor another

Latin American country, however. By this point, Fidel Castro's own economic experiment was draining Moscow of approximately one-half billion dollars annually.[50] "The Soviet Union was not in a position to support the Allende experiment in the way that Allende needed," Arrate remembered.[51]

So, how much support was the Soviet Union able to provide Chile? It is difficult for find a precise determination. We do know that trade between the Soviet Union and Chile grew from 300,000 rubles in 1969 to 7.8 million rubles two years later. The Soviets also offered to sell the Chileans 6.5 million rubles worth of tractors in 1971. As for financial assistance, Moscow furnished Chile with approximately 100,000 tons of wheat that same year. For the entire Allende presidency, estimates of Soviet aid ranged from $183 million to $340 million, with the higher end of the range bearing the most probability.[52]

On May 28, 1971, Chilean Foreign Minister Clodomiro Almeyda traveled to Moscow to work out an agreement on trade as well as technical and cultural assistance. Almeyda managed to renegotiate old Soviet credits from the Frei period that had been unexploited. Moscow also provided between $15 and $55 million dollars in additional credits for the sale of machinery and equipment, Soviet-made, of course. Surely Soviet sponsorship of plans for a basic oils plant and a prefabricated panel factory would have given the Nixon administration no cause for alarm! For the Chilean fishing industry, the USSR also promised in September to assist in the development of ports and make watercraft available for charter. In addition, the Soviet Union also dispatched twenty experts on the copper industry to Chile to provide help and advice.[53] When examined closely in detail, this assistance is not terribly impressive. It could not match the aid previously furnished by Washington, but then again, Moscow did not want to assume its rival's formal role. Interestingly, the Communist superpower felt obligated to assist the fledgling Socialist government in its nationalization programs, but the official Soviet organ *Pravda* cautioned Chile to preserve free enterprise "for a long time to come."[54]

Ideological attitudes inhibited the Soviets from offering the Chilean road to socialism their wholehearted support. Marxist-Leninist philosophy dictated that Third World countries had to complete two developmental stages before attaining socialist statehood. The anti-imperialist stage was the first one, which was then followed by the phase of socialist construction. Although Moscow regarded Cuba as an ideological work-in-progress, the beleaguered island had at least reached the second stage of development. Allende's Chile was barely in the first.[55] Accordingly, only Cuba merited the kind of special assistance to which a favored client was entitled. Moscow could only extend its generosity so far. A contemporary Soviet expert on the Third World, R. Ulyanovsky, baldly translated the Kremlin view: "In effect, assistance from the socialist community which actively opposes imperialism, is the foundation of non-capitalist development and the factor making this development possible. [However] assistance from the socialist countries necessarily bears the character of mutually beneficial cooperation, because the resources of one side obviously cannot satisfy the acute and growing requirements of the countries that have taken or are prepared to take the road of non-capitalist development."[56]

Indeed, the public pronouncements issued by the Kremlin about Chile indicated passive sympathy rather than active commitment. Speaking before the 24th Party Congress in 1971, General Secretary Leonid Brezhnev offered Chile nothing substantial even as he celebrated Allende's electoral triumph. "This has incensed domestic reaction and Yankee imperialism, which seek to deprive the Chilean people of their gains," Brezhnev declared. "However, the people of Chile are fully determined to advance along their chosen path."[57] In spite of this outward confidence, Brezhnev regarded Chile as too unstable for a substantial investment. The Chilean right wing was gaining too much force. According to Soviet Ambassador A.V. Basov in Santiago, "the political climate in the country was not conducive to the interests of . . . the rule of *Unidad Popular*."[58]

Like his diplomatic counterparts Richard Nixon and Henry Kissinger, Brezhnev was an accomplished practitioner of *realpolitik*. Chile simply was not part of the Soviet sphere of influence. "Foreign aid is a political-economic instrument that is used in conjunction with other techniques to gain power and influence in strategically vital areas," political scientists Joseph L. Nogee and John W. Sloan observed in 1979.[59] As much as the Soviets railed against Western imperialism, they had quietly resigned themselves to Latin America's unofficial status as a U.S. possession since the humiliation of the Cuban Missile Crisis. Furthermore, trade between the U.S.S.R. and Latin America was minimal because they offered the same products on the international market most of the time.[60] Since the Soviets did not expect Latin America to ever enhance its strategic or economic interests, they directed their beneficence elsewhere. "The bulk of Soviet assistance—about 80 percent—has gone to a narrow band of nations extending from the Mediterranean to China's southwestern borders," Nogee and Sloan pointed out.[61]

Documents show that analysts in the Nixon administration shared the conclusions of Nogee and Sloan. Nevertheless, the NSC's Senior Review Group had to speculate about every possible contingency: "In the future, should the Allende regime be receptive . . . the USSR might attempt to secure the use of facilities for the maintenance and replenishment of Soviet combatant ships and submarines.[62] Conjectures aside, the Senior Review

Group fully expected Chile to cultivate the Soviet Union. Acknowledging Allende's fiercely nationalist spirit, the analysts doubted that the Chilean president would ever permit Moscow to turn his country into a Soviet protectorate. Nor they did they believe that the Soviets had such a goal, because "they are more interested in using Chile as a cornerstone for the gradual long-term expansion of their interests in Latin America than in duplicating Cuba's total dependency."[63] The White House policy amounted to little more than an old fashioned defense of the Monroe Doctrine. The policymakers wanted to keep all outside powers, not just the Soviets, from their turf: "as U.S. influence declines, other powers, including Western Europe, Japan and some of the other larger Latin American countries themselves will seek to fill the vacuum. A greater role for these other countries may be the most effective way in which Soviet influence can be preempted. However, we have traditionally resisted the intrusion of extra-Hemispheric powers to prevent dilution of our political influence and loss of our markets for trade and investment."[64]

In contrast to Brezhnev in Moscow, Castro in Cuba demonstrated a heart-felt commitment to the Allende experiment. In a public address in Havana, Castro promised Allende's Chile "when you need it you can count on our sugar, and when you need it you can count on our blood, and when you need it you can count on our lives."[65] At the same time, he warned Allende not to "ignite" revolutions throughout Latin America. No doubt fearing for Allende's own political survival, the Cuban leader expressed the desire that "all the conflict situations in Latin America would continue to be attributed solely to him." Castro even encouraged Allende "not to worry if he had to wait six months, a year, or two" until commencing official diplomatic relations with Cuba. As it turns out, Allende did not even bother to wait to do so.[66] Moving beyond the ambassadorial-level exchanges, Allende also received Castro in Santiago in November of 1971. The Cuban leader feared that his Chilean counterpart was too attached to bourgeois modes of democratic governance. Such a system, Castro believed, was too vulnerable to violent takeover by reactionary forces. The Cuban leader tried to make his point to Allende by using his own island nation as an example: "In our country, men and women are willing to fight until the last drop of blood. And imperialism knows this. And that's why they respect us. And I don't believe they have a remote possibility of crushing the revolution."[67] In Castro's view, Allende was so ill prepared to do battle against the forces of imperialism that even the defenses for the Cuban embassy were inadequate: "I could take this embassy alone in 2 hours!" Obviously, he did not say this in the presence of Allende.[68]

Despite his own doubts about Socialist Chile's long-term survival, Castro dispatched an advisory team from the Cuban General Department of National Liberation to Chile to assist in the development of a presidential bodyguard for Allende. Luis Fernandez Oña, the head of this three-member team, had recently married Allende daughter Beatriz. When Oña first came to Chile, he was dismayed by the meager protection Allende already had. They "didn't have arms or anything! They had a little pistol, two little pistols!"[69] Thanks to Cuban training and generosity, Allende soon enjoyed his own highly competent bodyguard, known as the *Grupo de Amigos Personales*, or Group of Personal Friends. As 1971 came to an end, the CIA reported that "the haphazard collection of sidearms formerly used by GAP members has almost been totally replaced by Cuban-provided .45 caliber Colt automatic pistols, 9mm Browning automatic pistols and Czech 38 automatic pistols."[70] From 1970 to September 1973, Havana provided 3,000 pieces of weaponry to leftist factions in Chile. Although the Socialists and Communists took some arms, the revolutionary socialist group MIR or *Movimiento de Izquierda Revolucionario*, was the major beneficiary. Almost 2,000 Chileans, including many MIR members, also benefited from Cuban training.[71] Nevertheless, we shall see that Havana's relative generosity could not compete with Washington's exorbitant contribution to the Chilean military.

In order to reserve Latin America for the United States, the Nixon administration planned to solve the Chilean question by military means. In his memoir, Kissinger blamed Allende for the credit blockade: "A country defaulting on its foreign debts is scarcely creditworthy whatever its form of government."[72] Still, at the same time that the Chile's civilian sector suffered from Kissingerian stinginess, its armed forces reveled in Kissingerian benevolence.

On March 6, 1970, the Chilean military presented Washington with the following shopping list:

Airbase Ground Support Equipment
106 mm Recoilless Rifles
Gearing Class Destroyers
Jet Ranger Helicopters
105 mm Howitzers
C-130 Transport[73]

Roughly, the items were worth $7 million. Kissinger's National Security Council staff recommended offering credit adequate for the purchase of the most important items. Rejecting the request would "cause resentment in the Chilean armed forces and could sever our tenuous relations with them while there is still a possibility they might act against Allende."[74] The potential for action on the part of the Chilean armed forces was the foremost concern of the NSC, and was listed first, while the possibility that Chile would turn to Moscow for military hardware ranked last.[75] In the end, Kissinger approved granting the Chilean military $5 million in credit.[76]

This contradiction puzzled Senator J. William Fulbright, the distinguished chairman of the Senate Foreign Relations Committee. When the acting assistant secretary of state, John H. Crimmins, testified before the committee, Fulbright observed:

> I can only emphasize it seems to me a very ironic thing that you even question the sale of a 707 [Boeing jet] and yet you positively recommended an increase in military sales. It seems a very odd posture for the United States to be in of even having doubts about giving Chile the right to buy on the usual terms, with the Export Bank which was established for this purpose, a civilian transport which I am sure Boeing is most anxious to sell, and then without any hesitation apparently recommending a $6 million increase in the military sales. This just seems utterly inconsistent to what I thought was our policy.[77]

The arms sales and the financial quarantine would work in tandem, letting the Chilean officers understand that they could only benefit from a change in government. Although Washington had successfully estranged itself from the Chilean government, it maintained close contact with the Chilean military. Kissinger laughingly complained to Nixon: "The funny thing is that they have twisted your instruction to keep contact with the military into relaying it where we do more for the Chilean military than for any other military in Latin America. We have more admirals and generals in Chile than in Brazil."[78]

Obviously, Kissinger was referring to *Chilean* admirals and generals. The national security advisor as well as the president wished to keep their operation against Allende as low-key as possible. The presence of U.S. military officers of the highest rank in Chile would attract too much attention. Still, it is clear that the Nixon administration needed lower-ranking representatives of the U.S. military to maintain good relations with those Chilean admirals and generals.

Along with the attaché personnel at the U.S. embassies throughout Latin America, the Department of Defense assigned officers to a liaison service known as Milgroup. Charles A. Meyer, chairman of Interdepartmental Group for Inter-American Affairs, stressed the necessity of upgrading the qualifications of these personnel. Linguistic ability and a good education were imperatives.[79] In addition, Meyer recommended to Kissinger that "the freeze on further implementation of the MILGP study be lifted and that a new level of not to exceed 290 U.S. military spaces for the region be approved, leaving the detailed breakdown of each MILGP to be worked out among the Ambassadors, USCINCSO and Washington. In deciding upon the new levels for individual posts, the IG/ARA will oppose any increases that are not demonstrably contributive to the objective of increasing U.S. influence."[80]

For Chile, the IG/ARA favored the presence of thirteen Milgroup personnel.[81] Given the fixation of the White House on Allende, it is probable that this recommendation was fulfilled if not exceeded. Later, after the coup, the conduct of one Milgroup representative during the disappearance of an American expatriate, Charles Horman, would generate much suspicion.

Continuation of aid to the Chilean armed forces would prove effective, but Nixon understood that he could not accomplish his agenda without the CIA. The exposure of U.S. intelligence's shady dealings made this a precarious time for the Agency, but it still kept the president's trust. "I will not embarrass the CIA," Nixon insisted. "I will defend it."[82] His mind totally justified the covert operations in Iran, Guatemala, and Cuba that had been authorized by President Dwight D. Eisenhower. The resulting bloodshed had never tortured his conscience during his vice presidency, nor did the memory of it ever give him pause as he plotted Allende's destruction. "We did the Chilean things and we did a few other things and by God we won't need to do some more," Nixon admitted in the privacy of the Oval Office.[83] The National Archives has only recently declassified this last comment. Probably it was a reference to the aborted abduction of General Schneider.

Indifferent to the ugly consequences of Track II, the Nixon administration sanctioned continued contact between the CIA and the Chilean military. By this point, the prospects for a coup were not promising. Save for the cashiered Viaux and other officers on the fringe, the Chilean armed forces subordinated itself to civilian authority. "The Schneider assassination, and the repercussions, thereof, was a demoralizing development for the military and effectively braked whatever sentiment was developing for military action to prevent Allende's assumption of power," the Santiago station reported to the CIA director.[84] Still, the station remained hopeful as it forecast the long scheme of things: "The Chilean military probably would not oppose Allende, or, if developments should so dictate, plot his overthrow unless they were ignited by a political x opposition force with strong civilian support."[85]

Washington did not really care what political party presented the main challenge to the UP coalition, just as long as such a challenge existed. "Since the PDC may well be the largest party in Chile and therefore the most significant opposition force in the country, it merits the fullest possible support," the station argued.[86] Desperate that the Christian Democrats make a solid challenge in the municipal election in April of 1971, the 40 Committee extended substantial sums to the party. Since significant portions of the relevant documents are still blacked out, it is not absolutely clear how much money the Chrisitian Demociatic party received. A memorandum from the CIA chief of the Western Hemisphere Division mentioned that the 40 Committee had approved a total $1,240,000 for more than one opposition party, including the right-wing National party.[87] Another heavily censored cable from the Santiago station mentioned a contribution of $1,182,000 for fiscal year 1971.[88] Because the entire uncensored portion of the cable is devoted solely to the subject of the Christian Democrats, one can safely assume that their party received that amount.

If the socialist experiment in Chile had failed from the beginning, it is unlikely that its opposition would have required so much financial support from abroad. The Christian Democratic party was particularly weak. "It cannot carry out an opposition program based solely on the contributions from its party members or interested businessmen," the Santiago station acknowledged.[89] Therefore, the notoriously right-wing newspaper, El Mercurio, attracted Washington's attention. On September 14, Kissinger called CIA Director Richard Helms to inform him that "the President had just approved the proposal for supporting 'El Mercurio' in the amount of $700,000 . . . and wished to see the paper kept going and the amount stipulated could be exceed if it would usefully serve that purpose."[90] The weakness of Allende's opposition was an indication of his own political strength.

In the municipal election, the Christian Democrats won 25.6 percent of the vote. While that may not seem impressive, the CIA congratulated itself for providing the support essential for the propaganda and press campaign.[91] None of the documents indicated any expectation of an actual Christian Democratic victory. Apparently, what mattered was that the Christian Democrats remained a "leading opposition force to the Allende regime."[92] This brings us back to the Santiago station's prediction that the Chilean armed forces would not act "unless they were ignited by a political x opposition force with strong civilian support."[93] This did not necessarily mean a political opposition force that enjoyed majority support from the people; just a certain sector of Chilean society in collaboration with the military would suffice.

For the CIA, cultivating contacts within the Chilean military mattered far more than financing the opposition parties. Two years before the fall of Allende, the Agency set its sights on General Augusto Pinochet, the commander of the Santiago garrison. Oddly enough, the man who would later bear direct responsibility for the murder of thousands made little impression on Allende's circle. CODELCO's Arrate did not think Pinochet carried the weight of other Chilean generals:

> He was very servile . . . and he was a very obscure military man. The army had some very brilliant generals. Schneider, who was assassinated in 1970, was a very brilliant military man. And [General Carlos] Prats was a real intellectual . . . a man of a very high level of culture . . . who liked to write. Pinochet was the typical guy that was there and reached the position of general not menacing anybody and very obscure. I don't know really, why it took so long for him to [overthrow Allende] . . . probably because he wanted to act with no risks."[94]

Arrate remembered that Pinochet behaved in a sycophantic manner with General Prats, whom he later had killed. With great retrospective irony, the future tyrant of the right escorted Cuban leader Fidel Castro on his 1971 visit to Chile. "There are nice photographs of Pinochet with Castro," Arrate said.[95] This visit, of course, gave Washington another reason to hate Allende. U.S. policymakers feared that the Organization of American States, a deliberative body under Washington's unofficial control, would soon embrace Cuba. "Chile is leading the drive and Peru has the question of 'normalized' relations under active consideration," Charles A. Meyer informed Kissinger. "Chances are increasing that within eighteen months a majority of the OAS members will favor revision of OAS policy toward Cuba."[96]

As much as Pinochet and other disloyal generals probably despised Castro, and resented Allende's warm relationship with him, the CIA was having difficulty finding prospective leaders angry enough to stage a successful coup. The station in Santiago reported that "Pinochet would favor but would want to close eyes to events."[97] Yet the Agency seemed to sense some fascist potential in Pinochet. In an account of a dinner on August 5, the station observed that Pinochet "[censored portion] avoided making comments which would reveal his inner thoughts. This completely consistent with his known pattern: he is cautious and quiet on political subjects. Nevertheless his wife seconded comment by other guests to effect that government was getting in deep water with its present orientation."[98]

Although ideologically opposed to Allende, Pinochet was a curiously passive character. He was not an independent personality. He required the inspiration and even the permission of authority figures before he could act. Now, military and intelligence agents from Washington would become the authority figures. Interestingly, the other potential plotters seemed just as lacking in initiative. Colonel Paul Wimert, a U.S. military attaché and veteran of the Schneider affair, surely was annoyed after speaking with a

Chilean army contact. "He stated that the young officers (i.e. Lts and Capts) have organized themselves and have a plan to take control of the government," Wimert reported. "The drawback, however, is that they are lacking a leader – a recurring theme in discussions such as this."[99]

Clearly, Washington directed this sordid drama. U.S. policymakers wanted a coup, even if they opposed any premature action. When the Santiago station reported that some Chilean military officers planned a putsch for the spring of 1972, it was full of enthusiasm.[100] In its eagerness, the station offered many recommendations: "Choose one or two [censored] with whom we can talk frankly about the mechanics of a coup to be sure all significant aspects are thought through. Our input would be based on our own analysis of what tasks are necessary to ensure the coup would be successful."[101]

Kissinger was on the list of distribution for the reported plan for 1972, so he probably contributed to the response from CIA Headquarters, which was quite sharp: "There is of course a rather fine dividing line between merely 'listening' and 'talking frankly about the mechanics of a coup' which in the long run must be left to the discretion and good judgment of the individual case officer. Please err on the side of giving the possibly indiscreet and probably uncontrolled contact little tangible material with which to accuse us."[102]

Above all, Washington feared the exposure that would result from a hasty move. Opposition to civilian rule was not strong enough within the Chilean military at this point. The Agency's Western Hemisphere Division effectively scolded the Santiago station: "If and when Station reporting indicates a favorable political atmosphere and a serious military intent to take action against the Allende government, it will become the responsibility of other appropriate [censored] authorities to use this intelligence in reaching a policy decision."[103]

As the Nixon administration obsessively schemed, the Allende administration strove to improve the lives of the Chilean people. Specifically, the Chilean government planned to empower the workers by empowering itself. "State control is projected to destroy the entire economic base of imperialism and class domination by putting an end to private ownership of the means of production," pronounced the new minister of economics, Pedro Vuskovic.[104]

The Allende scheme, of course, offered a place for private enterprise, but the Chilean government did not stop with its takeover of the copper and communications industries. The regime also expropriated the top industrial companies, banking and distribution systems, and Chile's other important raw materials such as nitrates, coal, iron, and steel. Eventually, the UP government would nationalize 30 percent of Chilean industry.[105]

Nevertheless, Allende's policy of expropriation was neither arbitrary nor heavy-handed. The Chilean president relied on legal precedent for the most part. For example, when a terrified Ralston-Purina shut down all operations in Chile upon Allende's election, he relied on a law from 1943 to take control and save Chilean jobs. When it came to the Yarur textile factory, Allende turned to a decree from 1953 that permitted the Chilean president to seize closed factories that produced products key to the national economy.[106]

This new public wealth allowed more public spending for social welfare. The allotment of a half a liter of milk for every youngster, for example, was especially important in a country where malnutrition destined more than half a million children to physical and mental retardation.[107] Since the Chilean president was a medical man, it was perhaps inevitable that his government would socialize the national health care system.[108] Thanks to state subsidies, the common Chilean people now enjoyed greater access to public utilities. The real rate for electricity dropped by 85 percent, and the cost of telephone service decreased by 33 percent.[109]

Allende's attack on U.S. economic imperialism was important, but his redistribution of wealth within Chilean society mattered just as much. Agrarian reform drastically surpassed the program of the previous administration. The Frei government had legalized unionization of the rural labor force, but the Allende government ensured that 1971 would see an 82 percent jump in union membership. A new law restricted large estates from holding more than eighty hectares of land.[110] As a result of this new legislation, Allende confiscated almost as many *latifundia* in 1971 as Frei did during his entire six years in office.[111] This land was destined for peasant cooperatives.[112] Nevertheless, the UP government did not seize these estates in a lawless fit of revolutionary fervor. For instance, when a country gentleman and his sons fired their guns at peasants who had taken over their property, Allende responded with justice as well as promptness. In contrast to Frei, who would have charged the peasants with criminal trespass, Allende could appreciate history. The peasants, who were Mapuche Indians, had been defrauded of that very land three decades before. Therefore, Allende sided with the peasants.[113]

As with the expropriation of the copper mines, the agrarian reform established a fair system of compensation. Under this system, the dispossessed landowners received reimbursement mostly in the form of thirty-year bonds. In spite of this compensation, the wealthy planters must have been angry and fearful, for the agrarian reform begun by Frei and continued by his successor would ultimately cost them $1 billion.[114]

Ironically, while Allende helped improve the lives of the Chilean peasantry, he earned enmity from the left as well as the right for his agrarian policy. MIR tried to assume control of the policy by seizing large estates on its own. Accusing Allende of not moving fast enough, the MIR criticized the official agricultural agenda as "a bourgeois law that does not contribute to the improvement of the standard of living of the peasantry."[115] Despite MIR's criticism, rural support for the UP actually rose.[116] When asked to comment on Chile's new leader, one member of MIR had this to say: "That depends on which Allende you mean. Allende the man we like and respect. Allende the President of Chile, we are not sure."[117] Chances are that MIR would have opposed Allende no matter what his policy. They favored social transformation outside the established system. MIR had provided Allende critical support, but he had his own agenda. From the beginning, the conflict was a matter of style and values. When Allende began his administration, he rejected the request of the extreme left to reside in the squalid section of Santiago. As much as he sympathized with Chile's poor, Allende was markedly bourgeois in his personal tastes, with an appreciation for the finer things in life. He was not about to go slumming as a sign of solidarity.[118]

In any case, Allende encountered much fiercer opposition from the right. Wage increases for blue-collar workers undoubtedly enraged their wealthy employers. The UP government sought to correct the disparity in the minimum wages between blue-collar and white-collar workers. By guaranteeing the blue-collar sector a 39 percent pay raise as opposed to 10 percent for the white-collar one, Chilean economist Patricio Meller found, "the differential between minimum wages for white- and blue-collar workers narrowed from 49 percent (1970) to 35 percent in 1971."[119] While this may seem unfair on paper, the purchasing power of both groups increased almost equally, giving all workers a greater portion of Chile's gross domestic product.[120]

By the end of his first year in office, Allende felt unabashed yet justified pride. He had fulfilled most of his campaign promises. The Chilean president declared to his people: "We control 90 percent of what were the private banks . . . more than seventy strategic and monopolistic enterprises have been expropriated, intervened, requisitioned or acquired by the state. We are owners! We are able to say: our copper, our coal, our iron, our nitrates, our steel; the fundamental bases of heavy industry today belong to Chile and the Chileans."[121]

If Allende fulfilled many of his promises to the Chilean people, some aspects of the UP program did not work according to plan. The radical redistribution of income under Allende allowed working-class people to buy more than they ever had before. For the first time, the destitute of Chile added meat to their diets and now wore clothes instead of rags.[122] The dramatic rise in purchases of food and electrical appliances such as refrigerators and television sets boosted the amount of currency in circulation. For the first time, the workers had a taste of the good life, but that taste came with the price of inflation. The boost in state spending by 70 percent in 1971, also significantly contributed to the problem. While this governmental investment stimulated the economy, sharply reducing unemployment, it also required a great deal of credit. As a result, the government simply produced more money. Incredibly, Chile had more than twice as much money in circulation in 1971 than in 1970.[123] "In this sense, I think the economic policy of the Allende government had a weakness," conceded Arrate, an ardent UP partisan. "And I think the policymakers by the time did not deal adequately with this problem."[124]

Chile's economic troubles would worsen over the next two years, and the credit blockade deserves much of the blame. It is depressing now to speculate how far Allende could have guided his country's development with adequate financial support. Perhaps foreign credit, as well as unimpeded trade overseas, would have enabled Chile to better cope with inflation and other problems. While the White House arranged for Chile's destruction, a few North Americans could envision a humane policy alternative. A leading critic of the Nixon administration, Senator Edward M. Kennedy of Massachusetts, declared Chile had a right to determine its own political future. In particular, the senator resented the administration's discriminatory economic policies. "Those nations actively seeking to bring about social justice and political freedom are the nations whose efforts deserve our most generous bilateral assistance," Kennedy declared.[125] Indeed, the senator raised a valid and easily defensible point.

For its part, the Nixon administration used the Hickenlooper Amendment to justify the suspension of assistance to Chile.[126] Perhaps Washington interpreted the amendment to the Foreign Assistance Act too rigidly. The Hickenlooper Amendment required suspension of aid only if the expropriating nation "is not contrary to international law . . . or in any case with respect to which the President determines that application of the act of state doctrine is required in that particular case by the foreign policy interests of the United States and a suggestion to this effect is filed on his behalf in that case with the court."[127]

The Hickenlooper Amendment, therefore, did not bind Nixon absolutely. He could have taken a more compassionate course by conceding that Frei's Chileanization program had already overcompensated the copper companies. At the very least, the realm of international law has ample room for arbitration and compromise. The Allende administration was open to this; the Nixon administration was not.

In any case, Kennedy could see that the Exim Bank's abrupt rejection of the Chilean had backfired in many ways: "Now we find the government of Chile negotiating with the Soviet Union for those jets."[128] The senator challenged the illusion that corporate interests in Latin America coincided with the interests of the American people. "Private investment must come to terms with a changed environment, an environment dominated by the force of nationalism," Kennedy continued.[129] Unfortunately, Nixon lacked the insight of the progressive senator. As 1971 moved into 1972, the president preferred to maintain his own biased image of Latin America rather than accept its reality.

# Notes

1. Federico G. Gil, "Socialist Chile and the United States," *Inter-American Economic Affairs* 27, no. 2 (Autumn 1973): 32–34.

2. Gil, "Socialist Chile and the United States," 33.

3. Gil, "Socialist Chile and the United States," 33.

4. Conversation #245-6. 10:05a.m.–11:03a.m., Executive Office Building. April 6, 1971. *Nixon Tapes*, Nixon Presidential Materials Project, National Archives II, College Park, Maryland.

5. Richard R. Fagen, "The United States and Chile: Roots and Branches." *Foreign Affairs* 53, no. 2 (January 1975): 304.

6. Conversation #517-4. 9:37a.m.–10:36a.m., Oval Office. June 11, 1971. *Nixon Tapes*.

7. Fagen, "The United States and Chile," 305.

8. Tanya Harmer, "A Different 9/11: Cuba and the Chilean Coup of 1973," Annual Conference of the Society for Historians of American Foreign Relations, Chantilly, VA, June 21, 2007.

9. Gil, "Socialist Chile and the United States," 32.

10. Jorge Arrate, conversation with author, Santiago, Chile, June 20, 2005.

11. Hal Brands, "Richard Nixon and Economic Nationalism in Latin America: The Problem of Expropriations, 1969–1974," *Diplomacy and Statecraft*, 18, (2007) 222.

12. Brands, "Richard Nixon and Economic Nationalism in Latin America," 222.

13. 1971 Annual Report of the Kennecott Corporation and the 1972 Annual Report of the Kennecott Corporation, Historical Corporate Report Collection of the Walter A. Haas School of Business, University of California, Berkeley.

14. Arrate interview.

15. Gil, "Socialist Chile and the United States," 36.

16. Gil, "Socialist Chile and the United States," 37.

17. Cable #768 from Ambassador Korry to Secretary of State, February 1971. Senior Review Group Meetings, Box 52, Nixon Presidential Materials Project.

18. Arrate interview.

19. Hal Brands, "Richard Nixon and Economic Nationalism in Latin America: The Problem of Expropriations, 222.

20. Conversation #517-4.

21. Memorandum from John Connally to the President, August 10, 1971. H-Files, SRG Meetings, Box H-59, Folder 7, Nixon Presidential Materials Project.

22. Memorandum from John Connally to the President, August 10, 1971.

23. Conversation #517-4.

24. Fagen, "The United States and Chile," 308.

25. Fagen, "The United States and Chile," 308.

26. Conversation #510-5. 4:38a.m.–5:42a.m., Oval Office. June 2, 1971. *Nixon Tapes.*

27. Gil, "Socialist Chile and the United States," 43.

28. Conversation #593-10. 10:08a.m.–10:37a.m., Oval Office. October 15, 1971. *Nixon Tapes.*

29. Gil, "Socialist Chile and the United States," 43.

30. Aide-Memoire, "Purchase of Boeing Aircrafts for the Chilean Air Line "LAN-Chile," May 6, 1971. Attachment to *Confidencial 592/49, Embajada de Chile, Estados Unidos, 1971. Archivo General Histórico del Ministerio de Relaciones Exteriores*, Santiago, Chile.

31. Gil, "Socialist Chile and the United States," 36.

32. Memorandum of Meeting Held in Dr. Kissinger's Office, August 5, 1971. Participants: Dr. Kissinger, Chilean Ambassador Orlando Letelier, Pedro Valdes, and Arnold Nachmanoff. White House Special Files, [CF] CO 33 Chile [1971–1974], Box 28, Nixon Presidential Materials Project.

33. Memorandum of Meeting Held in Dr. Kissinger's Office, August 5, 1971.

34. Memorandum of Meeting Held in Dr. Kissinger's Office, August 5, 1971.

35. Memorandum of Meeting Held in Dr. Kissinger's Office, August 5, 1971.

36. Conversation #517-4.

37. Memorandum for the President from Henry A. Kissinger, June 9, 1971. H-Files, Box H-56, SRG Meetings, Chile 6/3/71, Nixon Presidential Materials Project.

38. Memorandum for the Files. "Multinational Corporations and United States Foreign Policy," *Appendix to the Hearings before the Subcommittee on Multinational Corporations of the Committee on Foreign Relations, United States Senate, Ninety-Third Congress, on the International Telephone and Telegraph, 1970–1971* (Washington: U.S. Government Printing Office, 1973), 1077.

39. Letter from L. Ralph Mecham of Anaconda to Chairman of the Board C. Jay Parkinson, February 10, 1971. "Multinational Corporations and United States Foreign Policy," *Appendix to the Hearings before the Subcommittee on Multinational Corporations of the Committee on Foreign Relations, United States Senate, Ninety-Third Congress, on the International Telephone and Telegraph, 1970–1971* (Washington, D.C.: U.S. Government Printing Office, 1973), 1009.

40. Memorandum for the President from Henry A. Kissinger, June 9, 1971.

41. Fagen, "The United States and Chile," 308.

42. Gil, "Socialist Chile and the United States," 41, and "Kennecott Declares War" in North American Congress on Latin America's *New Chile* (Berkeley, CA, and New York: Waller Press, 1973), 199.

43. Arrate interview.

44. Arrate interview.

45. Arrate interview and "The Blockade Takes Effect" in North American Congress on Latin America's *New Chile* (Berkeley, CA, and New York: Waller Press, 1973), 201.

46. Arrate interview.

47. Anthony Sampson, *The Sovereign State of ITT* (New York: Stein and Day, 1973), 263–64. ITT 1975 Annual Report.

48. Arrate interview.

49. Joseph L. Nogee and John W. Sloan, "Allende's Chile and the Soviet Union: A Policy Lesson for Latin American Nations Seeking Autonomy," *Journal of Interamerican Studies and World Affairs* 21, no. 3 (August 1979): 348–349.

50. Nogee and Sloan, "Allende's Chile and the Soviet Union," 348–49.

51. Arrate interview.

52. Nogee and Sloan, "Allende's Chile and the Soviet Union," 353–54. *Informe sobre la situacíon chilena elaborado por el Instituto de America Latina de la Academia de Ciencias de la URSS*, July, 1972 in "Chile en los Archivos de las URSS (1959–1973)," *Estudios Publicos* 72 (Spring 1998), 438.

53. Nogee and Sloan, "Allende's Chile and the Soviet Union," 354. *Informe sobre la situacíon chilena* in "Chile en los Archivos de las URSS, 438. Telex 55, Embajada de Chile, Moscu, May 29, 1971. *Archivo General Historico del Ministerio de Relaciones Exteriores*, Santiago, Chile.

54. Nogee and Sloan, "Allende's Chile and the Soviet Union," 355.

55. Nogee and Sloan, "Allende's Chile and the Soviet Union," 350–51.

56. Nogee and Sloan, "Allende's Chile and the Soviet Union," 352.

57. Nogee and Sloan, "Allende's Chile and the Soviet Union," 353.

58. Conversacíon del embajador A.V. Basov con representantes del Partido Socialists de Chile, December 26, 1971, in "Chile en los Archivos de las URSS (1959–1973)," *Estudios Publicos* 72 (Spring 1998), 417.

59. Nogee and Sloan, "Allende's Chile and the Soviet Union," 357.

60. Nogee and Sloan, "Allende's Chile and the Soviet Union," 357–58.

61. Nogee and Sloan, "Allende's Chile and the Soviet Union," 357.

62. Review of U.S. Policy Toward Latin America: Response to National Security Study Memorandum 108. March, 1971. H-Files, SRG Group Meetings, Box H-59, Folder 2, Nixon Presidential Materials Project.

63. Review of U.S. Policy Toward Latin America: Response to National Security Study Memorandum 108.

64. "Latin American-NSSM 108 and Military Presence Study," Senior Review Group Meeting, August 17, 1971. H-Files, SRG Group Meetings, Box H-59, Folder 2, Nixon Presidential Materials Project.

65. Harmer, "A Different 9/11: Cuba and the Chilean Coup of 1973."

66. Harmer, "A Different 9/11: Cuba and the Chilean Coup of 1973."

67. Harmer, "A Different 9/11: Cuba and the Chilean Coup of 1973."

68. Harmer, "A Different 9/11: Cuba and the Chilean Coup of 1973."

69. Harmer, "A Different 9/11: Cuba and the Chilean Coup of 1973."

70. Harmer, "A Different 9/11: Cuba and the Chilean Coup of 1973."

71. Harmer, "A Different 9/11: Cuba and the Chilean Coup of 1973."

72. Henry Kissinger, *Years of Upheaval* (Boston: Little, Brown and Company, 1982), 381.

73. Attachment: FMS-Options Paper, National Security Council Memorandum from Staff Secretary Jeanne W. Davis, February 16, 1971. NSDM 93, Box H-220, Folder 1, Nixon Presidential Materials Project.

74. FMS-Options Paper, February 16, 1971.

75. FMS-Options Paper, February 16, 1971.

76. NSC Memorandum by Henry Kissinger, "Chile—Agreements at Senior Review Group Meeting on February 17, 1971." February 25, 1971. Senior Review Group Meetings, Box H-52, Nixon Presidential Materials Project.

77. James Petras and Morris Morley, *The United States and Chile: Imperialism and the Overthrow of the Allende Government* (New York: Monthly Review Press, 1975), 195n.

78. Conversation #517-4.

79. "U.S. Military Presence in Latin America." Department of State Memorandum for Mr. Henry A. Kissinger, January 12, 1971. Box H-159, NSSM 68, Folder 3, Nixon Presidential Materials Project.

80. "U.S. Military Presence in Latin America."

81. "U.S. Military Presence in Latin America."

82. Conversation #587-7. 10:58a.m.–12:12p.m., Oval Office. October 8, 1971. *Nixon Tapes.*

83. Conversation #587-7.

84. Cable from Santiago Station to CIA Director, January 9, 1971. CIA Collection, Freedom of Information Act website, U.S. State Department.

85. Cable from Santiago Station to CIA Director, January 9, 1971.

86. Cable from Santiago Station to CIA Director, January 9, 1971.

87. CIA Memorandum from William Broe to Deputy Director of Plans, "Request for Approval of Project," February 12, 1971. CIA Collection, FOIA website.

88. Cable for Chief of Station to Chief, Western Hemisphere Division, June 18, 1971. CIA Collection, FOIA website.

89. Santiago Station to CIA Director, January 9, 1971.

90. "Authorization for 'El Mercurio' Support," Memorandum by William V. Broe, September 30, 1971. CIA Collection, FOIA website.

91. Cable from Chief of Station to Western Hemisphere Chief, June 18, 1971.

92. Cable from Chief of Station to Western Hemisphere Chief, June 18, 1971.

93. Santiago Station to CIA Director, January 9, 1971.

94. Arrate interview.

95. Arrate interview.

96. "U.S. Policy Toward Latin America." Memorandum to Mr. Henry A. Kissinger from Charles A. Meyer, September 3, 1971. Box H-178, NSSM 108, Folder 4, Nixon Presidential Materials Project.

97. Cable to CIA Director from Santiago, August 31, 1971. CIA Collection, FOIA website.

98. Cable to CIA Director from Santiago, August 6, 1971. CIA Collection, FOIA website.

99. Paul M. Wimert, Jr. "Young Chilean Officer Discusses Views on Chilean Government," Department of Defense Intelligence Information Report, February 26, 1971. DOD Collection, FOIA website.

100. "Preliminary Planning for an Eventual Military Move Against the Chilean Government." Intelligence Information Special Report, CIA Directorate of Plans, November 9, 1971. CIA Collection, FOIA website.

101. Cable from Chief of Station, Santiago to Chief, Western Hemisphere Division, November 12, 1971. CIA Collection, FOIA website.

102. Cable from Chief, Western Hemisphere Division to Chief of Station, Santiago, December 1, 1971. CIA Collection, FOIA website.

103. Cable from Chief, Western Hemisphere Division to Chief of Station, Santiago, December 1, 1971.

104. Patricio Meller, The Unidad Popular and the Pinochet Dictatorship: A Political Economy Analysis (London, United Kingdom: Macmillan Press Ltd., 2000), 30.

105. Meller, The Unidad Popular and the Pinochet Dictatorship, 29. Paul E. Sigmund, The Overthrow of Allende and the Politics of Chile (Pittsburgh: University of Pittsburgh Press, 1977), 209.

106. David J. Morris, We Must Make Haste Slowly: The Process of Revolution in Chile (New York: Vintage, 1973), 125.

107. Meller, The Unidad Popular and the Pinochet Dictatorship, 40, and Transcript of Address by Ambassador Letelier at American University Conference, April 30, 1971. Embajada de Chile, Estados Unidos 1971, Archivo, Santiago, Chile.

108. Barbara Stallings, Class Conflict and Economic Development in Chile (Stanford: Stanford University Press, 1978), 127.

109. Meller, The Unidad Popular and the Pinochet Dictatorship, 40.

110. Meller, The Unidad Popular and the Pinochet Dictatorship, 51.

111. See Table 1.19 in Meller, The Unidad Popular and the Pinochet Dictatorship.

112. Meller, The Unidad Popular and the Pinochet Dictatorship, 52.

113. Morris, We Must Make Haste, 197.

114. Meller, The Unidad Popular and the Pinochet Dictatorship, 53.

115. Jonathan Haslam, The Nixon Administration and the Death of Allende's Chile (New York: Verso, 2005), 94.

116. Edy Kaufman, Crisis in Allende's Chile: New Perspectives (New York and Westport, CT: Praeger, 1988), 73.

117. Morris, *We Must Make Haste Slowly*, 109–10.

118. Morris, *We Must Make Haste Slowly*, 109–10.

119. Meller, *The Unidad Popular and the Pinochet Dictatorship*, 33.

120. Meller, *The Unidad Popular and the Pinochet Dictatorship*, 33.

121. Peter Winn, *Weavers of the Revolution: The Yarur Workers and Chile's Road to Socialism* (New York: Oxford University Press, 1986), 227–28.

122. Edward Boorstein, *Allende's Chile: An Inside View* (New York: International Publishers, 1977), 111.

123. Arturo Valenzuela, *The Breakdown of Democratic Regimes: Chile* (Baltimore: The Johns Hopkins University Press, 1978), 151.

124. Arrate interview.

125. Address by Senator Edward M. Kennedy to the Chicago Council on Foreign Relations, October 12, 1971. *Oficio* 1202/798, *Embajada de Chile, Estados Unidos*, 1971, *Archivo*, Santiago, Chile.

126. Henry Kissinger, *Years of Upheaval* (Boston: Little, Brown and Company, 1982), 376.

127. Memorandum from William R. Joyce to Mr. Novarro, March 30, 1971. Attachment to *Oficio* 492/42, April 23, 1971, *Embajada de Chile, Estados Unidos*, *Archivo, Santiago, Chile*.

128. Address by Senator Kennedy.

129. Address by Senator Kennedy.

# CHAPTER FIVE

⸻⸻ ⚬❈❈❈⚬ ⸻⸻

# Allende's Fall: 1972–1973

More than anything, Kissinger and his staff feared the Chilean experiment as a potential inspiration for the rest of the hemisphere. As the Nixon administration faced the prospect of losing its inherited but needlessly protracted campaign in Vietnam, it could not accept failure in Latin America. "Its relative importance to us will grow rather than diminish as our commitments in other parts of the world decline," Nixon advisor Robert Finch wrote in a memorandum.[1] Damage to American "credibility" was simply unacceptable.

In the long twilight of the Cold War, Kissinger and other members of the administration often publicly linked the Allende presidency to Cuban and Soviet infiltration. To be sure, Allende and Castro enjoyed an ideological and personal rapport, dreaming the same dream of a Latin America free of U.S. domination. One indication of the closeness between Santiago and Havana was the wedding of Allende's daughter, Beatriz, to Luis Fernandez Oña, who became the second most important man at the Cuban embassy. "Since Allende's inauguration, the Cuban official presence has burgeoned from zero to 54 personnel," the CIA noted. "Almost one-third of these Cuban officials belong to the Cuban Intelligence Service and the so-called Directorate of Liberation." Allende's son-in-law, who had helped found the *Grupo de Amigos Personales*, was one of these intelligence officers.[2]

U.S. intelligence was also disturbed because the Chilean president made his nation a refuge for other Latin American radicals.[3] Because of this, the White House feared Allende would support actively subversive activities in other Latin American countries. "In the face of this threat *we should upgrade*

*our own intelligence and security liaison activities* with the emphasis on improved quality rather than great numbers," Finch insisted.[4]

Obviously, neither Allende nor Castro could have forced other Latin
American nations to rise up against U.S. imperialism. Any rebels who might
have fled to Chile had their own reasons of opposing their governments. As
in Vietnam, movements of national liberation in Latin America were home-
grown, indigenous to those particular countries. Washington, of course, did
not pause to consider the legitimate grievances of these Latin American revolutionaries. In any case, Cuba regarded Allende's Chile as too fragile to support any movement of national liberation, much less its own. "The Cubans
are convinced that Allende will be overthrown by a military or subversive
coup before the end of his term of office," the CIA reported to Kissinger,
questioning whether Castro would even help the Chilean president when
the time came.[5] The Agency believed that the Cuban leader would, at most,
offer counsel and moral support. "Cuba does not consider Chile a stable or
permanent base from which to export the revolution to the rest of Latin
America," the CIA concluded.[6] In reality, Cuban intelligence operations in
Chile gave U.S. intelligence little reason to worry: "Havana has been cir-
cumspect about trying to use Chile as a base for promoting revolutionary
movements elsewhere in Latin America, partly so as to not add to Allende's
problems and partly so as not to jeopardize the advantages offered by the
Cuban presence in Santiago. Cuban officials in Chile are now involved in assisting Latin American revolutionaries exiled in or transiting through Chile,
but on a fairly modest scale."[7]

The scale of Cuban involvement in Chile would indeed be modest, particularly when compared to the scale of other Cuban investments overseas.
One of Castro's most policies was his dispatch of 36,000 troops to the African
nation of Angola in 1975. By contrast, at the time of Allende's fall in September of 1973, there were fewer than 150 Cuban agents in Chile.[8]

In the end, the Allende regime was simply too conservative for either Castro or his patron, the Soviet Union. "Like Castro, Soviets probably do not
believe in the UP strategy of achieving socialism in a consumption economy," wrote Nathaniel Davis, Ambassador Korry's recent replacement, in a
dispatch home.[9] The Chilean president lacked the ruthlessness typical of
leaders in the Communist bloc. "Soviet and Eastern European ambassadors
make no secret to me of their conviction that 'Chileans do not like to work,'"
Davis continued.[10]

At the same time the Kremlin offered the Allende government moral and
political support, it held itself back. Moscow shared Havana's skepticism
about the survival of Socialist Chile. It also feared vexing Washington at this

time of détente. "To be sure, Moscow expresses *pro forma* sympathy and support for Chile's struggle to achieve 'independence' and implement 'progressive' changes," the CIA observed, "but references to the UP striving to achieve socialism are scrupulously avoided."[11]

By this time, Chile fully felt the effect of the Washington-imposed economic blockade. Ideology compelled the Soviet Union to help. Expanding the original offer of credit made to the Frei administration, in 1972 the Soviets extended an offer of $97 million for industrial purchases. They also made available an unconditional $37 million in bank credit.[12] Communist China also offered $65 million in credit to cover a five-year period. This modest assistance could hardly solve the Chilean impasse. As a Senior Review Group memorandum to Kissinger noted, "Regardless of the settlement arrived at by the Paris Club [an economic summit] Allende likely faces economic disaster in another 12 to 18 months—unless, of course, the Russians and Chinese undertake a massive bail-out operation. They seem reluctant in that direction. Moscow certainly does not want another Cuban rat-hole. A very tough settlement at Paris—along the lines we originally sought—would maximize the pressure on Allende and hasten economic collapse."[13]

Still, the Soviets did agree to buy 130,000 tons of Chilean copper in July of 1972, and also to spend $87 million on copper wares. Four months later, Moscow extended $103 million more in credits.[14] Even when the Chilean economy was in dire straits at the very end, the Kremlin offered little. "Soviet aid in 1973 was marginal; building a fishing institute and a fishing port at Colcura, expanding the Topcopilla Electric Plant, and constructing a wheat mill in Valparaiso," scholars Joseph L. Nogee and John W. Sloan wrote.[15]

In any case, Allende had his own reasons for not tightly embracing the Communist powers. A substantial sector of the Chilean electorate opposed close ties with the Soviet Union and China. Allende followed the principles of the non-aligned movement, and he wished to maintain Chile's independence. He also hoped to rely on Western nations for trade, credits, and technical know-how. "The difficulties inherent in forging new economic links between Chile and the Communist nations are manifested in Allende's slowness in utilizing the nearly $90 million in long-term credits proffered by the USSR over the years," the CIA observed.[16] In addition, Allende also had to consider the effect of such an arrangement on the rest of Latin America. "In any event, it would complicate his relationship with neighboring countries, which the USSR, PRC, and GOC would all prefer to avoid," the Senior Review Group found.[17]

Aversion to conflict did not prevent the Soviet Union from extending a proposal of $300 million in credits for the Chilean armed forces in 1972.

"Thus far, the military have resisted all blandishments as well as strong pressures from Allende on this issue," the CIA noted.[18] In order to avoid Soviet instruction, the military rejected any highly technologically complex armaments.[19] Nevertheless, the military did agree to make plans for a mission to the Soviet Union in June.[20] "They apparently are not as resistant to accepting less sophisticated equipment from Moscow that would not require Soviet advisors or extensive training," the CIA found.[21] At this time, a delegation of the Chilean Air Force visited the Soviet Union for technical information on MIG jets, which was hardly an indication of a major Soviet effort to uplift the Chilean military.[22]

Even if Allende had wanted to turn Chile into a Soviet satellite, his armed forces would not have let him. Indeed, the best way for Kissinger to keep the Chilean military independent of Soviet influence probably would have been to protect General Schneider. In any case, Allende did not wish to alienate the U.S. military. "He is anxious to maintain access to U.S. equipment and spare parts, and to keep U.S. credit channels open," the CIA's National Intelligence Estimate stated.[23] In fact, Allende heartily approved the joint maneuvers of the U.S. and Chilean navies.[24] One should also question why the Soviets waited so long to make such a generous offer. Through their own intelligence, the Soviets undoubtedly knew of their rival superpower's campaign to destabilize Allende. One might make the case that Moscow offered $300 million in military credits as a means for Allende's self-defense.

Just as U.S. aggression drove Castro into the Soviet camp, Allende was forced to look eastward for support. This did not mean that he favored an escalation of tensions between the United States and the Soviet Union. Indeed, the Chilean government looked upon détente favorably, and its urbane representative in Washington, Ambassador Orlando Letelier, reflected this view after the signing of the Strategic Arms Limitation Treaty. In a dispatch to the Ministry of Foreign Affairs in Santiago, Letelier expressed the hope that SALT would divert the greatest resources of the superpowers to peaceful ends. The Chilean diplomat also applauded SALT because it was "a formal recognition that both parties did not need to continue its armament spiral since it would not be fundamental to the real interests of such countries."[25]

As strained as the Chilean economy was, Washington could still privately acknowledge Allende's successes. "Growth rate under Allende is around 7 percent, twice the rate of the previous administration," a CIA document stated in 1972. "Unemployment has been drastically reduced."[26] Rather than impressing the Nixon administration, these statistics seemed to make it more determined to prevent the Chilean experiment from working.

The best way of ruining the Chilean economy was to deprive it of badly needed credit. As a Third World country, Chile had saved little and lacked internal sources of investment. Instead, it had relied on loans from wealthier nations such as the United States in order to finance its own development. Burdened by debts left over from the Alessandri and Frei administrations, Chile stagnated economically.[27] The foreign debt, which amounted to more than $4 billion, in fact, drained the nation of over 30 percent of all its export earnings.[28] In consequence, Chile's foreign exchange reserves declined.[29] The low supply of foreign currency made the purchase of desperately needed imports far more difficult.[30] Even the boost in agricultural production could not meet the demands of a hungry and increasingly demanding Chilean populace. As Nogee and Sloan pointed out, "When his regime collapsed, Allende was importing about $700 million a year in food alone."[31]

Washington took advantage of Chile's economic weaknesses. In particular, the secretary of the treasury saw an opportunity. "It is my understanding that you have made it very clear that we should keep maximum pressure on Chile," Connally reminded the president.[32] Connally wanted to maintain that pressure by denying Chile a chance to renegotiate its enormous foreign debt at the meeting of the Paris Club in February of 1972. The secretary of the treasury wanted the other creditor nations to negotiate with Chile on a multilateral basis. The United States, of course, would lead this international group. "If they were to go off and negotiate separately our leverage could be reduced substantially," Connally advised the president, recommending that his own department lead the U.S. delegation.[33] The Treasury secretary wanted to demolish any Chilean hopes that Washington would renegotiate. "As I understand it, this is not our intention and our principle purpose is to get broad creditor support to isolate Chile," Connally insisted.[34]

Ambassador Davis also favored this strategy, fully cognizant of the damage it would wreak. Davis argued, "There is no foreseeable way in which GOC would be able to finance a level of imports sufficient to fill domestic supply-demand gap, as long as U.S. and Europeans do not pull apart on debt renegotiation, relief will be insufficient to serve Allende's purposes."[35]

This refusal to relieve Chile of its burden of massive debt would help fulfill Washington's ultimate agenda. "Range of acute economic problems—inflation, declining agricultural production, squeeze on imports, difficulties with copper production—will have critical effect on political developments during coming year," Davis predicted.[36]

The Nixon administration found the Chilean terms unreasonable: "The Chileans want a three year consolidation period with relief covering 85 percent of principal *and interest*, a grace period of three years and repayment over seven additional years with interest at four per cent."[37] Despite the heavy hand of Washington, the Chileans managed to negotiate with the Western Europeans on a bilateral basis in April. The eventual deals rescheduled 70 percent of the payments that were owed by Chile that year for another three years.[38] Although this agreement must have helped, nearly three-fourths of the $97 million debt that Chile wished to reschedule had come from the United States.[39] As long as the Chilean government refused to compensate Kennecott and Anaconda for their copper mines, Washington would not budge. In addition to its concern about the copper companies, the Nixon administration was profoundly concerned about the old unpaid loans from Eximbank and the Agency for International Development, both U.S. government organizations. The Overseas Private Insurance Corporation, which insured U.S. corporate investments in foreign countries, was also a government agency that faced heavy loss. In total, the U.S. government risked losing $1.1 billion.[40]

Whether the U.S. taxpayers should support multinational corporations is a valid subject for debate, but Washington's credit blockade forced Chile to turn to the Soviets for more help. In early 1972, a Soviet delegation of economic specialists visited Chile. The Chileans asked for $30 million in annual credits for machinery, and between $100 and $200 million in credits for wheat, meat, butter, and other edible commodities. Normally, such credits were provided on a short-term basis, but the Chileans hoped to delay payment until 1976. In exchange, Santiago offered to sell copper, curing salt, iodine, fish, fish flour, and finished goods such as shoes and woolens: "Payment for Chilean exports would be paid in cash and in accepted currency. The Chileans based their position on both the monetary restrictions, as well as political reasons."[41] At a time when reactionary factions in Chile threatened Allende's hold on political power, he had to avoid any appearance of collusion. It is likely, however, that Santiago would not have made such an extravagant proposal if the situation had been less desperate.

For its part, the Soviet delegation considered the Chilean requests exorbitant: "The Soviet-Chilean plan for commercial development proposed by the Chileans implies that the Soviet Union would have to accept terms and conditions which have never been encountered in relations between the USSR and developing countries. . . . Meanwhile, it is assumed that the USSR would have to import products, which are of no immediate use, and pay for them immediately in accepted currency."[42]

Unfortunately for Chile, the parties failed to reach an agreement. Visiting Moscow in December of 1972, Allende tried again. The Chilean president asked the Soviets for a loan of $100 million as a counterweight to its negative balance of payments. When Allende offered copper as reimbursement for the credit, the Soviets responded: "And why does the USSR need copper, when we have invested extensively in the copper mines of Siberia and we have sufficient for domestic needs?" Grudgingly, the Soviets would only extend $40 million.[43]

His hopes for Soviet economic assistance in ruins, Allende knew that his only hope was a resolution of the controversy over the expropriation of the copper mines. Allende suggested settling the dispute by international arbitration. While the Nixon administration claimed to respect the principles and procedures of international arbitration, it dismissed the idea by referring to the 1914 U.S.-Chile Bilateral Treaty for the Advancement of Peace: "The Treaty expressly states that 'any question that may affect the independence, the honor or the vital interests of either or both of the countries, or the provisions of their respective Constitutions or the interests of a third nation, will not be subjected to such or any other arbitration.' In view of this obstacle to arbitration of the basic copper issues and the potential for delay, it would be best to consider other arrangements for international adjudication."[44]

In all probability, Nixon and his advisors avoided international arbitration because they did not have a case. Still, it is ironic that the White House would invoke an old treaty in its opposition to the arbitration proposal. A treaty is a binding contract in international law. Yet, the Nixon administration had shown little respect for the rule of law in Chile as it financed General Schneider's murder. At any rate, the Nixon administration did not manipulate the Chilean political process because it cared about "the independence, the honor, or the vital interests" of Chile.

In the fall of 1972, U.S. intelligence commenced an operation to influence the Chilean congressional elections that would take place the following March. The CIA station in Santiago found a reliable ally in Ambassador Davis. With the diplomat's support, the station requested that Washington appropriate $1,427,666 for the campaign. On a copy of one document relevant to this scheme, the space marked for approval was checked underneath with the following handwritten words: "WH [White House] notified 10/18."[45]

Obviously, a major portion of this fund went to the UP's political opposition. Ideologically indiscriminate, the Nixon administration subsidized the centrist Christian Democratic party, the conservative National Party, the Democratic Radical Party, and the Independent Radical Party. The latter two parties had defected from the Radical Party. Unlike the Democratic Radicals, though, the Independent Radicals belonged to the UP coalition. "The Station will also continue its efforts to influence the PIR and will be alert for opportunities for using the PIR to exacerbate tensions within the UP," the CIA noted.[46]

As with previous donations, the precise amount given to each party is blacked out. Still, information that is withheld on some declassified documents is available on others. Records indicate that the National Party, a faction dominated by wealthy landowners, businessmen, and the bourgeoisie, received $328,500 for Fiscal Year 1972 under the auspices of the 40 Committee.[47] The Committee also granted the Christian Democrats $587,000.[48] One can assume the remaining two parties received comparable amounts.

By strengthening the opposition parties in anticipation of the 1973 elections, Washington hoped to ultimately weaken Allende's ability to work with the Chilean Congress. If the opposition parties formed a workable coalition and then won a two-thirds majority in the legislature, they could "override presidential vetos of legislative bills and, if the situation should arise, give them the necessary votes to remove the president by office by impeachment."[49]

The CIA could dream, but it could also realistically estimate Allende's political clout. The Agency could hope for little more than a simple majority. "A 65/35 split would probably yield a two-thirds majority in each house," the State Department noted, "but CIA believes such a result to be highly unlikely."[50] Ambassador Davis offered the same prediction. "The Ambassador indicated that he believes a 60/40 split of the vote in favor of the opposition is a likely outcome for the March elections," the CIA reported.[51] Although Kissinger would later claim that Allende was a threat to Chilean democracy, the U.S. ambassador doubted there would be fraud to any significant degree.

If the Agency did not expect to reverse the Allende experiment through electoral means, why did it bother to subsidize the political opposition? One must take another look at the relevant documents. In collaboration with Ambassador Davis, the CIA had requested financial assistance for the private sector.[52] This support exploited the economic situation in Chile, which Washington had helped bring about in the first place. Facing a worsening economic situation, a sector of the bourgeoisie went on strike. Allende's radical policies had had no detrimental effect on the living standard of the middle class, but it felt the impact of shortages.

Thanks to the currency shortage, which existed because of Washington's credit blockade, the bourgeoisie could no longer buy the imported goods it enjoyed so much.[53] Professionals such as doctors openly expressed their desire that the Chilean president step down.

Conservative women also participated enthusiastically in demonstrations, with the full backing of the Christian Democrats and the National Party. Their most famous protest, the March of the Empty Pots and Pans, took place on December 1, 1971, in Santiago. The privileged marchers brought along their pots and pans to symbolize their alleged hunger. Representatives from the conservative parties accompanied the women, as did an escort of *Patria y Libertad*, the paramilitary group notorious for its involvement in the 1970 murder of General Schneider.[54] As the women made their way from the Plaza Italia toward their intended target of *La Casa Moneda*, the presidential palace, they repeated slogans intended to associate Allende with the primitive stereotypes of Communism:

Allende, listen, we women are many!
¡Chile *si!* ¡Cuba *no!*
Dungeon, dungeon, Fidel go home! [Castro was visiting at the time.]
There's no meat—smoke a Havana!
The left has left *us* without food!
There's not meat in the pot, and the government looks the other way![55]

The protest never made it to *La Moneda*. Very soon, fighting broke out between the conservative male escorts and young male members of the UP. By the time the marchers reached a park called Cerro Santa Lucía, the police were waiting with tear gas and water. The March of the Empty Pots and Pans ended ignominiously by leaving over one hundred people, mostly male, injured.[56]

The March of the Empty Pots and Pans was intended to create the impression *all* Chilean women opposed Allende. Even though some working-class women took part in the original March, ladies of privilege had been the principal organizers.[57] Moreover, the copycat demonstrations that immediately followed the disrupted march took place in Providencia, an affluent area of the city, before spreading over the rest of Chile.[58] The poor women who did protest in the pot-and-pan demonstrations had actually suffered the privations to which their wealthy counterparts had only pretended. Many years later, the veterans of these protests wondered if the upper class had not manipulated them. After all, many of the shortages and the accompanying long lines were the direct result of the machinations of Washington and the Chilean social elite.[59]

For example, the engagement of the truck industry owners in strikes in the fall of 1972 and the summer of 1973 had a devastating impact because Chile lacked an extensive railway system. By stopping the delivery of vitally needed goods such as food, the economy came to a standstill. The striking truckers needed to live on something, however: "A reporter asked a group of truckers who were camping and dining on 'a lavish communal meal of steak, vegetables, wine and empanadas' where the money came from. 'From the CIA,' they answered laughingly."[60]

Kissinger even admitted in his memoir that the CIA had contributed $2,800 to the truckers, but it is hard to believe that U.S. intelligence did not provide far more than that.[61] How else could the idle truckers have lived so well for so long? Tellingly, weapons of U.S. manufacture were even found in the truckers' headquarters. Corporate America had not abandoned the fight, either. ITT extended $400,000 to the strikers. [62]

The blue-collar employees of the copper mines also joined the economic resistance. When the workers at El Teniente wanted another pay raise to meet inflation, the Chilean government rejected the request in an effort to keep the currency depreciation under control. In any case, the income of the copper miners was already several times more than the minimum wage. In his policy of wealth redistribution, Allende had gravely erred by enriching the lower classes while failing to require sacrifices from their social superiors. With the exception of a very privileged few who possessed the most extreme wealth, all Chileans by October of 1972 enjoyed wages and salaries that were 99.8 percent higher than the year before. Surely the bourgeoisie did not urgently require further enhancement of their affluence. Yet this specific policy, which was well-intended and designed to assist the impoverished bulk of the population, hurt the Chilean economy as it coped with an international blockade at the very end. Further shortages and inflation followed.[63]

Therefore, the strike at El Teniente attracted many supporters. The strike, which began on April 18, 1973, cost Chile more than $1 million a day, further impeding an already crippled industry. By this point, the centrist Christian Democrats shared a common cause with the rightist National Party and *Patria y Libertad*. All three groups supported the strike. The workers from Chuquicamata engaged in a sympathy strike, attracting several thousand students. Unrest resulted in Santiago, leaving two dead and more than fifty people hurt.[64]

Strikes grew epidemically as democracy approached its end in Chile. In 1969, when Frei was still president, the economy sustained 977 strikes. By contrast, Allende had to cope with 3,287 work stoppages in 1972. This astronomical statistic merely followed a 170 percent increase in strikes in 1970–1971.[65]

U.S. intelligence reveled in the economic chaos, expecting much to come from it. "The situation as it has developed in the past 24 hours has undoubtedly put pressure on the Chilean military, and the outbreak of violence and a successful commercial strike will add to that pressure," the CIA reported on October 12.[66] To the probable disappointment of U.S. intelligence, this pressure did not suffice. The Agency realized that it needed more time to induce the Chilean armed forces to act: "This conclusion was based on the estimate that the country would have to suffer a little more under Allende before the kind of consensus which would provoke the military into deciding on a coup would be reached among the main elements of the opposition—hat is, the military, the political parties, and the private sector."[67]

This is precisely what happened. Political scientist Edy Kaufman speculated that the striking bourgeoisie had the most decisive impact on the Chilean armed forces: "While the upper class' open confrontation with the Allende regime from its very beginnings probably did not surprise the military, the active and gradual involvement of middle-class *gremios* [professional organizations]—increasing existing chaos and augmenting a perception of growing popular discontent, to the point of publicly asking for the resignation or overthrow of the president—may have been critical in forcing a decision of the military officers, who were vacillating between lack of action and participation in the inevitable coup."[68]

Indeed, the unrest cost Allende the support of Chile's centrist faction, the Christian Democratic party. Besides the economic uncertainty, the PDC was displeased with Allende's inability to contain groups on the extreme left. Groups such as the MIR, and *Movimiento de Accion Popular Unitario* (Popular Unity Action Movement), or MAPU, took expropriation of urban factories and large rural estates far beyond where the Allende government cared to go.[69]

Favoring a Cuban style rebellion, MIR particularly did not share Allende's respect for the conservatives' entitlement to political expression. When anti-UP groups planned a demonstration in Concepcíon in the fall of 1972, MIR and some UP partisans tried to stop it. The police stepped in, and the death of a radical student followed.[70] Allende who truly believed in the peaceful functioning of democracy, would not tolerate lawless violence even from the left. Months before the incident in Concepcíon, Allende had said, "I am one of those that is horrified when I hear certain people affirming irresponsibly that we are close to a civil war. Although we would win a civil war—and we would have to win it, the Chilean economy, human co-existence, and human respect would be affected for generations."[71]

Uninspired by Allende's attitude, extreme leftists in Santiago were outraged, chanting "Reformism opens the door to fascism" and "Down with the politics of conciliation."[72] They intuitively understood that the right wing exercised their democratic rights as the means to the end of undermining Chilean democracy. Remarkably, Allende could tolerate criticism to the point of libel from both political extremes. His respect for free expression and democratic procedures was that great. Rather than violently purging the

MIR, the Chilean president traveled to Concepcion to engage them in a debate. If Allende, with all his logic and shrewdness, could not dissuade them from the activities, it was only because they understood how violent the repression from the right would eventually be.[73]

Foreseeing a right-wing coup against the Chilean government, Havana provided MIR with philosophical and material support. Castro explained that "the Chileans would not be able to stay where they were," as a constitutional democracy, if they wanted to continue their socialist experiment. Once tensions between MIR and Allende approached the crisis point, however, Cuba took the Chilean president's side. Cuban Deputy Prime Minister Carlos Rafael Rodriguez scolded the more radical members of Allende's Socialist party who sympathized with the MIR. "There is no revolutionary alternative to the Popular Unity government and President Allende," the Cuban deputy prime minister said, insisting that proposing "policies that divide the working and popular forces that Socialists and Communists guide together, is not to open path towards a deeper revolution, but to open breaches where the enemy can penetrate."[74]

Furthermore, Havana promised Allende to cease the provision of weaponry to MIR. The Cuban training of MIR militants would continue, but Cuban arms would only be contributed in the event of a Chilean coup.[75] Perhaps Castro was more willing to accommodate the Allende government with this matter because his relationship with Moscow meant more to him than violent revolution in Chile, or the rest of Latin America. By this point, Cuba had joined the Council for Mutual Economic Assistance, an economic alliance led by the Soviet Union.[76]

Besides the radical Cubans, MIR had managed to alienate more conservative Chileans at home. Previously, the Christian Democrats saw that it was in their own interest to work with the UP coalition and make compromises. Now, MIR reflected poorly on the Allende government as it struggled with Chile's economic difficulties. The PDC's right wing had its heart set on the 1976 presidential election. What could possibly be gained from working Allende at such a turbulent time?[77] Eventually, the Christian Democrats came to favor a military coup as a means of restoring order. On August 22, the Christian Democrats helped guide a "Sense of the House" resolution through the Chamber of Deputies that declared the Allende regime unconstitutional, further diminishing its legitimacy to military eyes.[78] Of course, the Christian Democrats expected the military to swiftly transfer power to them. A dictatorship lasting seventeen years would have been unthinkable.

In sum, U.S. intelligence anticipated that the Chilean officers would soon make a move. By the summer of 1972, the CIA now viewed General

Augusto Pinochet as a potential leader. One record described Pinochet as "involved with coup preparations of General Alfredo Canales Marquez Army Chief of Staff."[79]

Many in Chile had regarded Pinochet as a non-entity, but he now emerged as a potent figure. As the CIA observed, "Pinochet, previously the strict constitutionalist, reluctantly admitted he now harboring second thoughts: that Allende must be forced to step down or be eliminated ("only alternatives"). Pinochet . . . believes Prats leading candidate to head new govt but admits that if coup is led by younger officers (far out possibility), Prats won't have chance because he too closely identified with Allende."[80]

Like the late General Schneider, General Carlos Prats believed in the subordination of the military to civilian authority. As the chief-of-staff of the Chilean Army, Prats stood in the way of Pinochet and the other mutinous officers. Pinochet, therefore, worked around Prats as he cultivated the U.S. military. Pinochet made a good impression during his visit to the U.S. Army School of the Americas in the Panama Canal Zone: "Pinochet was in Panama before coming to Mexico to negotiate purchase of tanks from U.S. Govt. He felt he was very well treated came away believing U.S. will supply tanks after all. (While in Panama, talked with more junior U.S. Army officers he knew from days at School of Americas and was told U.S. will support coup against Allende 'with whatever means necessary' when time comes."[81]

It appears that U.S. intelligence had to prod Pinochet and the other officers to act, even as planning on their part grew more active. During the Independence holidays, which lasted from September 16th to the 20th, the CIA seemed more eager for a coup than the Chilean military. The Santiago station was disappointed, as it reported to Washington: "It is station's opinion that possible coup attempt over the Chilean Independence holidays is now less likely than it appeared to be 48 hours ago. We will remain alert to developments and continue to keep HQs advise [sic]."[82]

In the midst of all this intrigue, the president of Chile decided to bring his case before the world. Addressing the General Assembly of the United Nations on December 4, 1972, Allende indicated that the Nixon administration had not fooled him. "We are having to face forces that operate in the half-light, that fight with powerful weapons, but that fly no identifying flags and are entrenched in the most varied centers of influence," he said.[83]

Allende regarded the economic conflict between his country and the U.S.-based multinational corporations as a struggle for sovereignty. Should power rest with the people or with the capitalist elite? The Chilean president then made a statement that still has relevance in this age of globalization: "Merchants have no country of their own. Wherever they may be they have no ties with the soil. All they are interested in is the source of their profits. Those are not my own words; they were spoken by Jefferson."[84]

The people exercised their power through their participation in democratic government. For U.S. corporations in possession of Chilean assets, however, the priority was the bottom line, and the empowerment of the Chilean people threatened profits. Certainly, Kennecott displayed little regard for the Chilean people when it flouted Chilean constitutional procedures. Allende pointed out that the corporation had appealed to a special Chilean tribunal after the expropriation. The tribunal decided in favor of Chile. Rather than accepting that decision, Kennecott pressured European countries not to purchase Chilean copper. "Such a pretension runs counter to fundamental principles of international law, according to which a country's natural resources—particularly when they are its lifeblood—belong to it and are freely utilized by it," Allende said.[85]

In an impressive use of statistics, the Chilean president made it obvious that the profits of Kennecott and Anaconda were indeed excessive. Kennecott had generated an average profit rate of 52.8 percent in Chile each year, but it accrued a profit rate of less than 10 percent abroad. Anaconda, for its part, collected a 21.5 percent profit annually in Chile from 1955 to 1970, compared to 3.6 percent elsewhere. Allende was angry: "Those same enterprises exploited Chile's copper for many years, in the last 42 years alone taking out more than $4,000 million in profits although their initial investment was no more than $30 million. In striking contrast, let me give one simple and painful example of what this means to Chile. In my country there are 600,000 children who will never be able to enjoy life in a normal human way because during their first eight months of life they did not receive the minimum amount of protein. Four thousand million dollars would completely transform Chile. A small part of that some would ensure proteins for all time for all children of my country"[86]

Allende saw his country's struggle as a symbol of the Latin American struggle, a struggle against economic imperialism. "This is something that is embodied in the conscience and determination of more than 220 million human beings who demand that they be listened to and respected," Allende said.[87]

Interestingly, the Chilean president did not once mention the names of Richard Nixon or Henry Kissinger. This was a delicate time in U.S.–Chilean relations, so it would have been impolitic for Allende to attack them directly. Even at this strained point, the Chilean government had not completely lost hope of reaching a modus vivendi with Washington. In anticipation of Allende's visit to the United States, Ambassador Letelier had written a cable exclusively for Foreign Minister Almeyda: "I believe we should not discard totally the possibility that President Nixon, in a surprise move that is characteristic of his personality, may form in a determined moment an invitation to President Allende. This invitation could have the purpose of sustaining an ample conversation on the relations between both countries or have a merely ceremonial character. It is most probable that this will not occur. In spite of that, I consider it prudent to be prepared for an alternative of this type. I believe if the invitation comes, it would be difficult to turn down."[88]

The invitation never arrived. Washington had corporate interests to serve. As Allende was appealing to the soul of the United Nations, Kissinger's staff not only planned for an eventual coup, but for its aftermath. The minutes of a meeting that Charles Meyer chaired on October 17, 1972, are heavily censored. Fortunately, a CIA report of an unidentified meeting, dated two days later, had similar wording: "In order to establish precisely what technical difficulties would be involved, working level members of the ad hoc committee on Chile are being asked to examine all possibilities for assisting any post-Allende Chilean government."[89]

The ad hoc committee did not debate whether the United States should sponsor a coup, only how it could help: "[censored, but probably U.S. intelligence] role will probably continue to be limited to strengthening the opposition and monitoring developments, if, however, contingency circumstances should lead to a military coup [censored] felt that military would then want: first, military hardware to maintain law and order; secondly financial assistance to achieve a level of liquidity which would permit the new government to function effectively: and thirdly the more traditional forms of aid in terms of food, loans, etc. on an accelerated basis."[90]

The legitimate government of Chile could never dream of such generosity. Even as the Nixon administration refused to reschedule Chile's general foreign debt, it extended almost endless forgiveness to Chile's military. The State Department noted, "With respect to Chilean delinquencies on its debt to the U.S., we have reached agreement in principle with the GOC on the terms of the rescheduling of the amounts due on the military credits, and have offered to sign the agreement immediately."[91]

After rescheduling the Chilean military's own debt, Washington offered credits for foreign military sales. The Chilean armed forces received $10 million in FMS credits for Fiscal Year 1972, and $12.4 million for Fiscal Year 1973. The State Department believed it was imperative that the U.S. government meet the needs of the Chilean military for FY 1973. "It would be harmful to U.S. interests if the Chilean military were to become committed to the UP revolution, which ARA [a policy-planning committee] believes

could well be a consequence of our reduction at this time of FMS credit below $12.4 million," the State Department warned.[92]

Collaboration between Washington and the mutinous officers became
even more urgent when the anti-UP coalition failed to win a two-thirds
majority of the Chilean Congress on March 4, 1973. Having won 54.7 percent of the vote, the opposition now controlled thirty of forty Senate seats,
and sixty-three out of 150 seats in the Chamber of Deputies. Despite pock-
ets of lower-class opposition, the UP's electoral share of 44 percent does not
seem impressive, but when one remembers the 36.4 percent share won by
the UP in 1970, this was a remarkable gain. Allende was more popular than
ever. The UP enjoyed even greater approval from the proletariat, both urban and rural.[93] Criticism from the ultra-radical MIR had not weakened
Allende from the leftward side at all. Furthermore, the enormous bourgeois
opposition turned out to be not quite so enormous, winning only 56 percent of the vote instead of the expected 67 percent.[94] "It was said to be the
largest increase an incumbent party had ever received in Chile after being
in power more than two years," wrote William Blum, a former State Department employee.[95] Essentially, Allende had the popular mandate to remain in control of Chile until 1976.

As in the plotting before Allende's accession in 1970, Washington's policy had two tracks: political and military. A few in the CIA opposed the implementation of the two tracks. Subsidizing Chile's armed forces and Chile's
political opposition simultaneously would ultimately work against each
other: "It is our understanding that a policy designed to provoke a military
coup in the next six months to a year must seek to increase political tensions
and to intensify economic suffering, particularly among the lower classes so
that a feeling of national desperation will impel the military to move. Financial assistance to opposition political parties, and particularly to the proposed mass activities of the PDC, will tend to dispel this feeling of desperation and to contribute to helping the economy."[96]

The author of this memorandum did not want to wait for the 1976 presidential campaign to unseat the UP. A coup would be the only alternative favorable to the Nixon administration: "It is true that the UP may well win
legally in 1976, and that even the prospect of a PDC victory in the 1976
elections leaves much to be desired. The Chilean situation may thus be considered desperate, and the U.S. Government must decide whether the risks
involved in desperate remedies are justified."[97]

Even though the 40 Committee continued the two-track policy by au-
thorizing $1 million in August for the political opposition as well as the pri-
vate sector, Nixon and Kissinger wanted Allende out in 1973, not 1976.[98]

Therefore, U.S. military and intelligence officers closely monitored the power struggle between the constitutionalists and the conspirators in the Chilean military. They were particularly concerned about stubborn loyalty of General Prats to the Allende government. Allende had appointed Prats defense minister instead of a civilian as a defensive measure. "He [Prats] charged his commanders, down to the company level, 'with their lives' to keep the troops out of political problems," the U.S. Defense Department noted.[99] By May, Prats felt enough pressure "and agreed to inform President Salvador Allende personally of the rising discontent of [censored] over government policies and actions."[100] At that point, the CIA found that most of the Chilean Army generals supported a coup.[101]

A failed mutiny, the so-called Tancazo, as opposed to General Roberto Viaux's Tacnazo of 1969, on June 29 did not discourage U.S. intelligence. "Flag rank officers of all three services are meeting regularly for this purpose," the CIA reported with likely satisfaction of this probable dry run by lower-ranking officers.[102] Since Prats stood in the way, the generals and their right-wing allies disposed of him in a petty manner.

The pretext was the most peculiar incident. Prats would recall that on July 25, 1973, he "was driving in military uniform in a military car . . . when people traveling in four or five cars repeatedly made disgusting gestures at me and yelled obscene epithets at me."[103] Well-aware of plotting within his own military, Prats was extremely tense.[104] He feared the people were all targeting him for a Schneider-style killing.[105] Suddenly, a mannish-looking woman, Alejandrina Cox, looked at him and put her tongue out. Assuming that the tongue-sticking stranger was a male member of a group of conspirators, Prats took out his pistol and shot at her car. Chile is a country with a grand tradition of chivalry, and the unfortunate general was mortified when he learned his mistake.[106] Although Cox was unhurt, Prats felt obligated to resign, but Allende would not hear of it.[107] "I would not have shot if I had known she was a woman," Prats said in a public statement. "I publicly repeat my apologies to Señora Cox, in her condition as a woman."[108] Interestingly, Cox, an aristocratic opponent of the UP government, would express remorse about her own behavior, but much too late for Prats to know.[109]

The generals would exploit Prats's shame to their own advantage. On August 21, their wives stood in protest outside the house of the commander-in-chief, a true humiliation in patriarchal Chile. They compounded the humiliation by persuading Señora Prats to accept a letter that urged the general to resign. Realizing that he had no support, he did just that on August 24, explaining that the generals "have not acted as they should. I could not divide the army."[110] He also left the civilian Ministry of Defense. Probably, Prats lacked the late General Schneider's fortitude and strength of character. One newspaper headline read: "Women Throw Out Prats."[111]

The women's husbands wanted to replace him with General Manuel Torres, who was third in command, when the coup began. The future despot of Chile still had not earned the total respect of his brother officers: "The plotters do not regard General Augusto Pinochet, who is the second most senior officer in the Army, as a suitable replacement for Prats under such conditions."[112]

When Prats resigned, Allende immediately appointed Pinochet commander-in-chief of the Chilean Army.[113] It has been suggested that Allende made a calamitous error by cultivating the armed forces instead of preparing the working classes for armed struggle, as MIR would have preferred.[114] One may never know for sure. Jorge Arrate, the chief executive officer of Chile's public copper company, CODELCO, wondered later if Allende should have fired the highest ranking military men, for the Chilean president knew about the close ties between the Washington and his own country's armed forces. He definitely had the constitutional right to do so: "If he would have done this, and used his faculties, his legal faculties, the question is: Would this have anticipated the military coup? It's something that you cannot answer. You can build a hypothesis, but I have no answer to that."[115]

Either way, Allende could sense the restiveness of his armed forces. After appointing his intimate associate, Ambassador Letelier, as minister of defense, Allende tried to establish a rapprochement with the military. In spite of the tension he felt, the Chilean president still believed that the stability of his government depended on the military. Again dangerously crossing the civilian line, Allende also gave the ministries of mines and finance to military officers.[116]

Those within the military's lower ranks perhaps suffered the tension even more than Allende did. One member of the Chilean Air Force tried to alert the UP activists among his friends of the impending coup. Disregarding what the airman had to say, few of those friends escaped later imprisonment or death.[117]

Unquestionably, the Air Force member took great risk himself in trying to help his friends, as did any member of the Chilean military who tried to prevent the coup. In August of 1973, the navy arrested more than hundred men, including civilian shipyard employees as well as sailors, with the charge of "insubordination." These unfortunate men were tortured for information on their alleged ties to the UP, but the Navy simply did not have a real case against them. Actually, it turns out that the naval authorities themselves were guilty of insubordination. They had targeted their victims for their opposition to the coup. When the naval prisoners were finally permitted to speak with a lawyer a week later, they wrote to Allende: "Is defending the government, the constitution, legality, and the people crime? Is overthrowing the government, violating the law, and ending the lives of thousands of human beings legal?" Unfathomably, Allende failed to repond.[118] Perhaps he simply felt trapped by circumstances. Whatever the reason, he now had few progressive friends left in the Chilean armed forces, whose reactionary commanders were now at the beck and call of Washington.

As beleaguered as his government was by the forces of reaction, Allende still must have drawn psychological sustenance from his supporters until the very end. Exactly a week before the coup, approximately one million Chileans marched past *La Moneda*, the presidential palace, and chanted: *"Allende! Allende! El pueblo te defiende!*—Allende! Allende! The people will defend you!" Chile had never seen a more heavily attended demonstration.[119]

Sadly, Allende's earnest working-class allies were no match for the military. The Chilean president's efforts to conciliate the generals were also futile. The planned coup faced no impediment, and Washington knew that the Chilean military would violently repress the left. "During a meeting [censored portion] General Pinochet included in his remarks the fact that he intended to take a very hard line in dealing with the MIR [group to the left of Allende]," the CIA reported less than a month before the coup. "He stated that the Army would in fact wipe out the MIR."[120] The Nixon administration was prepared to help Pinochet in this campaign of terror: "It is likely that any form of military intervention would result in a request to the U.S. for bilateral military assistance, particularly for riot control equipment, tear gas supplies and possible medical support and Mobile Training Teams. In fact, an interest in purchasing riot control equipment under FMS credits already has been communicated to us on an official basis. It might be useful to process this request before any change in government occurs, if the Chileans are willing to utilize unused past FMS credits or pay cash."[121]

Of course, Pinochet's forces could use this equipment not just against violent revolutionaries but also against law-abiding defenders of the Chilean constitution, but the Nixon administration did not see distinctions among the political left. All that mattered was that the Chilean military would reverse the Allende experiment. "After some, perhaps considerable bloodletting, Chile could eventually achieve a greater measure of political and social stability than had been the case under Allende," the CIA concluded about the possibility of a coup.[122] CIA agent Donald Winters recalled that "the understanding was they [the Chilean military] would do it when they were ready and at the final moment tell us it was going to happen." In any case, the CIA knew at least one day in advance "that a coup attempt will be initiated on

11 September. All three branches of the armed forces and the *carabineros* are involved in this action."[123]

Two days before the coup, Admiral José Toribio Merino, the commander of the Chilean Navy, wrote to General Pinochet and General Gustavo Leigh Guzman, the commander of the Chilean Air Force: "You have my word of honor that D-Day will be the 11 at 06:00 hours. If you cannot accomplish this phase with the total of the forces at your command in Santiago. . . ."[124]

Pinochet and Guzman had no objections. Interestingly, on September 9, Allende had informed Pinochet of his plan to hold a referendum on his own government; in effect, a national vote of confidence.[125] If Pinochet had truly believed that support for the UP government was weak, he could easily have cancelled the coup so he could gleefully witness the political undoing of Allende. Despite the anti-Allende sentiment among the socioeconomic elite and a segment of the middle class, however, the coup was an act of force rather than an expression of popular will.

Allende realized what was happening as the militarists conspired behind his back, and so did Castro. The Cuban leader informed Allende that the Cuban embassy had stored a number of "automatic weapons, antitank weapons" that would be adequate to sustain a battalion. Allende never took advantage of this offer. In those last chaotic days, Allende permitted the Chilean Communists to accept additional Cuban arms. When it came to his own Socialist party, however, Allende was less receptive to Havana's generosity because "he was afraid that they would one day take to the street with machine guns." Sadly, Castro recalled that the Socialists "took a few weapons, but far fewer than we wanted to give them."[126] Still, as disappointed as Castro was by Allende's reaction, he must have realized that the Chilean government had no chance against the upcoming coup. The force of the Chilean military, backed with U.S. support, would simply be too great. After the coup took place, the CIA determined that "Havana [saw] external military intervention—a war between Peru and Chile for example—as the only possible, though somewhat unrealistic way of unseating Chile's military government."[127] In reality, the Chilean government was entirely on its own.

On the morning of September 11, 1973, Allende learned by telephone of a naval uprising in the port town of Valparaiso. Rushing from his private residence to *La Moneda*, Allende then found that all the armed forces had risen.[128] The besieged president shortly afterward received a message from Pinochet, Admiral Merino, General Gustavo Guzman, and General Cesar Mendoza Duran, commander of the police: "The President of the Republic must resign from his high post immediately, in favor of the armed forces and the police; the armed forces and the police are united in their determination to assume their historic role of fighting to free their country from the Marxist yoke and to re-establish order and the rule of law."[129]

Another admiral, Gustavo Carvajal, followed this message with a telephone call, urging Allende to leave Chile. The president angrily refused: "Allende is not going to surrender, you military shit [milicos de mierde]!" Making a final radio address at 9:30a.m., Allende said:

> This is the last time I shall speak to you. The air force has bombed all our radio stations. My words flow more from disappointment than from bitterness— let them serve as a moral condemnation of those who betrayed their oath. . . . Faced with all these events, there is only one thing I can say to the workers: I shall not surrender. Radio Magallanes [pro-UP station] will be silenced very soon too, and my words will no longer reach you. Yet you will continue to hear them; I shall always be with you. At the very least I shall leave behind the memory of an honorable man, who kept faith with the working class. Long live Chile! Long live the people! Long live the workers![130]

In response to these moving words, Pinochet issued the following instruction to Admiral Carvajal: "Now, attack the Moneda! Give it to them!"[131] The Chilean Air Force complied with two Hawker Hunter jets. Amidst this aerial devastation, Allende commanded his loyal followers to leave the palace, including his personal physician. The doctor obeyed, but then returned to retrieve his gas mask to encounter a gruesome sight: "He saw the president sprawled in an armchair, the right of his skull smashed, the brain spilling out, his helmet on the floor, a machine gun still resting precariously on his knees."[132]

Allende's death has been a point of controversy ever since. Was he murdered or did he commit suicide? After the coup, future French President Francois Mitterrand recalled his 1971 visit to La Moneda. Mitterrand remembered that Allende had expressed his admiration for his predecessor, President Jose Manuel Balmaceda, who had killed himself in 1891. "If I am overthrown one day," Allende told the Frenchman, "I will do the same thing."[133]

The surviving members of the UP had a hard time accepting the idea that their leader had committed suicide. Arrate certainly found it difficult, but he said in the end it did not matter if Allende died either by his own hand or that of someone else: "He defended a building that was impossible to defend against Air Force and tanks, with a machine gun. So, he was in the position to give his life, and those who threw rockets against the building obviously were trying to kill the people who was inside. So, if he [committed] suicide or was murdered, it's the same. Those who threw the rockets wanted to murder him, and they were murderers."[134]

Allende probably never really had the option of escape. Had the Chilean president taken the plotters' offer of a flight out of the country, he would not have survived. When the offer had been made, Pinochet laughingly said "that plane will never land. Kill the bitch and you eliminate the litter."[135]

Thirty-two years later at the National Historical Museum in Santiago, I came across a poignant symbol of Allende's destruction: a fragment of his horn-rimmed glasses. Allende met a sad end, but the Chilean people have more than his broken eyewear for a memento. His statue now rests in an honored place outside the very palace where he took his own life. Salvador Allende is now a figure of respect as well as tragedy.

Back in the fall of 1973, however, Kissinger was not thinking of Allende's place in history. When hearing of the Chilean president's death, Kissinger was blasé. Conversing with Deputy Secretary of State Kenneth Rush two days after the coup, the national security advisor only expressed mild annoyance: "Well, now at the briefing today I think we can express regret at the personal fate of Allende. Of course, it's an absurd situation where we have to apologize for the overthrow of a hostile government—of a government hostile to us."[136]

Kissinger was still untroubled when he chatted with the president on September 16. "Nothing new of any importance or is there?" Nixon inquired of his conduit to international affairs. "Nothing of very great consequence," Kissinger answered.[137] The destruction of democracy in a Latin American country did not matter. Only four civilian democracies remained in South America: Argentina, Colombia, Venezuela, Guyana.[138] As much as Kissinger would have liked to see them fall, the collapse of Allende still pleased him immensely. "The Chilean thing is getting consolidated and of course the newspapers are bleeding because a pro-Communist has been overthrown," Kissinger said, puzzled by all the fuss.[139] In fact, the national security advisor was thinking about attending a football game that day. "I mean instead of celebrating—in the Eisenhower period we would be heroes," Kissinger complained. "We didn't—as you know—our hand doesn't show on this one though," Nixon replied, perhaps remembering that their conversation would be recorded. "We didn't do it," Kissinger agreed, also maintaining some level of plausible deniability. "I mean we helped them."[140]

Pinochet, who dominated the military junta by this point, understood this strategy of denial. Ambassador Davis reported to Washington about the Chilean dictator: "He showed understanding and was relaxed about matter of recognition and volunteered that obviously we should not be first to recognize. He showed same recognition of advisability of not too much public identification with us at moment."[141]

While Kissinger would only admit privately to assisting those who had betrayed Allende, it is inconceivable that they would have acted without his guarantees. If Washington had threatened the Chilean military with financial sanctions when it learned of their definite plan, Allende would have remained in power past September 11. Arrate argued that even though the Chilean political scene was sharply divided, with great support for both ideological extremes, policymakers in Washington decided Chile's fate. Arrate observed: "It's true that the country was polarized, but when countries are polarized the outcome can depend on a very decisive extent on influence. And I think that's what the U.S. did. The Chilean Right is very powerful. It's very powerful even today. It has always been powerful . . . but not the Chilean Right nor the militaries would have behaved as they did if they had not had the American support."[142]

Judge Juan Guzman, who later served as Pinochet's prosecutor, had collected enough information during his investigation to form a considered opinion. "I think, and many people here in Chile think, that the support given from the United States was fundamental," Guzman said.[143]

Profoundly culpable, Nixon and Kissinger rejoiced in Allende's fall, and regarded the bloodshed as a fair price to pay. For both psychological and economic reasons, the imperium in Latin America had to be maintained.

Pinochet, who ruthlessly and quickly seized unilateral control of the Chilean state, waged an effective war against his own country. Destroying a democracy that was a century and a half old, the new dictator dissolved the Chilean Congress. He outlawed political parties and the CUT labor organization. Martial law effectively brought an end to the true rule of law in Chile. The junta quickly dispatched its political opponents to detention centers such as the National Stadium, the Chile Stadium, the Air Force Military Academy, the Naval War Academy, and the infamous Villa Grimaldi complex.[144] These locations became factories of death.

The majority of the immediate victims were former government officials, political activists, and labor leaders. The very most prominent detainees were usually held at the Ministry of Defense before relocation elsewhere. Less prominent targets on the political left soon followed.[145] The agencies that directed this persecution were the intelligence services of the Chilean armed forces: the Navy, the Air Force, and the Army. The Army's *Direccion de Inteligencia Nacional*, better known as DINA, was the most notorious.[146] First established in 1973, DINA became an independent agency the following year.

These intelligence services either shot their victims or knifed them to death. Whatever method chosen, the victims endured torture before their execution. One such victim was Eugenio Ruiz-Tagle, who met his doom on

October 19, 1973. When his mother beheld his body, she knew he had not died a merciful death: "An eye was missing, the nose had been ripped off, the one ear visible was pulled away at the bottom, there were very deep burn marks as though done by a soldering iron on his neck and face, his mouth was all swollen up, there were cigarette burns, and judging from the angle of the head, his neck was broken; there were lots of cuts and bleeding."[147]

The beautiful folksinger Victor Jara was another victim. After his execution at the Chile Stadium, his wife found him with his hands broken, his face mutilated, and his body bearing forty-four gunshot wounds.[148]

By the end of 1973, 1,500 Chileans had perished. Thousands more had no choice but to seek refuge abroad. Favoring the affluent at the expense of the less fortunate, the military regime made Santiago's working-class neighborhoods a special target. "No one likes to have his house raided," one General Alejandro Medina said. "But if there are rats inside, you accept that someone comes in to get them out."[149]

Judge Guzman estimated that 3,500 Chileans were either killed or "disappeared" during the seventeen years of military rule, but the prosecutor hesitated to settle on a number as he discovered more and more remains from the period. Indeed, the death toll could have been as high as 4,000.[150]

Chilean bodies and souls were no longer sacred. Those lucky enough to escape death were not lucky enough to escape torture. According to the report by Chile's National Commission on Political Imprisonment and Torture, at least 28,000 people survived physical and psychological agony. Most of these victims of torture were young men between the ages of twenty and thirty. They were members of the Socialist and Communist parties, trade unions, organizations that were now all banned.[151]

All the standard techniques, too numerous and varied to fully list, were employed to inflict pain. Military authorities beat their victims with their fists, and kicked them for good measure. The captors took care to aim repeated blows at the eyes, nose, mouth, neck, knees, and sensitive private parts.[152] In addition, prisoners were forced to assume excruciatingly uncomfortable positions. The Chilean military also favored the application of electric shocks, and the all the main detention sites had equipment for this specific purpose. In September of 1973, one unfortunate man detained at the Air Force Academy had reason to regret the development of electric power: "With my eyes covered I was seated in a chair, simulating an electric chair because the hands and feet were tied to the chair, the torso was also tied down, then the eyes and mouth were also tied. The electric wires were put on my head; at the beginning of the sessions of torture my head and mouth lost control . . . I bit both sides of my tongue and the interior of my cheek."[153]

Afterward, water was sometimes applied to intensify the shock.[154] Prisoners were denied food, drink, and access to toilets. For example, a prisoner in the city of Chol Chol was crammed into a tiny cell: "The room was about two by two meters; we were one top of the other. I also remember they didn't allow us to go to the bathroom and we had to defecate right there. Many of us were throwing up because of the pain and because of the terrible smell that was in the place."[155] Asphyxiation was not unknown, nor was exposure to extremes in temperature.[156]

Torment of the mind can be more devastating than that of the body. Psychotherapist Otto Doerr-Zegers described psychological torture as an assault on "all the victim's possible existential platforms."[157] Political prisoners were subjected to extreme mental suffering: threats against themselves or their loved ones, simulated executions, and deprivation of sleep.[158] The captors made their captives kiss their boots, crawl on the floor, and even ingest bodily wastes. When one prisoner in the city of Contulmo did not answer a question to a lieutenant's satisfaction, he "ordered that excrement be brought from the stable and water in a bottle. Then he asks me the same and because I gave him the same answer they . . . hit me in the stomach and put the excrement in my mouth. Then they used the water to make me eat everything."[159] By humiliating their captives in unspeakable ways, the military authorities completely deprived them of any sense of themselves.

Not all the victims of torture were male. Women endured a special kind of degradation that had both psychological and physical consequences. Many years later, more than 3,000 testified about their rapes. Given the shame that surrounded sexual violence in a patriarchal culture, it is likely that even more women remained silent.[160]

In Santiago, a sergeant repeatedly attacked Luz Arce, a former member of Allende's *Grupo de Amigos Personales*, or personal bodyguard. During one sexual assault "he pushed my head underwater. . . . More water entered my mouth and nostrils as I fought him. I felt nauseous . . . and I ended up vomiting. I remember the sergeant's disfigured face through the water, and feeling of suffocation."[161]

During this time of mass slaughter and torment in Chile, the Nixon administration offered generous assistance from Washington: "On 17 September the Chilean Air Attache in Washington requested immediate delivery from the Canal Zone of the following items: 1 million rounds—7.62mm ammunition; 2,000 flares; 1 parachute; 1,000 steel helmets; 1,000 liners; 1,000 parkas. All of the above are available in the Canal Zone. Transportation to Chile will be via Chilean Air Force planes. Approval of sale of these items is recommended."[162]

Pinochet's actions gave many of his initial supporters pause. Surprisingly, even Judge Guzman had been a conservative in favor of the coup. "We thought that simply that Allende was not able to govern this country," Guzman explained, "and I believed that this was going to be a short, a very short period of . . . putting things in order to have the democratical system work again here."[163] Slowly, Guzman realized the true nature of the new regime. At first, he had thought that the military were merely fighting rebels "when I started realizing as a judge that most of the people that had been killed were paupers, very poor people, old women, old men, lots of outlaws also, some kids, then I realized that this was really a slaughter."[164]

Guzman also upgraded his opinion of Allende. "Well, I think he would have been a better president if he would have had the Congress on his side," Guzman said.[165]

Unfortunately, Allende was gone now, and as the atrocities in Chile continued to shock and disgust the entire world, Kissinger, who was now secretary of state, remained complacent. The new president, Gerald R. Ford, carried on the Chilean policy of his predecessor, who had resigned in disgrace during the Watergate scandal. Still, political pressure in his own country compelled Kissinger to speak about the issue before the Organization of American States in 1976. Meeting with Pinochet before his speech, Kissinger assured his client that he was only going through the motions: "I will say that the human rights issue has impaired relations between the U.S. and Chile. This is partly the result of Congressional actions. I will add that I hope you will shortly remove these obstacles . . . I can do no less, without producing a reaction in the U.S. which would lead to legislative restrictions. My speech is not aimed at Chile. . . . We welcomed the overthrow of the Communist-inclined government here. We are not out to weaken your position."[166]

For effectively reversing the progressive agenda of the Allende government, Pinochet had Washington's wholehearted support. Socialism in Chile was dead. Kissinger and his two presidential patrons thought they had won. Indeed, in the short-term, they certainly did. Yet, in the long-term, the United States lost. By maintaining U.S. hegemony over Latin America, they only made the entire Western Hemisphere less secure. Governments that deal aggressively with their people do not restrain their aggression in their dealings with other countries. As a result, even the capital of the United States felt the effects of the Chilean terror. Orlando Letelier, the former ambassador and Cabinet minister who had served under Allende, was living in exile in Washington, where he was a leading critic of the Chilean junta. He now worked at the Institute for Policy Studies, a progressive think tank. In September of 1976, a car bomb took his life. Ronnie Moffit, an IPS fundraiser who was in his car, died, while her husband, Michael, who was also Letelier's assistant, was injured in the blast. DINA had planted the bomb to eliminate Letelier.[167] In order to silence Letelier's effective lobbying against his dictatorship, Pinochet was willing to violate the territorial integrity of the United States. Kissinger and Ford may have believed that it was in the interests of the United States to support the Chilean dictatorship, but that dictatorship proved more harmful to our national security than the Allende government could ever have been. Perhaps Kissinger should have paid closer attention to an NSC memorandum produced months before the coup: "If we confine ourselves to reacting when a U.S. interest is in jeopardy, if we respond to each challenge to our interests with sharpness and force, political alienation will grow and conflicts and disputes will spread. A decade from now we will indeed have a new relationship, but it will be a generally hostile one."[168]

Chilean opponents of Pinochet never committed violent acts against the United States, but repressed people in other countries have. It is a truism that U.S. policies abroad have repercussions at home. On the twenty-eighth anniversary of the Chilean coup, Saudi and Egyptian terrorists crashed passenger jets into the World Trade Center and the Pentagon, two symbols of North American might and power. Numerology has no place in serious historical analysis, but the coincidence should make thoughtful Americans ponder to some extent. Like the murderous Pinochet in the 1970s and 1980s, the authoritarian rulers of Saudi Arabia and Egypt enjoy Washington's beneficence. One must remember that victims of tyrannies do not cower forever; eventually they fight back. The American people, or at least its more privileged sectors, cannot flourish at the expense of others and expect to live in a stable world.

In the case of Chile, our support for the junta had repercussions even greater than the horrifying murders of Letelier and Moffitt, when American citizens became the direct targets.

## Notes

1. Draft of Memorandum for the President by Robert Finch, December 2, 1971, attachment to Memorandum from Dr. Kissinger from Ashley C. Hewitt, January 18, 1972. NSSM 108, Box H-178, Folder 4, Nixon Presidential Materials Project, National Archives II, College Park, Maryland.

2. "Background for Chilean Hearings," March 22, 1972. CIA Collection, FOIA website, U.S. State Department. "Cuban Disappointment with the Chilean Experiment," CIA Intelligence Information Special Report, May 31, 1972. CIA Collection, FOIA website, U.S. State Department.

3. "Background for Chilean Hearings," March 22, 1972.

4. Draft of Memorandum for the President by Robert Finch, December 2, 1971.

5. "Cuban Disappointment with the Chilean Experiment," May 31, 1972.

6. "Cuban Disappointment with the Chilean Experiment," May 31, 1972.

7. "Chile: The Alternatives Facing the Allende Regime," National Intelligence Estimate, June 29, 1972. CIA Collection, FOIA website.

8. Tanya Harmer, "A Different 9/11: Cuba and the Chilean Coup of 1973," Annual Conference of the Society for Historians of America Foreign Relations, Chantilly, VA, June 21, 2007.

9. Cable from Ambassador Nathaniel Davis to Secretary of State, February 28, 1972. State Department Collection, FOIA website.

10. Cable from Ambassador Nathaniel Davis to Secretary of State, February 28, 1972.

11. "Chile: The Alternatives Facing the Allende Regime," June 29, 1972.

12. "Next Steps Options on Chile," April 4, 1972. H-Files, Box H-64, Senior Review Group meetings, 4/11/72–Chile, Nixon Presidential Materials Project.

13. Memorandum from William J. Jorden to Henry A. Kissinger, April 10, 1972. H-Files, Box H-64, SRG Meetings, 4/11/72–Chile, Nixon Presidential Materials Project.

14. Joseph L. Nogee and John W. Sloan, "Allende's Chile and the Soviet Union: A Policy Lesson for Latin American Nations Seeking Autonomy," *Journal of Interamerican Studies and World Affairs* 21, no. 3 (August 1979): 355.

15. Nogee and Sloan, "Allende's Chile and the Soviet Union," 355.

16. "Chile: The Alternatives Facing the Allende Regime," June 29, 1972.

17. "Next Steps Options on Chile," April 4, 1972.

18. "Background for Chilean Hearings," March 22, 1972.

19. "Chile: The Alternatives Facing the Allende Regime," June 29, 1972.

20. "Background for Chilean Hearings," March 22, 1972.

21. "Chile: The Alternatives Facing the Allende Regime," June 29, 1972.

22. Cable from the Chilean Embassy in Moscow to the Minister of Foreign Relations, May 25, 1972. *Oficio Ordinario 92, Embajada de Chile, Moscu 1972, Archivo General Historico del Ministerio de Relaciones Exteriores*, Santiago, Chile.

23. "Chile: The Alternatives Facing the Allende Regime," June 29, 1972.

24. "Chile: The Alternatives Facing the Allende Regime," June 29, 1972.

25. "*Pero mas que eso, estos acuerdos son importantes en cuanto dicen relacion con la possibilidad de destinar mayores recursos a fines pacificos y en cuanto son un reconocimiento formal de que ambas partes no necesitan continuar la espiral armamentista ya que ella no tendria fundamento en los intereses reales de tales paises.*"Cable from Ambassador Letelier to the Minister of Foreign Relations, October 6, 1972. *Oficio 01252/600, Embajada de Chile, Estados Unidos 1972, Archivo*, Santiago, Chile.

26. DCI Briefing Notes for Chairman Mahon, July 27, 1972. CIA Collection, FOIA website.

27. The author wishes to thank Erfaan Choudhry, M.B.A., for his economic insights. James Petras and Morris Morley, *The United States and Chile: Imperialism*

and the Overthrow of the Allende Government (New York: Monthly Review Press, 1975), 92.

28. Chile: No More Dependence! (Nottingham, UK: Bertrand Russell Peace Foundation, 1973), 3.

29. Petras and Morley, The United States and Chile, 98.

30. Erfaan Choudhry.

31. Nogee and Sloan, "Allende's Chile and the Soviet Union," 356.

32. Memorandum for the President from Treasury Secretary, January 15, 1972. White House Special Files, Central Files, Box 6, CO 33 Chile [1971–1974], Nixon Presidential Materials Project.

33. Memorandum for the President from Treasury Secretary, January 15, 1972.

34. Memorandum for the President from Treasury Secretary, January 15, 1972.

35. Cable from Ambassador Nathaniel Davis to Secretary of State, February 28, 1972. State Department Collection, FOIA website.

36. Cable from Ambassador Davis, February 28, 1972.

37. "Next Steps Options on Chile," April 4, 1972.

38. Federico G. Gil, "Socialist Chile and the United States," Inter-American Economic Affairs 27, no. 2 (Autumn 1973): 39. Petras and Morley, The United States and Chile, 116.

39. Petras and Morley, The United States and Chile, 116.

40. "Next Steps Options on Chile," April 4, 1972.

41. Informe sobre la situación chilena elaborado por el Instituto de America Latina de la Academia de Ciencias de la URSS, July, 1972 in "Chile en los Archivos de las URSS (1959-1973)," Estudios Publicos 72 (Spring 1998), 439.

42. Informe sobre la situación chilena elaborado por el Instituto de America Latina de la Academia de Ciencias de la URSS, 440.

43. Jonathan Haslam, The Nixon Administration and the Death of Allende's Chile (New York: Verso, 2005), 151–153.

44. "Chile Copper—Arbitration," Charles A. Meyer, April 13, 1972. H-Files, Box H-64, 4/11/72–Chile, SRG meeting, Nixon Presidential Materials Project.

45. "Covert Support for Chilean Opposition Looking to March 1973 Congressional Elections," State Department Memorandum for Ambassador Johnson. State Department Collection, FOIA website. Cable to Santiago Station, October 12, 1972. CIA Collection, FOIA website.

46. "FY 1972 Amendment No. 1 to Project [censored]," Memorandum for Deputy Director of Plans, March 9, 1972. CIA Collection, FOIA website. "Briefing on Covert Operations," Memorandum for the Deputy Secretary, October 11, 1972. State Department Collection, FOIA website.

47. Project Approval Notification, March 17, 1972. CIA Collection, FOIA website.

48. Memorandum for Assistant Deputy Director for Plans, November 18, 1972. CIA Collection, FOIA website.

49. Cable from Santiago to CIA Director, September 24, 1972. CIA Collection, FOIA website.

50. "Briefing on Covert Operations," October 11, 1972.

51. "Meeting with Ambassador Nathaniel Davis–10 January 1973," Memorandum for the Record, January 11, 1973. Attachment to Dispatch to Chief, Western Hemisphere Division from Chief of Station, Santiago, January 12, 1973. CIA Collection, FOIA website.

52. Cable to CIA Director, September 26, 1972. CIA Collection, FOIA website.

53. Elizabeth Farnsworth, Richard Feinberg, and Eric Leenson, "The Invisible Blockade: The United States Reacts" in *Chile: Politics and Society*, ed. Arturo Valenzuela and J. Samuel Valenzuela (New Brunswick, NJ: Transaction Books, 1976), 367.

54. Margaret Power, *Right-wing Women in Chile: Feminine Power and the Struggle against Allende, 1964–1973* (University Park, PA: The Pennsylvania State University Press, 2002), 147–52.

55. Power, *Right-wing Women in Chile*, 153. For a map of the March of the Empty Pots and Pans, see page 154.

56. Power, *Right-wing Women in Chile*, 155.

57. Power, *Right-wing Women in Chile*, 148.

58. Power, *Right-wing Women in Chile*, 155–56, 156n.

59. Power, *Right-wing Women in Chile*, 10.

60. William Blum, *Killing Hope: U.S. Military Interventions and CIA Interventions since World War II* (Monroe, ME: Common Courage Press, 1995), 213.

61. Henry Kissinger, *Years of Upheaval* (Boston: Little, Brown and Company, 1982), 395.

62. Haslam, *The Nixon Administration and the Death of Allende's Chile*, 193. Edy Kaufman, *Crisis in Allende's Chile: New Perspectives* (New York and Westport, CT: Praeger, 1988), 81.

63. Arturo Valenzuela, *The Breakdown of Democratic Regimes: Chile* (Baltimore: The Johns Hopkins University Press, 1991), 61.

64. Kaufman, *Crisis in Allende's Chile*, 78–79.

65. Valenzuela, *The Breakdown of Democratic Regimes*, 61.

66. Information Report to CIA Directorate of Plans, October 12, 1972. CIA Collection, FOIA website.

67. "Meeting on Current Chilean Situation at Department of State, 1630–1830, 17 October 1972." State Department Collection, FOIA website.

68. Kaufman, *Crisis in Allende's Chile*, 80.

69. Valenzuela, *The Breakdown in Democratic Regimes*, 67. See also Peter Winn, *Weavers of Revolution: The Yarur Workers and Chile's Road to Socialism* (New York: Oxford University Press, 1986), 228.

70. Valenzuela, *The Breakdown in Democratic Regimes*, 67.

71. Harmer, "A Different 9/11: Cuba and the Chilean Coup of 1973."

72. Harmer, "A Different 9/11: Cuba and the Chilean Coup of 1973."

73. Harmer, "A Different 9/11: Cuba and the Chilean Coup of 1973."

74. Harmer, "A Different 9/11: Cuba and the Chilean Coup of 1973."

75. Harmer, "A Different 9/11: Cuba and the Chilean Coup of 1973."

76. Harmer, "A Different 9/11: Cuba and the Chilean Coup of 1973."

77. Valenzuela, *The Breakdown in Democratic Regimes*, 77.

78. Valenzuela, *The Breakdown in Democratic Regimes*, 104.

79. Document Identification, Augusto Pinochet, June 27, 1972. CIA Collection, FOIA website.

80. "Chile: Likelihood and Possible Consequences of a Military Coup," September 13, 1972. CIA Collection, FOIA website.

81. Ibid. Apparently, the CIA was mistaken. According to Mr. Lee A. Rials, Public Affairs Officer of the Western Hemisphere Institute for Security Cooperation, formerly the U.S. Army School of the Americas, Pinochet never studied there. Still, some of his brother officers had. Lee Rials, June 9, 2008, exchange by electronic mail.

82. Cable from Santiago to CIA Director, September 15, 1972. CIA Collection, FOIA website.

83. Salvador Allende, *Chile: No More Dependence!* (Nottingham, UK: Bertrand Russell Peace Foundation, 1973), 7.

84. *Chile: No More Dependence!*, 11.

85. *Chile: No More Dependence!*, 10.

86. *Chile: No More Dependence!*, 6.

87. *Chile: No More Dependence!*, 20.

88. "*Creo que no debíeramos descartar totalmente la posibilidad de que el Presidente Nixon, en un movimiento sorpresivo y caraterístico de su personalidad, decidiera formular en un momento determininado una invitación al Presidente Allende. Esta invitación podría ser el próposito de sostener un conversacion amplia sobre las relaciones entre de los dos países o incluso de carácter meramente protocolar. Lo mas probable es esto no ocurra. Con todo, considero que es prudente estar preparando para una alternativa de este tipo. Creo que si esta invitación llegara a producirse, resultaria muy difficil declinarla.*"

Cable from Ambassador Letelier to Foreign Minister Almeyda, November 8, 1972. *Telex N-838, Embajada de Chile, Estados Unidos 1972*, Archivo, Santiago, Chile.

89. Cable to Santiago, October 19, 1972. CIA Collection, FOIA website.

90. Cable to Santiago, October 19, 1972.

91. "Unclassified," State Department Document from Santiago, February 22, 1973. State Department Collection, FOIA Collection.

92. "Unclassified," February 22, 1973, and "FMS Credits for Chile," Department of State Action Memorandum, February 22, 1973. State Department Collection, FOIA website.

93. Valenzuela, *The Breakdown of Democratic Regimes*, 86.

94. Barbara Stallings, *Class Conflict and Economic Development, 1958–1973* (Stanford: Stanford University, 1978), 146.

95. Blum, *Killing Hope*, 213.

96. "Policy Objectives for Chile," Memorandum for Chief, Western Hemisphere Division, April 17, 1973. CIA Collection, FOIA website.

97. "Policy Objectives for Chile."

98. CIA Cable to Santiago Station, August 21, 1973. CIA Collection, FOIA website.

99. "General Prats' 13 Apr Meeting with Santiago," National Military Command Center, April 26, 1973. Department of Defense Collection, FOIA website.

100. CIA Report, May 2, 1973. CIA Collection, FOIA website.

101. CIA Report, May 2, 1973.

102. CIA Report, July 7, 1973. CIA Collection, FOIA website and Kaufman, Crisis in Allende's Chile, 252.

103. Power, Right-wing Women in Chile, 223n.

104. Power, Right-wing Women in Chile, 223.

105. Power, Right-wing Women in Chile, 223n.

106. Power, Right-wing Women in Chile, 223.

107. Power, Right-wing Women in Chile 223–24.

108. Power, Right-wing Women in Chile, 226.

109. Power, Right-wing Women in Chile, 225.

110. Kaufman, Crisis in Allende's Chile, 286–87. Power, Right-wing Women in Chile, 228.

111. Power, Right-wing Women in Chile, 228.

112. CIA Report, July 7, 1973.

113. Hugh O'Shaughnessy, Pinochet: The Politics of Torture (New York: New York University Press, 2000), 46.

114. Winn, Weavers of the Revolution, 240.

115. Jorge Arrate, conversation with author, Santiago, Chile, June 20, 2005.

116. Kaufman, Crisis in Allende's Chile, 291. Margaret Power, "We Opposed the Coup: Chilean Military Resistance to the Overthrow of Salvador Allende," Annual Meeting of the American Historical Association, Washington, D.C., January 5, 2008.

117. Power, "We Opposed the Coup: Chilean Military Resistance to the Overthrow of Salvador Allende," 9.

118. Ibid., 11–13.

119. Winn, Weavers of the Revolution, 243.

120. Information Report, August 24, 1973. CIA Collection, FOIA website.

121. Chile Contingency Paper: Possible Chilean Military Intervention," State Department Memorandum for Brig. General Brent Scowcroft, September 8, 1973. Box H-172, NSSM-97, Folder 1, Nixon Presidential Materials Project.

122. "Consequences of a Military Coup in Chile," Intelligence Memorandum, August 1, 1973. CIA Collection, FOIA website.

123. CIA Information Report, September 10, 1973. CIA Collection, FOIA website. Peter Kornbluh, The Pinochet File: A Declassified Dossier on Atrocity and Accountability (New York: The New Press, 2003), 112.

124. Haslam, The Nixon Administration and the Death of Allende's Chile, 219.

125. Kaufman, Crisis in Allende's Chile, 296.

126. Harmer, "A Different 9/11: Cuba and the Chilean Coup of 1973.

127. Ibid.

128. O'Shaughnessy, *Pinochet: The Politics of Torture*, 54.

129. Ibid.

130. Haslam, *The Nixon Administration and the Death of Allende's Chile*, 222, and O'Shaughnessy, *Pinochet: The Politics of Torture*, 56–58.

131. O'Shaughnessy, *Pinochet: The Politics of Torture*, 58.

132. Haslam, *The Nixon Administration and the Death of Allende's Chile*, 222.

133. Associated Press, "Socialist Says Allende Once Spoke of Suicide," *The New York Times*, September 12, 1973.

134. Arrate Interview.

135. Peter Kornbluh, *The Pinochet File*, 113.

136. Telephone Conversation, Ken Rush/Henry Kissinger, 9:03a.m., September 13, 1973. Courtesy of John Powers, Nixon Presidential Materials Project, National Archives II, College Park, Maryland.

137. Telcon, President Nixon/Henry Kissinger, 11:50a.m., September 16, 1973. Courtesy of John Powers, Nixon Presidential Materials Project.

138. "Junta in Charge," *The New York Times*, September 12, 1973.

139. Telcon, President Nixon/Henry Kissinger, 11:50a.m., September 16, 1973.

140. Ibid.

141. Cable from Ambassador Davis, September 1973. Washington Special Action Group Meetings, Box H-94, Nixon Presidential Materials Project.

142. Arrate interview.

143. Judge Juan Guzman, conversation with author, Santiago, Chile, June 13, 2005.

144. *National Commission on Truth and Reconciliation*, authorized by Chilean President Patricio Aylwin in 1991, Part Three: Chapter One. Truth Commissions Digitial Collection, United States Institute of Peace, www.usip.org/library/tc/doc/reports/chile/chile_1993_toc.html: Accessed April 23, 2008.

145. Ibid.

146. Professor Margaret Power, Illinois Institute of Technology. Electronic Mail Exchange, June 22, 2008.

147. *National Commission on Truth and Reconciliation*. Part Three: Chapter One.

148. Ibid.

149. Pamela Constable and Arturo Valenzuela, *A Nation of Enemies*: Chile Under Pinochet (New York: W.W. Norton & Company, 1993), 20.

150. Presentation by Elizabeth Farnsworth on her documentary on Judge Juan Guzman, University of California, Berkeley, March 6, 2006. Larry Rohter, "The Saturday Profile: Shining a Light Into the Abyss of Chile's Dictatorship," *The New York Times*, February 25, 2006.

151. *"Para Nunca Mas Vivirlo, Nunca Mas Negarlo,"* Prologo: *Informe de la Comision Nacional Sobre Prision Politica y Tortura*. Chilean Interior Ministry, 2004–2005, pge 5.

152. *"Metodos de tortura: definiciones y testimonios," Capitulo V: Informe de la Comision Nacional Sobre Prision Politica y Tortura*, 226.

153. "Metodos de tortura," 232–35.

154. "Metodos de tortura," 232–35.

155. "Metodos de tortura," 248.

156. "Metodos de tortura," 248.

157. Alfred W. McCoy's A Question of Torture: CIA Interrogation from the Cold War to the War on Terror (New York: Metropolitan Books, 2006), 10–11. I would highly recommend Professor McCoy's excellent study.

158. "Metodos de tortura," 236–39, 248–49.

159. "Metodos de tortura," 240.

160. "Metodos de tortura," 242–44.

161. Luz Arce, The Inferno: A Story of Terror and Survival in Chile (Madison: University of Wisconsin Press, 2004), 59.

162. "Actions vis-à-vis Chile: Military," September 17, 1973. Washington Special Action Group Meetings, Box H-94, Nixon Presidential Materials Project.

163. Guzman interview.

164. Guzman interview.

165. Guzman interview.

166. Christopher Hitchens, The Trial of Henry Kissinger (New York: Verso, 2002), 70.

167. John Dinges, The Condor Years (New York: The New Press, 2004), 191.

168. "Review of U.S. Policy Toward Latin America," Memorandum for Mr. Henry A. Kissinger from John Hugh Crimmins, Acting Chairman, Interdepartmental Group for Inter-American Affairs, May 29, 1973. Box H-178, NSSM 108, Folder 2, Nixon Presidential Materials Project.

# Afterword: Two American Victims

In the aftermath of the coup, observant Americans instantly assumed the complicity of their own government. They did not require declassified documents to confirm their suspicions. Still, whether approving or repelled by the Chilean junta, these sharp surveyors of the international scene felt safely removed from its brutality. Even though the Nixon administration had immediately embraced General Pinochet, a man with an almost Hitlerian disregard for human rights, Americans were confident of their own safety. After all, they were citizens of the most powerful nation on earth.

What should have challenged this complacency were the deaths of two young Americans shortly after the destruction of democracy in Chile.

On September 17, 1973, soldiers raided the Santiago home of Charles Horman and dragged him away. For a month, his family frantically searched for him until the confirmation of his death. Six months later, Horman's grief-stricken parents, Ed and Elizabeth, received a telegram from Secretary of State Henry Kissinger. "In order for the American Embassy at Santiago to arrange shipment, you will recall that a deposit of nine hundred dollars (900) is required to cover the estimated cost for preparation of the remains and transportation to New York City," the telegram read. "Funds and instructions should be sent to the office of Special Consular Services, Department of State. Please accept our deepest condolences in this tragic affair."[1]

Kissinger's condolences did not satisfy Ed Horman. Anxious to publicize what had happened to his son, Ed discussed his own investigation. "I began my own ad hoc review expecting only arrogance and absence of care," Ed said. "Then, as things progressed, I became aware of something far more serious. I am now convinced that the United States government had foreknowledge of and possibly planned my son's execution."[2]

On September 20, soldiers also forced their way into the Santiago apartment of David Hathaway and Frank Teruggi. The soldiers took them to the National Stadium, which served as a concentration camp and interrogation center for Chilean leftists.[3] The Chilean authorities then released Hathaway on condition that he leave Chile within forty-eight hours, but he could not make his departure without trying to determine the fate of his roommate. After touring a morgue, Hathaway though he had spotted a body that resembled Teruggi. Having little time, Hathaway asked a friend, Steven Volk, to take a second look. Volk studied the nameless, numbered bodies, finally recognizing one that bore a slashed throat and two or three bullet wounds in the torso: "This is him."[4]

Like Ed Horman, Teruggi's father did not trust the integrity of the United States government. "I served 40 months in the infantry," Frank Teruggi, Sr., said. "I used to have a lot of respect for our men in Washington, but now."[5]

The fathers of the two victims did not contrive conspiracy theories for fun. Indeed, the evidence strongly suggests that the intelligence arm of the United States government bore responsibility for the deaths of two American citizens, Charles Edmund Horman and Frank Randall Teruggi.

---

A Harvard graduate and journalist by profession, Charles Horman represented the best of American youth. He was intellectually gifted and idealistic. He participated in the civil rights movement, even briefly going to jail in Louisiana for his efforts.[6] Horman was also a true prose stylist, writing with great lyricism and beauty. In the most tragically ironic way, his own words later could have comforted his own family, who were inexplicably tormented by the guilt of survivors: "We have no more right to accuse ourselves than to accuse others. Guilt feelings are like fear—given us for survival, not destruction."[7]

Avid for new experiences, Horman journeyed to South America in 1971 with his wife, Joyce. First-hand, the couple saw the poverty and devastation of Latin America. They witnessed an especially gruesome sight as they traveled through Ecuador. "In the back of the bus, an Indian family sat huddled together—a mother, father, and three children," Joyce recalled. "They had a big tin can with jagged edges which they passed among them, and each person spat blood and phlegm into it. The whole family was dying of tuberculosis."[8] Chile provided a pleasant contrast, however. "Several weeks later, we passed into Chile, where health care was free and every child received a half liter of milk a day," Joyce said. "We reached Santiago, and Charles said, 'This is where I can write. This is where I want to be.'"[9] Joyce pointed out that her husband was not an extreme leftist, but did approve of Allende's social reforms. "People were taking a hold of their future," Joyce said. "Everybody was talking about politics 100 percent of the time. It was vibrant, electric."[10]

Frank Teruggi came to Chile for the same reasons. An alumni of both the California Institute of Technology and the antiwar movement, Teruggi enrolled as an economics student at the University of Chile. Teruggi supported Allende, but like Horman, was no fanatic. "While the rest of us were marching and shouting at the rallies, I knew I would find Frank back at the edge of the crowd, observing," a Chilean friend remembered.[11]

Both Horman and Teruggi worked for *Fuente de Información Norteamericana* (FIN), a progressive media organization. Marc Cooper, an American who worked as a translator for Allende, found most of his fellow expatriates abrasively left-wing, but he liked the two men. Cooper "thought fondly of the spry and witty Teruggi, who was clearly the brightest among his friends."[12] Horman was a complete stranger when he came to Cooper's apartment to make his acquaintance: "That was sufficient basis for us, fueled by a couple of liters of rich Chilean red wine, to talk of politics and life deep into the night."[13]

Cooper later wished he had known them better. "I would next see them a decade later and then only as celluloid ghosts conjured up in the Costa-Gavras film *Missing*."[14] Horman and Teruggi should have survived the coup in a form far more substantial than celluloid. What went wrong? Given the greater complexity of the Horman case, this chapter will focus first on him.

On September 10, 1973, Horman took his friend Terry Simon, a visitor from America, to the coast town of Viña del Mar for sightseeing. Leaving behind Joyce, who had to renew her resident's visa, they only intended to spend the day in Viña del Mar. The coup that took place the next morning trapped Horman and Simon at the Miramar Hotel for four days. The highways were all closed.[15] On the afternoon of September 12, they encountered an American, Art Creter, on the hotel terrace. Creter laughingly identified himself as a "naval engineer . . . retired, of course," based in Panama, who came to Chile for a short assignment with the Navy."[16] Creter told Horman and Simon that they would probably be stuck in Vina del Mar for several more days. Nevertheless, he assured the two friends that they were not in any danger, and that the coup had gone very smoothly."[17]

Creter seemed to have some inside knowledge about the coup, so Horman and Simon probed him further. "We asked if it had been planned far in advance, and he replied that that 'it never goes this smoothly unless it's planned in advance,'" Simon stated.[18] "He went on to explain that around 4:30 in the morning of the 11th the military began mobilizing, and soldiers were placed on street corners throughout the country, and 'about half an hour later all Chile was under military control.'"[19]

The naval engineer then mentioned the close presence of a cruiser, two destroyers, and a submarine from the coast, indicating the involvement of the U.S. military in the coup. Furthermore, Creter showed a comfortable acquaintance with U.S. foreign policy when Horman and Simon asked if their own government would recognize the regime: "Well, it's all up to the politicians, but I don't think there's any doubt about it."[20]

Anxious to return to Santiago, the pair asked if they ought to go to the U.S. Consulate in nearby Valparaiso, if one existed. Creter assented. "When we invited him to come with us, he laughed and said that the Consulate was the 'last place he'd go' because the Consulate didn't like to know too much about the activities of the U.S. military in the country," Simon recalled.[21]

She provided writer Thomas Hauser a more dramatic account of the conversation with Creter. In this retelling, Simon asked what Creter, as an American, was doing in Chile. "I'm here with the United States Navy," Creter replied with a smile. *"We came here to do a job and it's done."*[22] When Creter walked away, Horman could not help but express his amazement. "That was incredible," Horman said to Simon. "I don't believe he said all that to us."[23]

Reflecting more deeply that night, Horman now fully realized that the United States was behind the coup. "We've stumbled upon something very important," he told Simon. "I think we should keep a record of everything we see and hear in Viña."[24]

Although Simon's affidavit and the account by Hauser differ to a certain extent, it is apparent that Creter revealed more than he should have. Creter displayed an easy intimacy with U.S. military personnel before Horman and Simon, who both later spotted him entering the local headquarters of the Chilean military with Roger Frauenfelder, an American officer.[25]

The next day at the hotel, Horman and Simon came across Colonel Patrick Ryan, the deputy chief of the United States Naval Mission in Valparaiso. They explained their predicament to him, and he promised to try to assist them. Like Creter, Ryan displayed inside knowledge of the coup. "He told us that he had information 24–48 hours in advance of things happening, and he would know when the roads and borders opened," Simon stated. "He also offered the information that Allende was buried in Viña, and that we wouldn't see that in the newspapers for a long time, if ever."[26]

After Ryan went on his way, Horman and Simon looked for the U.S. Consulate. They found the British Consulate instead, where they learned that the United States did not even maintain a consulate in Valparaiso. A security attaché from the British Embassy in Santiago advised them "that the North Americans had prior knowledge of the coup and they were the people with the most accurate information, and that we should contact them."[27]

On September 14, Ryan offered the stranded tourists a ride so they could radio their parents back home in the United States. On the way, the three Americans discussed the coup. Simon recalled that "Col described the truck drivers as the 'real heroes of the thing . . . they brought the government down.'"[28] Adding that "we wouldn't have had all these problems in Chile if it hadn't been for Cuba," the colonel went on to give them even more revealing information. "Ryan told us that he personally had taken a Chilean Navy general [Admiral Sergio Huidobro Justiano] . . . to the United States in July on a $1 million military shopping trip," Simon stated.[29]

They reached Ryan's office at United States Naval Mission in Valparaiso, where they first encountered Frauenfelder. The officer informed the tourists of the presence in the harbor of two destroyers, two destroyer escorts, and a submarine from the United States. They questioned Frauenfelder about his own personal reaction to the coup. "He said, 'Since I've been here I've become a real supporter of that cause,'" Simon remembered. "Before Charles and I left to have lunch, Frauenfelder told us that the former mayor and governor of Valparaiso were being held prisoner on a naval training ship that we could see from his window."[30]

Ryan drove the pair to the home of a colleague who had the Naval Mission radio. Simon dictated a message for transmission through the U.S. Southern Command in Panama: "I'm safe and well. Delay leaving Chile. Tell Dad. Contact Charlie's parents at (212) RH 4-2339. Tell them all OK. Love, Terry."[31]

On the morning of September 15, Ryan picked them up at the hotel for lunch at his home. Yet again, Horman and Simon saw evidence of U.S. involvement in the coup. "At one point during the drive, we were stopped by a Chilean soldier at a checkpoint and Col. Ryan was asked for identification," Simon stated. "He produced (and afterwards let us examine) an identification card which identified him as a Lieutenant Colonel in the *Armada de Chile*."[32] Ryan arranged an afternoon ride for Horman and Simon with Captain Ray Davis, commander of the United States Military Group in Santiago. "We left Vina with a good feeling about Pat Ryan," Terry recalled. "Of course, we didn't realize that what we had learned from him would probably contribute to Charles's murder."[33]

Two months after the death of Charles Horman, Ryan sent a statement to his superior, the chief of the Navy Section of the U.S. Military Group, Chile. In the statement, Ryan denied revealing sensitive information to Horman and Simon: "I am absolutely positive, that at no time did I discuss, or did I overhear in any member of the Navy Mission discuss in a more than passing manner the military/political situation with the couple. Quite obviously, in that we were experiencing a coup de etat [sic], such matters may have been mentioned in passing, but primarily they were addressed in relation to their impact on the couple's personal problem."[34]

If Ryan had revealed embarrassing information to Horman and Simon, it is unlikely that he would have made a full confession to his commander. Ryan would have gained far more from misstating the facts than Simon. As Ed Horman sought answers about his son's death, Ryan and other U.S. personnel, military and civilian, felt pressure to present their actions in a favorable light. Ryan's letter to Fred Purdy, the consul at the U.S. Embassy in Santiago, was heatedly defensive. In short, he called Simon a liar: "I might very well have said 'Chile would not be where it is today if it hadn't been for Cuba.' I believe that statement is true. Some other quotes Miss Simon attributes to me and various Navy Mission members contain some truth, half truths, or no truths at all."[35]

Although Ryan acknowledged that he might have discussed the truckers' strike, he denied speaking "so disrespectfully or condescendingly of Almirante Huidobro as to say 'I took him on a shopping trip to CONUS.'"[36] The accusation of the shopping trip particularly incensed Ryan: "Those are Miss Simon's words, not mine, and like her recollection of where we met, they are *embellished* to suit her purposes!"[37] Additional evidence will reveal the likely truth-teller.

Turning back to the narrative, Captain Ray Davis drove Horman and Simon back to Santiago. Davis did not care for Horman: "For some reason, I don't know why, he chose of his own volition to sit in the back seat and not the front with Terry and myself. Normally, when three people ride in a car, everyone gets in front. I can't drive and talk to someone in back very well."[38]

Like Ryan, Davis displayed an *Armada de Chile* card at a military roadblock. Unlike Ryan, however, Davis avoided discussing American involvement in the coup. Perhaps listening to his own intuition, Horman also had little to say. When they finally reached Santiago, Davis offered to drive them home, but Horman directed him to the Hotel Carerra instead. Davis gave Simon his card, asking her to contact him if she needed assistance. At the hotel, Simon asked Horman why he did not want Davis to take them home. "I didn't want Davis to know where we live," Horman replied. "I don't trust him, and there wasn't time to get home on our own before curfew."[39] The next morning, they reached home, joyfully reuniting with Joyce after a dramatic week's absence.

Unfortunately, that joyful reunion did not end the story. Horman feared that the information they had about the coup, as well as their foreign status, marked them as targets for new regime. They wanted to leave Chile. As Joyce checked on their friends and stocked food, Horman and Simon took a hotel room by the embassy in case one of them could not reach home in time for the military-imposed curfew. They also tried to arrange a flight out of Chile. At the Braniff Airlines office, the ticket agent informed them that the airports were closed for civilian use. He suggested going to the embassy, where a lady named Mrs. Tipton was making a list of two hundred Americans who had to leave Chile immediately.[40]

Writer Thomas Hauser nicely captured their encounter with a switchboard operator at the embassy:

> "Could we speak with Mrs. Tipton?" Charles asked.
>
> "No one by that name works here," the operator answered.
>
> "Okay! Could we speak with whoever's in charge of helping Americans leave Chile?"
>
> "That's not our job. You'll have to talk with someone at the Consulate."
>
> As Charles began a slow burn, Terry interrupted. "We were told two days agothat the Consulate was closed because of gunfire and the Consul was working here. Is that still true?"
>
> "I really don't know."
>
> "Could you call and find out?"
>
> "Look, lady, if you want to know whether or not the Consulate is open, you'll have to go to the Consulate. It's lunch time, so nobody would be there now anyway."
>
> "Do you know if a Mrs. Tipton works at the Consulate?"
>
> The operator stared at the switchboard as if to ignore their existence.
>
> "No, I don't," he answered when it became clear they would stand over him until he replied.[41]

Frank Manitzas of CBS News witnessed the exchange. The newsman advised them to insist on speaking with the ambassador, but Horman thought the consulate was the better option. Fearing the approaching curfew, Horman decided to go home, so Simon went to the consulate by herself. Mrs. Tipton proved as helpful as the operator.

Explaining that she was a tourist visiting two American friends, Terry recounted her experience at Braniff and asked that their names be put on the list of people seeking priority return to the United States.

> "Well," Mrs. Tipton answered, "the gentleman at Braniff gave you incorrect information. As you can see, I work at the Consulate, not the Embassy. And, if

you want to leave, you'll have to go back to the airline when the borders are open. We handled two emergency cases here at the Consulate, but everyone else is on their own. We're not responsible for people who want to leave, and I have no information about the necessary procedures."

"That's not much help," Terry noted.

"I'm sorry. There's nothing more I can do for you. You'll simply have to go back to your hotel room and wait."[42]

The U.S. embassy may have done little to help American citizens stranded in Chile, but public relations became top priority after Horman's death. In March of 1974, Deputy Chief of Mission Herbert B. Thompson wrote a memorandum to Consul Fred Purdy. "We may need a concise statement at some point," Thompson wrote. "Perhaps you could amend the following to make it completely factual."[43] Thompson favored a denial that Horman had ever come to the embassy. Apparently, the deputy chief of mission did not regard Horman's encounter with CBS's Manitzas as evidence. If Horman had come, Thompson wanted it known that the embassy would have "properly referred" him to the Consulate. "Between the time of Charles Horman's reported inquiry at the Embassy and the time of his arrest, there were several hours during which he could have sought assistance at the Consulate," Thompson wrote, overlooking the fact that the curfew had forced Horman to return home.[44]

Thompson noted that the consulate had helped thirty-one American citizens find seats on a UN charter flight on September 19. "It is plain that if Charles Horman had informed the Consulate of his urgent need to depart Chile, efforts would have been made to include him on that flight," Thompson insisted.[45] Given the dismissive treatment of Simon by Mrs. Tipton, it is unlikely that Horman would have received any special consideration. He hardly could have approached the consulate with the line: Please help me. I have come across U.S. involvement in the coup, and my life is in danger. Furthermore, given the violence in Chile at the time, every American had an "urgent need" to leave the country.

We need not rely solely on Hauser's account in *Missing*. Marc Cooper, who had worked for Allende as a translator, endured similar treatment from the embassy. On the day of the coup, Cooper telephoned the embassy for guidance. "No special orders," a woman answered laughingly. "Just stay off the streets. I'm looking out of the window now with binoculars. Looks like Mr. Allende is finally going to get it."[46]

Cooper's ties to the Allende regime were close, so he rightly feared for his own life. On September 14, he spoke on the telephone to Mrs. Tipton at the consulate, explaining his situation and asking for help. Mrs. Tipton asked if he had a U.S. driver's license, and he responded in the affirmative. "Good," Mrs. Tipton said. "Don't bother to come in today because we're about to close. But come in Monday. Bring your license and ten dollars and we'll expedite you a new passport. Should take about a week, maybe ten days."[47] Cooper protested, but Mrs. Tipton would not listen. "Just stay away from the shooting and obey the authorities," she said.[48] Cooper and his American friends then tried confronting Consul Fred Purdy, demanding help. Purdy lamely advised them to act with caution, and then dismissed them. Cooper believed that the embassy was simply indifferent to the fact that their safety was at stake. "It was more important to give political support to the new dictatorship that it was to undermine its credibility by suggesting that American citizens need protection against it," Cooper noted sadly.[49]

No thanks to the U.S. consulate, Cooper eventually found his way out of Chile, but Horman was not so lucky after he left Simon. His race against the curfew cost him his life. Around 5:00 in the afternoon of September 17, 1973, twelve to fifteen soldiers came in a truck and arrested him.

What happened after Horman's arrest? The evidence indicates that once Horman was in military custody, he said that his friends could vouch for the fact that he was not an extremist. Two friends were reached. One friend, Warwick Armstrong, received a call telling him to report to the nearest police station. Armstrong called the consulate instead. Consul Fred Purdy's own chronology of events acknowledges this call: "September 18—about mid-day, U.S. Embassy's Consulate received a call from Mr. Warwick Armstrong reporting Horman missing since late September 17 and possibly detained."[50]

Even though the consulate knew of Horman's arrest one day later, it took no effective steps to save his life. Certainly, Purdy's strange behavior suggests profound negligence on his part. Joyce Horman and Terry Simon did not even learn of the calls made to the consulate until they insisted on seeing the consulate's notecards.[51] When Horman's father Ed confronted Purdy about these calls, the consul initially denied any knowledge about them.[52]

According to the chronology, the consulate at least went through the motions by calling police stations and the Chilean Department of Investigations. Apart from Purdy's own failings, Ambassador Nathaniel Davis also behaved in an unconscionable manner. He easily could have applied pressure to the ruling junta itself for information about Horman, but did not. The failure of the consulate to act doomed Horman. The exact circumstances of his death remain a mystery, but a Chilean refugee at the Italian embassy provided some possible answers three years afterward.

Rafael Gonzalez spoke to Joanne Omang, a reporter for the *Washington Post*, and Frank Manitzas, the CBS stringer who had seen Horman at the U.S. Embassy. For more than twenty years, Gonzalez had worked for Chilean intelligence. After the coup, Gonzalez had grown disgusted by the methods used by the newly formed Directorate of National Intelligence, or DINA. "I was told I would be shot because I complained of the economical new way of the government and the way in which they were acting," Gonzalez told the reporters. "DINA is like a Gestapo or whatever you want to call it, but not an intelligence service."[53]

Haltingly, Gonzalez explained to Omang and Manitzas that he had heard the order for Horman's execution given on the ninth floor of the Ministry of Defense. "I . . . I . . . I . . . knew that Charles Horman was killed," Gonzalez told the reporters. "Because he knew too much. And this was done between the CIA and the local authorities."[54] Manitzas asked for proof. "Because Charles Horman was brought from Valparaiso to Santiago, and I saw the guys that brought them here to Santiago," Gonzalez replied. "And he disappear later on. I knew that . . . that they receive the order to shoot him . . . and he was dis . . . because I heard that order."[55] Manitzas asked for clarification. "General Lutz was the Army intelligence director and the number two Colonel Barria were . . . was with some American that his name I don't know, and they decided this guy was supposed to disappear," Gonzalez said.[56] In addition, Gonzalez said he had seen Horman when he was still alive.

The reporters took pains to clarify everything Gonzalez said. Again, they asked him if he had seen Horman at the Ministry of Defense in September of 1973. Gonzalez said he had. The reporters asked Gonzalez to repeat his story. He complied, explaining how he knew that he had seen Horman. "And I asked the guy who was there who he was and they told me the guy is an American whose name is Charles Horman," Gonzalez said. "Who was in the room when the order was given?" Omang asked.[57] General Lutz, Colonel Barria, and another American, Gonzalez answered. Although Gonzalez never spoke to the strange man, he guessed that he was an American. Manitzas asked why. "Because of the way that he behaves, I mean he was dressing the shoes, you know, and everything," Gonzalez responded.[58]

Anyone inclined to doubt Gonzalez must consider three things. When the U.S. government, thanks to Senator Jacob Javits of New York, finally pressured Chile into releasing Horman's body, Gonzalez had the task of looking for it. Because Gonzalez had seen Horman before, he was able to identify him.[59] Secondly, given the deep involvement of the CIA in the coup, Gonzalez probably came into frequent contact with U.S. personnel, and knew an American when he saw one. In addition, Gonzalez had nothing to gain by coming forth with this story. He hoped to move to the United States, and it hardly helped his case to suggest that a CIA operative was behind Horman's murder.

Naturally, the assertions made by Gonzalez did not please the State Department. Although the U.S. consul in Santiago also interviewed Gonzalez, the State Department officially dismissed his testimony. To the embassy in Santiago, the office of Secretary of State Henry Kissinger cabled talking points for State Department spokesmen. Kissinger wanted spokesmen to mention that the consul had interviewed Gonzalez, and that the embassy had asked the Chilean Foreign Ministry to conduct an inquiry of the former intelligence officer's claims. The secretary of state publicly took the conclusions of the Foreign Ministry at face value. State Department spokesmen were instructed to say: "The Chilean note stated that Colonel Barria, reportedly present in General Lutz's office, when consulted by the Chilean government emphatically stated that Mr. Gonzalez's accusations were absolutely false. The note also pointed out that General Lutz has since died."[60]

As for the possibility that an American was with Lutz and Barria, the State Department already had a response in stock: "We state categorically that no U.S. intelligence representative was present when this alleged order was given, nor was the USG aware of or in any way involved in any Chilean interrogation of Horman."[61]

Privately, the State Department had doubts. Prompted by the embarrassment of the Gonzalez affair, State began a secret investigation. In August of 1976, Rudy V. Fimbres, the department's regional director for Bolivia and Chile, submitted a report to Harry W. Shlaudeman, the assistant secretary of state for inter-American affairs: "This case remains bothersome. The connotations for the Executive are not good. In the Hill, academic community, the press, and the Horman family the intimations are of negligence on our part, or worse, complicity in Horman's death."[62]

Fimbres believed it was imperative not only to defend innocent U.S. officials, but to hold the culpable ones accountable: "Based on what we have, we are persuaded that:—The GOC [Government of Chile] sought Horman and felt threatened enough to order his immediate execution. The GOC might have believed this American could be killed without negative fall-out from the USG."[63]

Fimbres charged the U.S. government with far more than negligence: "There is some circumstantial evidence to suggest:—U.S. intelligence may have played an unfortunate part in Horman's death. At best, it was limited to providing or confirming information that helped motivate his murder by the GOC. At worst, U.S. intelligence was aware the GOC saw Horman in a rather serious light and U.S. officials did nothing to discourage the logical outcome of GOC paranoia."[64]

Contrary to the State Department's official line, Fimbres was one government bureaucrat who regarded Rafael Gonzalez as neither delusional nor prone to telling tall tales. "If he is unbalanced, it is for Chilean intelligence to explain why he kept him on the payroll for so many years and used him as contact with us on Horman," Fimbres pointed out, adding that Gonzalez later helped the consulate locate Horman's body.[65]

That December, a State Department lawyer named Frederick Smith, Jr., completed another review for Shlaudeman. Like Fimbres, Smith concluded that Gonzalez was a reliable, consistent witness. Clearly, the Chilean was well acquainted with the Horman case. Smith noted that a man named Rafael Gonzalez appeared at the consulate on March 21, 1974, requesting that an American official come with him as he worked to send Horman's body home. "The return of Horman's remains was accomplished shortly thereafter," Smith wrote.[66]

During his interview with the U.S. consul, Gonzalez mentioned his intelligence work for the Chilean Air Force, or FACH, where he remained a civilian for twenty years until his appointment as captain in 1974. He retired from the service the following year. Gonzalez also lived off and on in the United States, first as a student and then as a permanent resident. For a time, he was an employee at the Chilean Consulate General in New York. Smith observed, "Documents presented to the consular officer by Gonzalez apparently substantiated his military service. Visa Office records confirm several aspects of his claimed status and presence in the U.S. do not contradict any of Gonzalez's statements in this regard."[67]

The Chilean government denied that Gonzalez was a retired FACH officer, but Smith found that the U.S. embassy "considered this a largely technical distinction and concluded, from official documents produced by Gonzalez, that he worked in the U.S. and other countries in a covert capacity and in a similar or somewhat more public capacity for the GOC in Chile."[68]

In addition, Smith pointed out that the statements made by Gonzalez about his employment history to the press and to the U.S. consular officer largely matched each other. There was no indication that he embellished his story. The director of the Chilean foreign ministry had labeled Gonzalez a psychopath, and the U.S. embassy felt somewhat uneasy about him as well. Still, Smith observed that even though the embassy believed that Gonzalez "probably has some kind of mental imbalance or fixation," it also acknowledged "he has shown a sharp intelligence and lucidity in his interviews with consular officer, and on July 16 he showed him a letter from two psychiatrists attesting to his mental stability."[69]

If U.S. intelligence did have a role in Horman's death, then who exactly was responsible? Because the State Department did not follow the suggestions made by Fimbres and Smith to pursue an investigation, it is impossible to say with certainty who passed the word to the Chilean military. A great deal of evidence points to Captain Ray Davis, even if that evidence would never have convicted him in a court of law. Gonzalez said that he had seen the men who had brought Horman from Valparaiso to Santiago, and the only man who did that was Davis.[70] Moreover, Davis was the head of the United States Military Group in Chile, whose office was located on the ninth floor of the Ministry of Defense. If Gonzalez was right, the order for Horman's execution was given just down the hall from Davis's office. Journalist Frank Manitzas observed, "That's significant in the extreme. There must have come a time when Charles knew he was labeled for execution. At that point, if not before, he would have told his captors, 'Call Ray Davis. He'll vouch for me. The Chilean military would never had executed an American citizen under those circumstances – unless, of course, it believed that it already had American consent."[71]

Manitzas did not automatically assume that Davis issued a kill order. "In talking with the Chileans, he might have spoken in such a way that they took something he said as an order with no trouble at all," the newsman speculated. "Just mentioning Charles's name could have been enough to spur those guys into action."[72] Nevertheless, Davis behaved in ways that did not suggest complete innocence. When Joyce and Simon frantically searched for Horman after his disappearance, Davis invited them to spend the night at his house. As the two women prepared for bed, he made a pass at both of them.[73] Afterward, Davis called Joyce and made a cruel remark which implied that her husband was dead: "Look, you're an intelligent, young, pretty girl with your whole life ahead of you. Look forward, not back."[74]

Judd Kessler, who served as acting director of the Agency for International Development's Chilean mission, had his suspicions about Davis: "My understanding is that, at the point the Embassy believed a coup was inevitable, it called the CIA off of any contact with the [Chilean] military. The guys who still did have contact with the military were guys like [Ray] Davis, who saw them all the time, were well-informed, buddy-buddy with them, and were opposed to the Allende government. I'm sure that these guys in their own personal way let them know what they thought."[75]

As for Davis himself, his attitude toward Charles Horman was callous: "If I go to New York City, I don't go messing around with the Mafia. You play with fire, you get burned."[76] One must remember that Davis had little to say to Horman and Simon on the road. Perhaps he knew how indiscreetly

Colonel Ryan and Art Creeter had behaved with them. It is unlikely that Ryan and Creter wished the tourists any harm. Ryan, whose concern for their safety was remarkable, had warned them not to return to Santiago because of the violence.[77]

One should not only point a finger at Ray Davis. A fair investigator would also interview the CIA agents who were stationed in Santiago such as James Anderson, Ray Warren, John Devine, and Donald Winters.[78] There is a chance, however small, that Horman's trip to Vina had nothing to do with his death. U.S. intelligence may have already determined his fate. This probably explains what happened to Frank Teruggi, who has been long-neglected in this essay. In 1975, the Senate Select Committee on Intelligence published a report on covert action in Chile: "During 1970–73, the Station collected operational intelligence necessary in the event of a coup—arrest lists, key civilian installations and personnel that needed protection, key government installations which need to be taken over, and government contingency plans which would be used in case of a military uprising. According to the CIA, the data was collected only against the contingency of Future Headquarters requests and was never passed to the Chilean military."[79]

The CIA's claim that it never gave its arrest lists to the Chilean military is implausible. Furthermore, it seems likely that Horman and Teruggi were on those arrest lists. The Federal Bureau of Investigation kept a file on Teruggi because of his politics. More likely than not, the FBI passed on its information to the CIA. One FBI document dated December 14, 1972, mentioned a conference held by the Committee of Returned Volunteers the year before in Allenspark, Colorado: "The name Frank Teruggi appeared on a list which indicated that Frank Teruggi attended the above conference as a delegate. CRV is a national group composed primarily of returned Peace Corps volunteers who espouse support of Cuba and all Third World revolutionaries and oppose United States 'Imperialism and Oppression' abroad."[80]

The FBI report also noted the Chicago Area Group on Latin America, or Chicago Action Group for the Liberation of the Americas, an organization that supported the leftist media. "A news letter dated August, 1971, issued by the Chicago Area Group on Latin America . . . set for that FRANK TERUGGI, member of the CAGLA, would be going to Santiago, Chile in October, 1971," the report continued.[81]

Another FBI document, dated October 25, 1972, is blacked out to such an extent that it is difficult to decipher. Apparently, a source for the 66th Military Intelligence Group in Bonn, West Germany, knew an American who was dedicated to helping dissident servicemen stationed in that country or those who were absent without leave. "The nature of this source should be protected," the report stated.[82] Somehow, the informant claimed that Teruggi was an important person to know.

The report, which describes Teruggi as a subversive, included the address where he was later arrested: Hernan Cortes 2575, Santiago, Chile. "He described TERUGGI as an American then in Chile editing a newsletter 'FIN' of Chilean information for the American left," the report continued, noting his involvement with CAGLA.[83] According to the report, this American had interest in contacting Teruggi.[84] It is hard to imagine Teruggi harboring AWOL servicemen from West Germany in his Santiago home. Steven Volk, Teruggi's friend, found the idea ridiculous: "I was never able to find the slightest bit of evidence that Frank was ever associated with any such group, that even if he was involved in work that broadly opposed the war in Vietnam and encouraged opposition to that war, it was not in the least connected with either promoting desertion from the military (except in the most general terms of opposing the war) or, much more specifically, with the issue of military deserters in Germany."[85]

Perhaps the AWOL organization was just simply aware of Teruggi's reputation as an activist, and nothing more. In any case, this incriminating report might have doomed Teruggi.

In his study, Frederick Smith suggested that Horman had also been under surveillance. Indeed, Horman's activities might have attracted the wrong kind of attention. At Chile Films, Horman worked as a cartoonist for Eduardo "Coco" Parades Barrientos, an associate of Allende who later died with the Chilean president. In addition, Horman was also writing about Spanish and U.S. imperialism in Chile, Chilean socialism, and the participation of the CIA in the Schneider assassination. He also worked with associates on *Chile: With Poems and Guns*, a pro-Allende film. "Along with Teruggi," Smith wrote, "he was associated with North American News Sources [FIN], a clipping service that also reportedly published a small, leftist, pro-Allende magazine."[86]

The State Department lawyer then made a crucial observation: "According to Mrs. Horman, Sr., she and her husband would clip stories on Chile from U.S. newspapers and mail them to Charles. She said Charles reported receiving them resealed."[87]

Smith speculated on why only Horman and Teruggi were killed, since the Chilean government had detained twenty or thirty U.S. citizens. The lawyer indicated that he had no hard evidence that Horman had known too much. "It is, therefore, not possible to say to what extent Horman's (and Teruggi's) activities may have set them apart, in the eyes of the GOC, as special threats," Smith concluded.[88] He conceded that Chilean intelligence could have gathered data on Horman and Teruggi before the coup, since their politics were no secret. Still, Smith wonders how Chilean operatives, employed by the Allende government, could have done so before the coup. This leaves the idea that American intelligence in Chile had been tracking the two men beforehand. Smith acknowledged "it appears strange that, given the obvious and important political considerations involved, the GOC would believe it could kill Horman and Teruggi without serious repercussions with the U.S."[89] Smith concurred with Rafael Gonzalez's assertion that the Chilean government "wouldn't go and race to kill an American . . . because here they would have been very careful of the lives of an American citizen."[90]

Why was Teruggi singled out for execution? The Chilean military arrested and then released other American expatriates with more intense political commitments. The military did not even bother to detain Steven Volk, the man who later identified Teruggi's body, for his own involvement with the FIN news service.[91] In his State Department report, Frederick Smith made an interesting observation about David Hathaway, Teruggi's roommate and FIN colleague, whom an Army officer interrogated at the National Stadium. "Hathaway was asked little about himself but mainly about Teruggi including about Teruggi's membership in a leftist (but unspecified) political party," Smith reported. "But Teruggi was not asked similar questions about Hathaway."[92] Six days after his arrest, Hathaway was released, and then expelled from Chile.[93] Obviously, the Chilean military did not like the staff at FIN. By detaining the other Americans before deporting them, the new regime could scare them away from Chile for good. Yet, the other Americans survived the coup.

Clearly, the Chilean military classified Teruggi as a special case. General Lutz, the director of Chilean Army Intelligence who allegedly ordered Horman's execution, claimed to the defense attaché at the U.S. embassy that Teruggi had come to his country "to spread false rumors to the outside world about Chile and the situation there."[94] Although Lutz also ridiculously charged Teruggi's leftist friends with his murder, the general added that the American belonged to a radical organization dedicated to damaging the junta and its dealings with the U.S. embassy.[95] Perhaps Teruggi's involvement in CAGLA set off the Junta. Moreover, it is very likely that the new military regime felt threatened by Teruggi's alleged connection to a movement to help AWOL servicemen or extremists. In the words of the State Department's Rudy Fimbres, Teruggi's possible antiwar activism may have triggered the junta's profound "paranoia."

As for the execution of Charles Horman, the search for truth continues. Chileans themselves are now conducting the investigation that Fimbres and

Smith had advocated three decades ago. Judge Juan Guzman has confronted the past with a bravery that the veterans of the Nixon administration do not yet have. Recently retired as Pinochet's prosecutor, Guzman holds Horman's own country responsible for his killing: "I have the sensation that you know, judges cannot decide on impressions. They have to have evidence. I have the sensation that, in one way or another, the government of the United States had to do with Horman's death. The Chilean government, or let's say, the military here couldn't have the least interest in this person. They knew that he had nothing to do with terrorism. They knew a little bit of his background, but the truth is that he had heard too much in Viña del Mar."[96]

The judge found Rafael Gonzalez to be a credible source on what exactly happened to Horman: "So I thought it was very reasonable to think that he was taken to the Ministry of Defense."[97] Clearly, the junta regarded Horman as a special situation. Guzman subpoenaed Henry Kissinger because of his involvement in the coup, but "I had questions regarding Charles Horman also for Mr. Kissinger."[98] The former secretary of state never responded to Guzman's inquiry. The judge is right; no evidence directly implicates the former secretary of state in the murder of Charles Horman. As Nixon's deputy, nevertheless, Kissinger fomented the bloody conditions that precipitated Horman's death. If Kissinger had no tolerance for Chileans with leftist beliefs, his diplomatic service would have had no reason to extend care and concern to Charles Horman, a man who thought differently from other Americans. By disregarding the rights and lives of the Chilean people, he devalued American life itself.

"Covert action should not be confused with missionary work," Kissinger once sniffed.[99] Yet, morality in foreign policy is not a luxury. The secretary of state did not fully grasp that cynical interventions by Americans overseas eventually hurt Americans themselves. Whether two Americans died in September of 1973, or 3,000 in September of 2001, the cost is too great.

## Notes

1. Telegram from Secretary of State Henry Kissinger to Mr. and Mrs. Edmund Horman, March 23, 1974. State Department Collection, FOIA Website, U.S State Department.

2. Hauser, *Missing: The Execution of Charles Horman* (New York: Simon & Schuster, 1988), 185.

3. Hauser, *Missing*, 138.

4. Hauser, *Missing*, 140–42. Steven Volk, "Seeking Justice in Chile: A Personal History," June 26, 2002. Oberlin College Faculty Observations: www.oberlin.edu/newsinfo/observations /observations_steven_volk1.html, accessed June 7, 2008.

5. Lewis H. Diuguid, "A Student's Disputed Death," *The Washington Post*, June 20, 1976.

6. Hauser, *Missing*, 6.

7. Hauser, *Missing*, 176.

8. Hauser, *Missing*, 29–30.

9. Hauser, *Missing*, 30.

10. Itay Hod, "The End of a Nightmare," *Salon.com*, October 19, 1999.

11. Diuguid, "A Student's Disputed Death."

12. Marc Cooper, *Pinochet and Me* (New York: Verso, 2001), 49–50.

13. Cooper, *Pinochet and Me*, 50.

14. Cooper, *Pinochet and Me*, 50.

15. Statement of Terry Simon, April 11, 1974. State Department Collection, FOIA website.

16. Statement of Terry Simon, April 11, 1974.

17. Statement of Terry Simon, April 11, 1974.

18. Statement of Terry Simon, April 11, 1974.

19. Statement of Terry Simon, April 11, 1974.

20. Statement of Terry Simon, April 11, 1974.

21. Statement of Terry Simon, April 11, 1974.

22. Hauser, *Missing*, 65.

23. Hauser, *Missing*, 67.

24. Hauser, *Missing*, 68.

25. Statement of Terry Simon.

26. Statement of Terry Simon.

27. Statement of Terry Simon.

28. Statement of Terry Simon.

29. Statement of Terry Simon and Hauser, *Missing*, 77.

30. Statement of Terry Simon.

31. Hauser, *Missing*, 78.

32. Statement of Terry Simon.

33. Hauser, *Missing*, 83.

34. Deputy Chief Navy Section Lieutenant Colonel P.J. Ryan, USMC to Chief Navy Section/Commander U.S. Military Group, Chile. "Supplementary Statement concerning my Conversation with Mr. Charles Harmon and his Female Companion in Vina del Mar during the period 11–15 September 1973," November 16, 1973. State Department Collection, FOIA Website.

35. P.J. Ryan, Lieutenant Colonel, USMC to U.S. Consul Fred Purdy, U.S. Embassy, Santiago, Chile, October 8, 1974. State Department Collection, FOIA website.

36. Ryan, Lieutenant Colonel, USMC to U.S. Consul Fred Purdy, U.S. Embassy, Santiago, Chile, October 8, 1974.

37. Ryan, Lieutenant Colonel, USMC to U.S. Consul Fred Purdy, U.S. Embassy, Santiago, Chile, October 8, 1974.

38. Hauser, *Missing*, 241.

39. Hauser, *Missing*, 87–88.

40. Hauser, *Missing*, 90–93.

41. Hauser, *Missing*, 93.

42. Hauser, *Missing*, 95.

43. Deputy Chief of Mission Herbert B. Thompson to Consul Fred Purdy. "Discussion of Story that Charles Horman was 'Turned Away' by Embassy," March 12, 1974. State Department Collection, FOIA website.

44. Thompson to Purdy, "Discussion of Story that Charles Horman was 'Turned Away' by Embassy."

45. Thompson to Purdy, "Discussion of Story that Charles Horman was 'Turned Away' by Embassy."

46. Cooper, *Pinochet and Me*, 38.

47. Cooper, *Pinochet and Me*, 44.

48. Cooper, *Pinochet and Me*, 44.

49. Cooper, *Pinochet and Me*, 50.

50. "Chronology of Information Received and Actions Taken Concerning Welfare and Whereabouts in Chile of Charles Edmund Horman," State Department Collection, FOIA website.

51. Hauser, *Missing*, 129–30.

52. Hauser, *Missing*, 150–51.

53. "Interview with Rafael Agustín Gonzalez Verdugo in the Italian Embassy," June 7 and 8, 1976. State Department Collection, FOIA website.

54. "Interview with Rafael Agustín Gonzalez Verdugo in the Italian Embassy."

55. "Interview with Rafael Agustín Gonzalez Verdugo in the Italian Embassy."

56. "Interview with Rafael Agustín Gonzalez Verdugo in the Italian Embassy."

57. "Interview with Rafael Agustín Gonzalez Verdugo in the Italian Embassy."

58. "Interview with Rafael Agustín Gonzalez Verdugo in the Italian Embassy."

59. "Interview with Rafael Agustín Gonzalez Verdugo in the Italian Embassy."

60. Cable from Secretary Kissinger to U.S. Embassy in Santiago, DOC_Number: 76STATE168348. July 7, 1976. State Department Collection, FOIA website.

61. Cable from Secretary Kissinger to U.S. Embassy in Santiago.

62. R.V. Fimbres, R.S. Driscoll, and W.V. Robertson to Harry W. Shlaudeman, "Charles Horman Case," August 25, 1976. State Department Collection, FOIA website.

63. Fimbres, Driscoll, and Robertson to Shlaudeman, "Charles Horman Case."

64. Fimbres, Driscoll, and Robertson to Shlaudeman, "Charles Horman Case."

65. Fimbres, Driscoll, and Robertson to Shlaudeman, "Charles Horman Case."

66. Frederick Smith, Jr., to Mr. Harry W. Shlaudeman, "Further Steps in the Case of Charles Horman," December 29, 1976. State Department Collection, FOIA website.

67. Smith to Shlaudeman, "Further Steps."

68. Smith to Shlaudeman, "Further Steps."

69. Smith to Shlaudeman, "Further Steps."

70. Gonzalez interview.

71. Hauser, *Missing*, 242.

72. Hauser, *Missing*, 242.

73. Hauser, *Missing*, 120–24.

74. Hauser, *Missing*, 131.

75. Hauser, *Missing*, 241.

76. Hauser, *Missing*, 241.

77. Hauser, *Missing*, 81.

78. Peter Kornbluh, *The Pinochet File: A Declassified Dossier on Atrocity and Accountability* (New York: The New Press, 2003), 287.

79. *Covert Action in Chile, 1963-1973: Staff Report of the Senate Select Committee to Study Governmental Operations with Respect to Intelligence Activities*. United States Senate (Washington, D.C.: U.S. Government Printing Office, 1975), 38.

80. "Frank Teruggi," Chicago, Illinois, December 14, 1972. Federal Bureau of Investigation Collection, FOIA website.

81. "Frank Teruggi."

82. FBI Memorandum from Legation in Bonn, Germany to Director, October 28, 1972. Courtesy of the National Security Archive.

83. FBI Memorandum from Legation in Bonn, Germany to Director, October 28, 1972.

84. FBI Memorandum from Legation in Bonn, Germany to Director, October 28, 1972.

85. Professor Steven Volk, June 9, 2008. Exchange by electronic mail.

86. Frederick Smith, Jr., December 29, 1976.

87. Smith, December 29, 1976.

88. Smith, December 29, 1976.

89. Smith, December 29, 1976.

90. Smith, December 29, 1976.

91. Hauser, *Missing*, 228.

92. Frederick Smith, Jr., December 29, 1976.

93. Hauser, *Missing*, 138–140.

94. Frederick Smith, Jr., December 29, 1976.

95. Smith, December 29, 1976.

96. Judge Juan Guzman, conversation with author, Santiago, Chile, June 13, 2005.

97. Guzman conversation, June 13, 2005.

98. Guzman conversation, June 13, 2005.

99. William Blum, *Killing Hope: U.S. Military and C.I.A. Interventions Since World War II* (Monroe, ME: Common Courage Press, 2004), 244.

# Bibliography

## Primary Sources

### Documents

*Archivo General Historico del Ministerio de Relaciones Exteriores*, Santiago, Chile.

"*Chile en los Archivos de la URSS*," eds. Eugenia Fediakova and Olga Ulianova, Estudios Publicos, Spring 1998.

"The Interim Report: Alleged Assassination Plots Involving Foreign Leaders," The Select Committee to Study Government Operations with Respect to Intelligence Activities. Washington, DC: U.S. Government Printing Office, 1975.

The National Security Archive, Washington, D.C., www.gwu.edu/~nsarchiv.

Nixon Presidential Materials Project, National Archives II, College Park, Maryland.

U.S. State Department Freedom of Information Act website. Collections of the State Department, Defense Department, National Security Council, Central Intelligence Agency, and the Federal Bureau of Investigation. www.foia.state.gov.

U.S. State Department, *Foreign Relations of the United States, 1964-1968, Volume XXXI, South and Central America; Mexico*. U.S. State Department website.

### Interviews

Arrate, Jorge. Conversation with author. Santiago, Chile, June 20, 2005.

Guzman, Judge Juan. Conversation with author. Santiago, Chile, June 13, 2005.

### Tapes

Nixon Presidential Materials Project. National Archives II. College Park, Maryland.

## Transcripts of Telephone Conversations

Nixon Presidential Materials Project. National Archives II. College Park, Maryland.

## Publications

Allende, Salvador. *Chile: No More Dependence!* Nottingham, UK: Bertrand Russell Peace Foundation, 1973.

Anaconda *Annual Report.*

Anderson, Jack, with George Clifford. *The Anderson Papers.* New York: Random House, 1973.

Arce, Luz. *The Inferno: A Study of Terror and Survival in Chile.* Madison: University of Wisconsin Press, 2004.

Chilean Interior Ministry. *Informe de la Comisión Nacional Sobre Prisión Política y Tortura.* 2004–2005.

Cooper, Marc. *Pinochet and Me.* New York: Verso, 2001.

Dean, John. *Blind Ambition: The White House Years.* New York: Simon & Schuster, 1976.

Debray, Regis. *Conversations with Allende.* Bristol, United Kingdom: NLB, 1971.

Frost, Sir David, with Bob Zelnick. *Frost/Nixon: Behind the Scenes of the Nixon Interviews.* New York: Harper Perennial, 2007.

Helms, Richard. *A Look over My Shoulder: A Life in the Central Intelligence Agency.* New York: Random House, 2003.

Kennecott *Annual Report.*

Kissinger, Henry A. *A World Restored: Metternich, Castlereagh and the Problems of Peace, 1812–22* (Boston: Houghton Mifflin Company, 1957.

——. *White House Years.* Boston: Little, Brown and Company, 1979.

——. *Years of Upheaval.* Boston: Little, Brown and Company, 1982.

*National Commission on Truth and Reconciliation,* authorized by Chilean President Patricio Aylwin, 1991. Truth Commissions Digital Collection, United States Institute of Peace.

Nixon, Richard M. *RN: The Memoirs of Richard Nixon.* New York: Grosset & Dunlap, 1978.

North American Congress on Latin America. *The Rockefeller Empire: Latin America,* April-June 1969.

*Pepsico Annual Report.*

Persico, Joseph. *The Imperial Rockefeller: A Biography of Nelson A. Rockefeller.* New York: Simon and Schuster, 1982.

Rockefeller, Nelson A. *The Rockefeller Report on the Americas: The Official Report of the United States Presidential Mission for the Western Hemisphere.* The New York Times ed. Chicago: Quadrangle Press, 1969.

*Rome Statute of the International Criminal Court.*

Rostow, Walt. *Stages of Economic Growth.* Cambridge: MIT Press, 1960.

*United States Senate, Hearings before the Subcommittee on Multinational Corporations of the Committee on Foreign Relations, Ninety-Third Congress, on the International Telephone and Telegraph, 1970–1971.* Washington: U.S. Government Printing Office, 1973.

United States Senate Select Committee to Study Governmental Operations with Respect to Intelligence Activities, *Covert Action in Chile: 1963–1973*. Washington: U.S. Government Printing Office, 1975.

Volk, Steven. "Seeking Justice in Chile: A Personal History," June 26, 2002. Oberlin College Faculty Observations, www.oberlin.edu/news-info/observations/observations_steven_volk1.html. Accessed June 7, 2008.

## Secondary Sources

### Books

Ambrose, Stephen E. *Nixon: The Education of a Politician, 1913–1962*. New York: Touchstone, 1987.

———. *Nixon: The Triumph of a Politician, 1962–1972*. New York: Simon and Schuster, 1989.

Blum, William. *Killing Hope: U.S. Military Interventions and CIA Interventions since World War II*. Monroe, ME: Common Courage Press, 1995, 2004.

Boorstein, Edward. *Allende's Chile: An Inside View*. New York: International Publishers, 1977.

Brodie, Fawn M. *Richard Nixon: The Shaping of His Character*. New York: W. W. Norton & Company, 1981.

Collier, Ruth Berins, and David Collier. *Shaping the Arena: Critical Junctures, the Labor Movement, and Regime Dynamics in Latin America*. Notre Dame, IN: University of Notre Dame Press, 2002.

Constable, Pamela, and Arturo Valenzuela. *A Nation of Enemies: Chile Under Pinochet*. New York: W.W. Norton & Company, 1993.

Cusack, David F. *Revolution and Reaction: The Internal and International Dynamics of Conflict and Confrontation in Chile*. Denver: University of Denver Graduate School of International Studies, 1977.

Dallek, Robert. *Nixon and Kissinger: Partners in Power*. New York: HarperCollins Publishers, 2007.

Dinges, John. *The Condor Years*. New York: The New Press, 2004.

Faundez, Julio. *Marxism and Democracy in Chile: From 1932 to the Fall of Allende*. London: United Kingdom: Yale University Press, 1988.

Gaddis, John Lewis. *Strategies of Containment: A Critical Reappraisal of American National Security Policy During the Cold War*. New York: Oxford University Press, 2005.

Garcia, Pio. *Las Fuerzas Armadas y El Golpe de Estado en Chile*. Mexico, Spain, and Argentina: Siglo Veintiuno Editores, 1974.

Gilman, Nils. *Mandarins of the Future: Modernization Theory in Cold War America*. Baltimore: The Johns Hopkins University Press, 2003.

Gustafson, Kristian. *Hostile Intent: U.S. Covert Operations in Chile, 1964–1974*. Washington, D.C.: Potomac Books, 2007.

Haslam, Jonathan. *The Nixon Administration and the Death of Allende's Chile*. New York: Verso, 2005.

Hauser, Thomas. *Missing: The Execution of Charles Horman*. New York: Simon & Schuster, 1988.

Hersh, Seymour M. *The Price of Power: Kissinger in the Nixon White House*. New York: Summit Books, 1983.

Hitchens, Christopher. *The Trial of Henry Kissinger*. New York: Verso, 2001.

Hogan, Michael J. and Thomas G. Paterson, eds. *Explaining the History of American Foreign Relations*. New York: Cambridge University Press, 1991.

Isaacson, Walter. *Kissinger: A Biography*. New York: Simon & Schuster, 1992.

Kaufman, Edy. *Crisis in Allende's Chile: New Perspectives*. New York and Westport, CT: Praeger, 1988.

Kornbluh, Peter. *The Pinochet File: A Declassified Dossier on Atrocity and Accountability*. New York: The New Press, 2003.

Logevall, Fredrik. *Choosing War: The Lost Chance for Peace and the Escalation of War in Vietnam*. Berkeley, Los Angeles: University of California Press, 1999.

Loveman, Brian. *Chile: The Legacy of Hispanic Capitalism*. New York: Oxford University Press, 2001.

Lowenthal, Abraham. *Partners in Conflict: The United States and Latin America in the 1990s*. Baltimore: The Johns Hopkins University Press, 1990.

McCoy, Alfred. *A Question of Torture: CIA Interrogation from the Cold War to the War on Terror*. New York: Metropolitan Books, 2006.

Meller, Patricio. *The Unidad Popular and the Pinochet Dictatorship: A Political Economy Analysis*. London, United Kingdom: Macmillan Press Ltd., 2000.

Moran, Theodore H. *Multinational Corporations and the Politics of Dependence: Copper in Chile*. Princeton, New Jersey: Princeton University Press, 1974.

Morris, David J. *We Must Make Haste—Slowly: The Process of Revolution in Chile*. New York: Vintage, 1973.

North American Congress on Latin America. *New Chile*. Berkeley, CA, and New York: Waller Press, 1973.

O'Shaughnessy, Hugh. *Pinochet: The Politics of Torture*. New York: New York University Press, 2000.

Petras, James, and Morris Morley. *The United States and Chile: Imperialism and the Overthrow of the Allende Government*. New York: Monthly Review Press, 1975.

Power, Margaret. *Right-wing Women in Chile, 1964–1973*. University Park, PA: The Pennsylvania State University Press, 2002.

Rabe, Stephen G. *The Most Dangerous Area in the World: John F. Kennedy Confronts Communist Revolution in Latin America*. Chapel Hill: The University of North Carolina Press, 1999.

Sampson, Anthony. *The Sovereign State of ITT*. New York: Stein and Day, 1973.

Sater, William F. *Chile and the United States: Empires in Conflict*. Athens: The University of Georgia, 1990.

Schoultz, Lars. *Beneath the United States: A History of U.S. Policy toward Latin America*. Cambridge: Harvard University Press, 1998.

Shlaim, Avi. *The Iron Wall: Israel and the Arab World*. New York: Norton, 2001.

Sigmund, Paul E. *The Overthrow of Allende and the Politics of Chile*. Pittsburgh: University of Pittsburgh Press, 1977.

———. *The United States and Democracy in Chile*. Baltimore: The Johns Hopkins University Press, 1993.

Smith, Peter H. *Talons of the Eagle: Dynamics of U.S.-Latin American Relations*. New York: Oxford University Press, 2000.

Sobel, Robert. *I.T.T.: The Management of Opportunity*. New York: Times Books, 1982.

Stallings, Barbara. *Class Conflict and Economic Development in Chile, 1958–1973*. Stanford, California: Stanford University Press, 1978.

Treverton, Gregory F. *Covert Action: The Limits of Intervention in the Postwar World*. New York: Basic Books, 1987.

Valenzuela, Arturo. *The Breakdown of Democratic Regimes: Chile*. Baltimore: The Johns Hopkins University Press, 1978.

Valenzuela, Arturo, and J. Samuel Valenzuela, eds. *Chile: Politics and Society*. New Brunswick, NJ: Transaction Books, 1976.

Wallerstein, Immanuel. *The Modern World-System: Capitalist Agriculture and the Origins of the European World-Economy in the Sixteenth Century*. New York: Academic Press, 1974.

Winn, *Weavers of the Revolution: The Yarus Workers and Chile's Road to Socialism*. New York: Oxford University Press, 1986.

Woodward, Bob. *Veil: The Secret Wars of the CIA 1981–1987*. New York: Simon & Schuster, 1987.

## Periodicals

*Contemporanea*
*Diplomacy and Statecraft*
*Foreign Affairs*
*Inter-American Economic Affairs*
*Journal of Interamerican Studies and World Affairs*
*New York Times*
Newsletter of the *North American Congress on Latin America*
*Salon.com*
*Washington Post*

## Television Program

"Schneider v. Kissinger." *60 Minutes*. Columbia Broadcasting System. September 9, 2001.

## Presentations

Farnsworth, Elizabeth. University of California, Berkeley, March 6, 2006.

Harmer, Tanya. "A Different 9/11: Cuba and the Chilean Coup of 1973." Annual Conference of the Society for Historians of American Foreign Relations. Chantilly, VA, June 21, 2007.

Power, Margaret. "We Opposed the Coup: Chilean Military Resistance to the Overthrow of Salvador Allende." Annual Meeting of the American Historical Association. Washington, D.C., January 5, 2008.

### Electronic Mail Exchanges
Anonymous Law Professor, Spring 2008.
Choudhry, Erfaan. January 2006.
Hamp, Julie, Pepsico Communications. April 22, 2008.
Power, Margaret. Illinois Institute of Technology. June 22, 2008.
Rials, Lee A. Western Hemisphere Institute for Security Cooperation. June 9, 2008.
Sands, Philippe. University College, London. Spring 2008.
Volk, Steven. Oberlin College. June 9, 2008.

# Index

# About the Author

Lubna Z. Qureshi earned her doctorate in history from the University of California–Berkeley in 2006. She also holds an M.A. from Temple University and a B.A. from the University of Wisconsin–Madison. Her areas of research are U.S. diplomatic history and international history.

Printed in Great Britain
by Amazon